Norway and
Europe
in the 1970s

Volume No. 27 in the Series
Norwegian Foreign Policy Studies

HILARY ALLEN

Norway and Europe in the 1970s

Universitetsforlaget
Oslo — Bergen — Tromsø

© Universitetsforlaget 1979

ISBN 82-00-05230-3

Cover: Bjørn Roggenbihl

Printed in Norway by
Tangen-Trykk

Distribution offices:

NORWAY
Universitetsforlaget
P. O. Box 2977, Tøyen
Oslo 6

UNITED KINGDOM
Global Book Resources Ltd.
109 Great Russel Street
London WC1B 3Nd

UNITED STATES and CANADA
Columbia University Press
136 South Broadway
Irvington-on-Hudson
New York 10533

Contents

PART TWO

Preface

This book tries to answer two questions. Why did a majority of those who voted in the referendum of September 1972 reject membership of the European Economic Community? And how have Norway's relations with the EEC developed since then? The first part is therefore concerned with the reasons why three successive governments applied for membership negotiations; with the negotiations themselves between 1970 and 1972, which were successfully concluded by the signing of a treaty of accession in January 1972; and with the referendum campaign which ended in a defeat for the Labour government in the following September. The second part of the book looks at the free trade agreement which replaced membership; at the policies pursued towards the EEC by the two governments which held office between the referendum and the election of September 1977; and at the impact of the EEC issue on domestic politics after September 1972, which goes far to explaining those policies.

These are important questions in Norway's relations with the rest of Europe, and whether or not to join the EEC was probably the hardest fought political issue in the country this century. Yet in Norway itself little has been written about the events which led up to the referendum since the commentaries and interpretations which appeared immediately afterwards. Since September 1972 there has been hardly any serious political or academic discussion about the economic and political consequences of being outside the enlarged EEC, or about Norway's long-term future outside it. This is partly because the question was quickly overshadowed by others: by Norway's new position as an oil producer, by the extension of the country's sea limits, and by developments in the northern regions. Partly the explanation lies in politics: in the pro-market parties' interest in burying the subject, and the more widespread desire to put aside an issue which had divided the country so deeply. But another reason is that many Norwegians — though certainly not the most convinced anti-marketeers — now seem to regard the question of membership as having been of only marginal importance for their country after all. Much has changed since 1972, both in Norway and the EEC. Oil has altered Norway's

5

economic prospects. Some of the main predictions of both sides have been proved wrong or grossly exaggerated: the EEC, for example, hardly appears to be developing into a full economic and political union as the opponents of entry insisted it would, nor has a free trade agreement been economically disadvantageous, as the pro-marketeers argued it would be. So in retrospect the passions aroused by the debate appear to have been out of proportion to the real importance of the decision they had to take, and many of the arguments employed in it largely irrelevant to Norway's present situation and therefore of merely historical interest.

In addition many former supporters of membership now think that in some ways the 'no' was perhaps even a good thing for Norway. Oil, prosperity, their economy's comparatively good performance during at least the first two years of the international recession since 1974, the fact that staying outside the EEC did not weaken Norway's position within the Atlantic alliance (as many pro-marketeers had argued it would), the EEC countries' economic difficulties and failure to realise the ambitious objectives of the early 1970s: all have contributed to vindicating the voters' verdict as far as many former pro-marketeers are concerned. So they have no wish to keep alive public memories of their former advocacy of membership by dwelling on the subject. And the anti-marketeers, of course, are just as interested in closing the debate about Norway's relations with the EEC (apart, that is, from those who still hope to reap domestic political advantages from the issue), for they want to avoid any discussion which might perhaps reveal that there are after all some disadvantages for Norway in not being inside the EEC. Indeed this vindication of the referendum result has gone so far that something resembling a myth of inevitability has grown up to envelop it, in public at least: as though it was inevitable from the outset that the Norwegian people would reject this departure from the course of their national history.[1] The myth has advantages for both sides. The former supporters of membership can be portrayed as having struggled vainly against invincible historical forces, rather than as having perhaps been merely tactically inept. Combined with the pro-marketeers' concern to avoid the subject and the unanswerable argument that the people's democratically expressed wish must be respected, the aura of inevitability is the anti-marketeers' best defence against the subject being re-opened in the foreseeable future.

Yet there was nothing inevitable about the outcome of the long referendum campaign. It owed something, of course, to the strong urge for national independence and the sense of remoteness from Western Europe which are natural consequences of Norway's history and geographical position. It owed as much perhaps to the particular social and intellectual climate of the late 1960s and early 1970s in which the last application was submitted and the campaign took place. But the result also owed much to the campaign tactics of each side, to political miscalculations and chance events, to personalities, and to actions and decisions abroad which influenced the course of the debate in Norway. This seems to be widely forgotten now: partly as a consequence of neglecting to piece the story together afterwards, partly because of the way the events have been relegated to the category of subjects which are not openly or frankly discussed in public, partly because those who very nearly won have joined with those who only just won to portray the result as primarily due to deep historical and social forces beyond mere politicians' control. As the verdict of the referendum has come to seem the right one, indeed almost the inevitable one, the details of how it came about appear almost irrelevant. In this atmosphere it is difficult to consider objectively the possibility that the majority against membership in September 1972 might in large measure have been the outcome of a hard political battle: that the result might have gone the other way if, for example, certain leading politicians had behaved differently or taken different decisions at certain critical moments, or if one or other side had adopted a different campaign strategy.

Nor has the result been of merely marginal significance. It has affected Norwegian politics and Norway's foreign policy, especially of course its relations with Western Europe. Most of the politicians and civil servants who worked for membership have remained active and influential. Within three years the Labour party had begun to recover some of the votes it lost in 1973 as a consequence of trying to take Norway into the EEC. In the general election of September 1977 Labour and the Conservatives, the other party supporting membership in 1972, emerged the clear victors. But in the intervening five years, the groups which had won the referendum — the primary sector, the left socialists, the radically inclined section of the academic community and politically active youth, the populists and environmentalists, the cultural and moral movements of rural Norway — enjoyed a greater influence on Norwegian policy than previously. In some cases this seems to have been a short-term phenomenon attributable to the political upheavals of the referendum campaign and its immediate aftermath. In others the influence may be longer lasting. Thus at home the farmers and fishermen have gained large tangible benefits from their victory, while the positive words in the political vocabulary of the late 1970s — 'national control', 'decentralisation', 'conservation of the environment and resources' — echo the slogans of the anti-marketeers in 1972.[2] The Labour party leadership still sometimes hesitates to implement policies strongly opposed by the groups which defeated it in 1972, even when it judges these policies to be in the national interest.[3] In relations with foreign countries the insistence on national sovereignty and national control of Norwegian resources, although nothing new, has gained even greater legitimacy as an argument for particular policies; the decision not to seek full membership of the International Energy Agency (IEA) in 1974 was a case in point.[4] There are now very definite limits to the type of co-operation a Norwegian government can be seen seeking with the EEC if it wants to avoid political embarrassments at home. Above all there has been a diversion of political and academic interest away from Western Europe. Instead of being active participants like the Danes or even very aware of EEC affairs like the Swedes, the Norwegians have remained aloof observers on the periphery, much more interested in what is happening in the Barents Sea to the north, in the North Sea and Atlantic to the west, even in the developing countries outside Europe. Oil, fisheries, shipping and trade all tie their economy to western Europe, especially to the EEC, of course. But beyond those economic matters which directly touch their own interests, concern about Western Europe is on the whole slight and an attitude of detached non-involvement widespread.

So in order to understand Norway's relations with Europe it is necessary to see how and why the decision was reached which set Norway on its present course, and to chart that course during the years since the referendum. The decision to remain outside the enlarged EEC was a major event in Norway's post-war relations with Europe. Norwegians, and the EEC, need reminding that Norway's present position on the fringe of Western European politics was not somehow predestined and natural, that indeed at the time many Norwegians wanted their country to participate fully in the mainstream of European affairs and regarded the rejection of membership as a break with the main direction of Norwegian foreign policy since the second world war. It is also worth recalling the arguments, now forgotten or considered irrelevant or too politically inconvenient to mention, for choosing membership. Not because it is a realistic political option for any Norwegian government in the foreseeable future. But because although some of the pro-marketeers' predictions have not materialised, others do still possess some validity and ought not to be forgotten. It is a commentary on the present situation, and a reason for making this effort of recall, that even those Norwegians who recognise this would not say so in public six years after the referendum.

This book has been made possible by a grant from the Social Science Research Council, while holding a Visiting Research Fellowship at the Centre for International Studies at the London School of Economics and Political Science. I am most grateful to both. The Institute for International Affairs in Oslo, where much of the research and writing was done, has given me more practical help, advice and friendship than I can ever repay. I am indebted also to those many Norwegian politicians, civil servants, diplomats and academics who have spoken so frankly, and been so helpful, to a foreigner trying to understand their country. The interpretation of the events described here is, of course, entirely my own. If it will encourage Norwegians, who are so much better qualified than I am, to attempt the same task, then the book will have amply repaid the writing.

November 1978

PART ONE

Introduction

In a consultative referendum on 24 and 25 September 1972 a small majority of those who voted — 53.5 per cent — rejected membership of the EEC. All previous public opinion polls had shown a majority against joining the EEC.[1] Yet still the result came as a surprise to many: in Norway as well as abroad, on the 'no' side as well as the 'yes' side. Many leading opponents of membership had been uncertain of victory until the end; not a few had anticipated defeat. Similarly most of those campaigning for entry had remained convinced until the outcome was known that somehow their minority in the polls would be transformed into a majority in the referendum itself.

These expectations were based on some widely accepted ideas about Norwegian politics. One of these was that on such major political and economic issues the great majority of voters habitually followed the advice of the leaders of the established political parties and the economic organisations to which they belonged.[2] Another was that the renowned discipline and loyalty of Labour party members and voters could almost always be relied on to produce the support a Labour government asked for, however unenthusiastically or reluctantly that support might at times be given.[3] And on this particular issue not only had a large majority of the country's political and economic leadership — in parliament and the political parties, in industry and the trade unions — been campaigning for membership, but the Labour prime minister had made the referendum a question of confidence in his government, thereby turning a Labour vote against EEC membership into a vote against his government. Yet still some 35 per cent of those Labour party supporters who voted, voted 'no'.[4]

No sooner was the referendum over than the interpretations began. How was it to be explained that a normally malleable electorate had rejected a policy advocated by the country's two largest political parties (which between them had won some 66 per cent of the votes in the previous election), by influential sections of other parties, by both sides of industry, and by most of the media? How could Norway's political and economic leadership have suffered such a defeat? How had it come about that a Labour government was able to rally the support of no more than 65 per cent of its own voters even when its continuation in office depended on the outcome?

According to one of the (frequently overlapping) explanations advanced, the result simply reflected the inadequacy of most professional politicians when confronted by this highly controversial and emotive issue, which had cut across the normal political dividing lines and overturned normal political loyalties. The reasons given for their failure on this occasion varied however. Some pro-marketeers regarded it as a culpable failure:[5] the pro-market politicians had been defeated because they abandoned their responsibility to give leadership in a question which, however difficult for some of the political parties to handle, was of vital national importance. The first step in this abdication of responsibility had been their decision to permit a referendum on a question of such magnitude and complexity at all. The next had been the 'wait and see' attitude which many adopted for party political reasons, despite the fact that their duty had been to give public opinion a clear lead. The final step had been the way in which they eventually surrendered even their constitutional function, by permitting a merely consultative referendum to acquire a binding character.

According to another version of this 'failure of the politicians' interpretation, their failure lay rather in having lost control of the situation.[6] This had happened partly because, once the question had been made the subject of a referendum, the campaign increasingly developed outside the normal political organisations, and the control of events passed from the professional politicians to the non-professional activists in the large *ad hoc* campaign organisations. More fundamentally however, the politicians lost control according to this view because the conflicts and alliances unleashed by the issue cut across the parties themselves. Their organisations were neutralised. Politicians grown accustomed to regarding normal politics as taking place along a left-right axis were at a loss in a campaign in which this proved an incomplete guide to voters' reactions.[7]

Others stressed the pro-market politicans' tactical mistakes and errors of judgement. They had been so sure of winning that their campaign tactics and arguments had been tailored more to party political considerations than to actually winning the campaign. The Conservatives, for example, were criticised for having tried too long to maintain in office a coalition which was deeply split: as a consequence they had been unable to give public opinion a strong lead at an early stage. Labour's leaders were said to have been primarily concerned to minimise the internal party damage caused by this question. So they too had held back for too long, given priority to the wrong arguments, and lost control of the party because of their fear of splitting it.[8]

Some commentators attached as much or more importance to the allegedly superior campaign organisation of the 'no' side, and to the type of propaganda it had used. Pro-marketeers were particularly inclined to give this as as an explanation for their defeat. The anti-marketeers' tactics had been brilliant, they said, at the same time implying that somehow normal politicians and parties were handi-capped in adopting extraordinary methods when confronted by an extraordinary issue. That applied even more to the anti-marketeers' propaganda. Their propaganda (so this line of argument continued) had been of a kind that responsible politicians were unable to use, had they even wished to do so: deliberately designed to arouse and exploit people's deepest fears, it had been the type of irresponsible propaganda which could be used only by those who could not be called to account afterwards and would bear no responsibility for dealing with the consequences of the policies they advocated.[9]

A rather different interpretation of the referendum result took as its starting point not the apparently overwhelming unity of Norway's political establishment assumed in this first set of explanations, but instead the deep divisions within it. This second interpretation, which might be labelled the 'elite divided', regarded the real conflict over EEC membership as being between major sectors of the Norwegian economy. On the one side were the primary producers and their poli-tical allies (including on this issue the left socialists). The farmers were non-exporting, high cost producers requiring tight import controls, high prices, and large subsidies to survive; the fishermen, although interested in free trade as exporters, were concerned above all else to protect their resource base and the control of production and marketing at home. On the other side were the economic organisations and political parties primarily concerned about the modern sectors of the economy — industry, commerce and shipping — which were heavily dependent on exporting and free trade, and served by lower food prices, both as consumers and in order to hold industrial wages at internationally competitive levels. According to this explana-tion, the victory of the primary producers was due to their success in mobilising other sectors of society to their side by playing on broader ideological and national themes, which veiled this core of sectional self-interest at the heart of the campaign against EEC member-ship.[10]

Closely related to this interpretation, with its emphasis on economic factors, was yet a third. This placed more weight however on historical and political factors in seeking to explain the winning alliance between the primary producers and radical left, whether liberal or socialist,

12

and might be called the 'national-patriotic' explanation. In Norway the radicals in the towns had traditionally been national standard bearers, partly no doubt because of the country's long history of subservience to foreign powers. Their equally traditional allies in domestic conflicts over relations with the outside world, especially with Sweden in the late nineteenth century, had been the politically organised farmers. The referendum campaign had merely revived this old national-patriotic coalition, this time over the question of Norway's relations with the EEC. It was a winning coalition because of the strong emotional force which its appeal to national independence possessed in a country that had regained it only sixty-seven years before, after being submerged in so-called unions with its Scandinavian neighbours for over 500 years.[11]

This interpretation had links with two others, which could be grouped together under the heading of 'centre versus periphery', and which both saw the result as a victory of the latter over the former. In the first version the 'centre' stood for all the normally predominant elements in Norwegian political and social life: the capital (despite its extreme south-east location), the political and bureaucratic establishment, the leaders of both sides of industry, and the media. The 'periphery' meant the regions, especially the distant ones in the north, ordinary voters, ordinary party members, ordinary workers, small coastal fishermen, small farmers up country. The 'no' majority represented these people's demand for a greater say in the conditions of their own lives: for more open government, more internal party democracy, more decentralisation of power to the communities where they lived. It was a rejection at home of all those features of modern society which such people regarded as even more pronounced in the EEC, into which the 'centre' wanted to take Norway: features like bigger bureaucracies, more distant government, centralisation of power, concentration in large urban and industrial centres, efficiency and rationalisation pursued at the expense of the 'small man' and established ways of life.[12] The notion of 'centre versus periphery' thus had a variety of territorial, political, economic and social connotations. But it was a dichotomy the reality of which seemed borne out by the referendum result, which showed opposition to EEC membership to have a close relationship to social status and income level and as increasing in proportion to the distance from Oslo and the few other towns of any size in Norway.[13]

This last phenomenon could also be used, however, to support the second version of the 'centre versus periphery' theme. According to this the fundamental division revealed by the referendum result was none other than the old and deep conflict in modern Norwegian history between town and country.[14] At one level this was an economic conflict

between the food producers and consumers, between the primary producers on the one side and business and industry on the other.
At another level it was the political division which in Norway had
prevented the creation of a broadly based conservative party in which
agricultural interests could be balanced against those of other sectors
of the economy. But it was also a deep cultural division in which
language, religion, and social outlook separated the country from the
town in a way that immeasurably hardened the lines created by
economic and political differences. This town-country axis had dominated Norwegian politics until the economic changes of the early
twentieth century introduced into the towns, and even large areas of
the countryside, the class conflicts and political parties characteristic
of industrial society. But although overlaid by these it had never
disappeared. What the referendum produced, according to this interpretation, was a revival of the traditional rural opposition to the policies
and interests and values of modern industrial Norway, and especially
of Oslo and all that the capital stood for in modern Norway.

These various explanations of the referendum result were not mu-
tually exclusive. Indeed they had many features in common, pointing
to the same phenomena but emphasising one rather than another,
depending on the observer's view of Norwegian history and politics —
and in some cases where he himself had stood in the campaign just
ended. Nor were these the only interpretations put forward. But they
did indicate what some commentators at the time regarded as having
been the main factors at work, and also some of the arguments used
during the debate about membership. For it was a characteristic of this
campaign of extraordinary emotional intensity that analysis and
special pleading became so intermingled as to be inseparable for many
Norwegians — at the time and afterwards.

1. Norway in 1970

The Economy[1]

Norway is a long strip of a country stretching some 1 000 miles from north to south, and for much of its length little more than a coastline with a narrow hinterland. Halfway up the coast it enters the Arctic circle; its capital, Oslo, lies on the same latitude as southern Alaska. Much of the country consists of mountainous plateaux cut by deep valleys and rivers, the mountains and rivers falling steeply to the sea in the west. So communications were difficult until the building of railways and coming of air travel. Even now northern towns and many of the small communities in the provinces remain far from Oslo in travelling time and in other things that shape peoples' outlook: economic activities, climate, and the social and cultural milieu.

With a land area as large as Britain's, Norway had less than four million inhabitants in 1970, and these were very thinly spread, especially in the north. Rather more than a third lived in communities with less than 200 people, and only three cities had more than 100 000 inhabitants — Oslo, Bergen and Trondheim.[2] All three lie on the coast, like most of the larger communities and many of the smaller ones. They have been drawn there by access to the economic opportunities offered by the seas and rivers: fishing, shipping, trade and the industries powered by hydro-electricity from the waterfalls. Inland, especially in the west and north, the economic basis for settlement has always been poor: small scale agriculture, forestry, some small industry in the twentieth century. But only about 3 per cent of Norway's land is suitable for agriculture, and only the southeast for the larger scale agriculture of Western Europe. Along the coast and fjords small farming can be supplemented by fishing, but even together they provide an inadequate basis for settlement. So by 1970 there had for some years been a twofold movement of population within the country: southwards, away from the north with its harsher economic conditions, and a general one away from the small rural communities to the larger, more urbanised ones with their better employment opportunities.

This population movement, a problem for the north for many

15

years, had been recognised as one of Norway's major economic and social problems by the late 1950s. How to halt it, or at least slow it down, and keep alive the tiny communities scattered in the valleys and on the mountains had become a prominent subject of economic planning and political debate.[3] Regional policy in Norway therefore did not mean what it usually meant in the older industrial economies to the south, namely the modernisation of dying industrial areas. It meant maintaining in areas still largely dependent on primary economic activities an adequate economic basis to sustain viable communities. Ultimately it meant being able to maintain a population in the far northern parts of the country at all. So although generally referred to as a regional problem, it was one which also had national dimensions because it affected vital national interests, not least the credibility of the country's security policy in an area bordering the Soviet Union.

Until the beginning of the twentieth century Norway had been a predominantly agricultural country, lacking the large coal reserves and accumulations of capital that provided the basis for early industrialisation in Britain and on the continent. At the time it gained its independence from Sweden in 1905 Norway was still one of the poorest countries in Europe. Two things changed this during the years that followed, and by 1970 had turned it into a prosperous industrial economy with one of the world's highest per capita incomes.[4] The first was shipping, the second hydro-electricity.

Geography and the poor quality of their land had already made the Norwegians into a maritime nation when the liberalisation of the world's sea-carrying trade in the middle of the nineteenth century threw open to free competition an activity in which they proved to have all the natural advantages for success. By 1880 their merchant fleet was the third largest in the world,[5] and despite the heavy losses of two world wars in the twentieth century it still ranked fourth in 1970.[6] From the outset this fleet depended on carrying the trade of other countries because the volume of Norway's own trade was so small. Particularly important was the trade of Western Europe, including after the second world war oil from the Middle East. By 1970 the six countries of the EEC and Britain were together employing some 60 per cent of Norway's shipping.[7] Both economically and politically shipping has been of fundamental importance for modern Norway's development. It provided the economic basis and self-interest, and probably also the boost to national self-confidence, which enabled them to seize their independence in 1905. In most years its earnings covered a large part of the country's almost permanent deficit on current trade.[8] And both before and after independence shipping drew Norwegians into world affairs in a way that the country's geographical remoteness might otherwise have precluded.

Independence coincided with the harnessing of Norway's water resources.[9] From being a country poor in energy, its major industrial advantage became its abundant and cheap supplies of the form most suitable for modern industrial production. Industries were established close to the hydro-electric plants along the coast and fjords. Some, like wood processing and steel, were able to exploit the country's own natural resources. Others, notably the electro-chemical and electro-metallurgical industries, were heavily dependent on imported raw materials. All produced overwhelmingly for export, giving yet another powerful stimulus to Norway's integration into the world economy, and especially that of Western Europe, their major market and the main source of Norway's own imports.

Foreign capital played an important part in establishing the energy-intensive industries, and even in 1970 the share of foreign ownership in them was still relatively high.[10] Half the shares in Norway's largest aluminium plant, Aardal and Sunndal Verk, for example, were owned by the Canadian company Alcan.[11] Foreign capital had also been important in developing the water resources, but in that case the Norwegians had early placed strict controls on the extent and duration of such ownership. As a small, newly independent nation, they had from the beginning been aware of the dilemma of wanting to retain full national control over the country's resources, yet of being too poor to exploit them without foreign finance. Then, as since, their solution was to import the capital, but to erect very careful regulations in order to minimise the threat to independence.

During the first two-thirds of the twentieth century hydro-electricity changed Norway's economic and social structure, its prospects as a nation, and its relations with Western Europe as profoundly as the exploitation of off-shore oil and gas is likely to do in the last third of the century. Exploration for oil has been under way in the Norwegian sector of the North Sea since the mid-1960s, and the first substantial find was made in December 1969.[12] But the size of the reserves is not clear. Nor did the probable economic impact of oil seem as great as four years later, after the profound changes in the international oil market had enhanced the competitiveness and revenue-earning potential of North Sea oil. Only then — after the referendum — were most Norwegians to begin to realise that the developments off their coast compared in importance with the exploitation of their on-shore water resources some seventy years earlier.

Despite the industrialisation based on hydro-electricity, Norway was still mainly an exporter of primary products and semi-processed raw materials in the 1950s.[13] In 1950 these still made up some 80 per cent of its commodity exports. Norwegian agriculture did not produce for export and had no ambition to do so, preferring the security of its own heavily protected home market. But the fishing industry, the forestry, electro-metallurgical and electro-chemical industries were all heavily represented in Norwegian exports. Little contribution was made to exports by the small industrial plants established after the war in the shelter of the protected domestic market. But they provided employment, in particular bringing at least some alternative employment opportunities to regions previously entirely dependent for settlement on agriculture, forestry and fisheries.

Twenty years later, in 1970, some 78 per cent of Norway's exports still went to Western Europe's two trading blocs, the European Free Trade Association (EFTA) and the EEC.[14] The importance of foreign trade was greater than ever, supplying some 40 per cent of Norwegian gross national product.[15] Shipping remained a vital foreign exchange earner, net freight earnings equalling in 1968, for example, some 40 per cent of the exports of goods and services.[16] But there had been considerable changes in the composition of Norwegian exports, in the relative importance of different markets within Western Europe, and in the country's economic structure. Two-thirds of its exports were still primary products and semi-processed raw materials, but the share of machines and of finished and semi-finished manufactures had risen from 13 per cent in 1960 to 25 per cent. And among primary products and semi-processed raw materials, the share of fish and forest products had fallen, while that of the electro-metallurgical industries had expanded as a result of heavy investment in hydro-electricity and productive capacity.[17] By the late 1960s Norway was producing 5 per cent of the world's raw aluminium and 15 per cent of its magnesium. Within Western Europe it shared with France the position of the largest producer and exporter of aluminium, and it was the largest exporter of magnesium and certain ferro-alloys. These changes in the composition of its exports had been reflected in structural changes in the economy. By 1970 industry was employing 35 per cent of the working population, while the primary sector's share had fallen from 30 per cent in 1950 to 15 per cent.[18]

The main stimulus to these developments had been changes and opportunities in Norway's international markets. Participation in the freeing of industrial trade within EFTA in the 1960s had stimulated Norway's small manufacturing industry into exporting, and by sharpening competition in its home market had turned exporting into a necessity.[19] Its products went mainly to the other Nordic members of EFTA, especially Sweden, where proximity, language, and the already well-established Nordic economic co-operation eased the way for small firms just venturing out. By 1970 the Nordic area was taking a quarter of Norway's exports.[20] Britain, the major EFTA market, was less important as a stimulus to growth in Norway's modern manufacturing sector. But it remained the country's largest single export market, and a very important one for the traditional exports of fish, paper, ores and metals. In the late 1960s it was taking a third of Norway's aluminium exports, half its pulp, a large share of its fish meal and fish oil exports, and by 1970 had also opened a duty-free market to Norway's important frozen fish exports.[21]

The importance of the EFTA market was increased by the relatively high tariffs which the EEC imposed on both Norway's traditional and modern manufacturing exports.[22] Norway had remained outside the EEC in 1957 along with Britain and the rest of Scandinavia, although in 1962 and again in 1967 it had followed Britain and Denmark in unsuccessfully applying for membership. By 1970 the much bigger EEC market was taking no larger a share of Norwegian exports than the Nordic one, and a mere 7 per cent of these were manufactures, three-quarters still coming from the traditional export industries.[23] Within the latter group however the EEC had become a very important market for Norwegian metals, helped by its system of zero or low duty tariff quotas;[24] and metals by then accounted for a third of Norway's exports to the Six. Thus the EEC took some 40 per cent of Norway's raw aluminium exports (slightly more than the EFTA market) and half its ferro-alloys.[25] The prospects for even further expansion looked good — providing that Norwegian products could compete on equal terms and the uncertainties of the annually fixed quota system were removed.

Indeed the EEC offered a generally attractive market for future export growth if its tariffs were lowered or removed. Manufacturing industry would gain a larger market than that offered by EFTA, and the traditional export industries would be able to sell a larger share of their products in a more highly processed and thus more profitable form, which was an important consideration as the supplies of water, timber, and fish on which they were based began to dwindle. That was one reason why most of industry and commerce supported the official policy of seeking membership negotiations along with Britain and Denmark and perhaps even Sweden, which had also asked for negotiations about its relationship with the EEC. There were other reasons as well why industry and commerce supported EEC membership. If Norway did not enter along with these countries it would be put at a competitive disadvantage in the enlarged EEC's markets, which in 1970 were taking, for example, 80 per cent of its aluminium and ferro-silicon exports, 60 per cent of its paper exports and 42 per cent of its fish exports.[26] Denmark was also a major fish exporter, while Sweden was a competitor in the supply of ores, pulp and paper to the industrial economies of the Six. The Norwegians also feared that they would lose the advantages of EFTA's free trade if the other three EFTA members joined the EEC and Norway did not. A complicating factor in these calculations was what would happen if Britain and Denmark entered but Sweden decided to remain outside after all, raising the prospect of new tariff barriers between Norway and Sweden. The Swedish market was by then too important to be put at risk. But the open Swedish application of 1967, which had not specifically ruled out membership, gave some hope that this problem would not arise, and if it did, then Norway would have to seek some other means of preserving free trade between them.

The one major sector of Norway's economy not interested in foreign markets was agriculture. Faced by the rapid modernisation and industrialisation of the Norwegian economy, the farmers' overriding concern was a defensive one, namely to maintain their already shrunken relative position in the economy by keeping the protection they enjoyed against imports and their producer organisations' control over the domestic market. Indeed by 1970 the general outlook of Norwegian agriculture was a deeply defensive one, and this was an essential ingredient in its response to the question of EEC membership. There had been a steady decline in the number of small farms over the previous twenty years, while the agricultural labour force had declined by nearly half and was forecast to decline by a similar percentage in the coming twenty years.[27] It contributed less than 4 per cent to gross national product, employed only 13 per cent of the working population, and was dependent for a substantial part of its income on subsidies from the state, principally in the form of price subsidies tied to sales of milk and grain.[28] Home production did not even cover the major part of Norway's food requirements despite the protection and large financial transfers. It more or less met the country's need for dairy products (the sector from which the small hill and coastal farms derived practically their entire income), but a high proportion of the cereals consumed, especially animal feed grains, had to be imported.

Despite this relative decline as a sector of the national economy, and the fact that domestic production supplied less than half the country's food, agriculture's interests still carried considerable political weight in the formulation of national policy, including trade policy. One reason for this was its crucial importance for regional settlement. Successive governments had encouraged a certain degree of rationalisation, but there was a limit to how far and how fast such a process could go if a population was to be maintained in those large areas of the country where it was the sole or main economic activity. The large income transfers showed the importance all post-war governments had attached to this aspect of agricultural policy, as did the all-party commitment eventually to establish parity between the average agricultural and industrial wage.[29] Another reason why agriculture enjoyed an influential voice in Oslo was that in Norway, as in Sweden and Finland, it had its own political party to protect its interests at the national level.[30] Agriculture had not been submerged in a broad conservative party within which its demands would have to be balanced against those of industry and trade. In 1970 the agrarian Centre party was not only participating in the coalition government, which had been office since 1965, but was providing the country's prime minister. The farmers' producer organisations further helped to ensure them a disproportionate influence in national policy formulation. Nearly all farmers belonged to the co-operatives established for all the main agricultural products. These co-operatives — with their 17 000 full time employees,[31] their legally guaranteed control over most buying, processing, and sale of agricultural products, and their role as the government's negotiating partner in the biennial fixing of price and subsidy levels — represented a national pressure group to be reckoned with by any government.

It was the same concern about maintaining the pattern of settlement which gave the fishermen a disproportionate influence at national level. There were other parallels. There were the same shrinking numbers (down to 3 per cent of the working population) and declining contribution to national income (just over 2 per cent in 1970).[32] There was the same dependence on large income transfers and subsidies, and in the north there was the same predominance of vulnerable small producers. The fishermen also had strong producer organisations, membership of which in their case was compulsory, which controlled access to the industry and all buying and selling of landed fish, and like their counterparts in agriculture set price and subsidy levels in direct negotiations with the government.[33] In other words there was the same combination of a threatened economic position and defensive outlook, on the one hand, and on the other, the existence of powerful producer organisations and a strongly entrenched position in national policy formulation, which the producers themselves regarded as essential bulwarks against any further deterioration in their situation.

Where the parallels ceased was that the fishermen were primarily exporters. So in certain circumstances they might be expected to range themselves alongside industry in favour of trade liberalisation, even if it included primary products. EEC membership, for example, would open a large market for the fresh and frozen fish exports on which the Six maintained high tariffs,[34] while staying outside an enlarged EEC which included Britain and Denmark would put Norwegian fishermen at a serious disadvantage in EEC markets as well as cost them, it was feared, their duty-free access to the important British market. But two things could cut across such an alliance between the interests of industry and fishing. One was that many small fisher-men were still part-time farmers or lived in communities which had close connections with agriculture. The other was uncertainty about how any future EEC fisheries policy would affect Norwegian fishermen's resource and marketing position at home. If it were to threaten the exclusive twelve-mile fishing limit introduced in 1961, or the legal position and powers of their producer organisations, then the trade benefits to be gained from EEC membership might not be worth the sacrifice. The fishermen, although exporters, would be united with the farmers in opposing any international agreements that involved surrendering either the protection they already enjoyed in Norway or the control of production and marketing which gave them a lever on prices and a strong bargaining position in Oslo.[35]

That was an important consideration in Norway, where state control of the economy was extensive. The tradition of public planning went back at least to the 1930s and the impact of the depression, a Labour government and the new econometrics developed at Oslo University's Institute of Economics. Labour's almost unbroken hold on office for the first twenty years after the second world war had ensured the continuation of state intervention during that period. After 1965 the non-socialist coalition which replaced Labour had left its predecessor's objectives and economic policies basically intact be-cause by then their success had won them broad national support. The stable post-war political framework, combined with the homoge-neous character of a state economic administration staffed mainly by men trained in the same school of economics, had enabled the Norwegians to follow consistent policies over a long period. The basic objectives of these policies were a high and stable rate of growth, very low unemployment, and an equalisation of incomes as between social groups and regions.[36] One of the major constraints on the Norwegians' freedom to pursue them had always been their small economy's extreme exposure to international developments over which they had little influence. The perennial problem was how to gain the maximum benefit from an open international economy while simultaneously minimising the loss of independence to pursue na-tionally set objectives. Their solution had been to liberalise industrial trade but retain a tight control on capital movements in and out of the country and on the establishment of foreign firms in Norway. They imported large amounts of capital, but they did so to a con-siderable extent in the form of loans which involved no transfer of ownership.

The loans were used partly to help cover the balance of trade deficits and partly to finance a high rate of capital formation. High rates of personal taxation, low long-term domestic interest rates and state control of credit were other means used to keep investment levels high and concentrate it in sectors approved by the state planners. Steeply progressive rates of direct taxation, income transfers, and a variety of regional policies were used to equalise incomes. A series of four-yearly economic forecasts and programmes had provided the overall medium term framework for economic management since the late 1940s. The success had been impressive. Using an array of policies designed by Norwegians for Norway's peculiar natural and social conditions, they had gone a long way towards achieving many of their objectives. If the growth rate in the 1960s had been no more than average by international standards, it had remained stable.[37] Unemployment had been kept down to a national average of 1 per cent. Rising living standards had been accompanied by greater social and regional equality. Primary sector incomes had risen relative to those of other economic sectors, even if parity was still some way off.[38]

So in Norway in 1970, unlike for example Britain, there was a solid confidence in their ability to manage their own economy. They did not have that record of repeated failures which was causing some people in Britain to look hopefully to the stimulus of a new institutional framework such as the EEC. In Norway there were quite a number of arguments which could be advanced for membership. But a poor performance in handling their economy was not one of them. Rather the reverse. There were not a few Norwegians, inside and outside the economic administration, for whom this success was itself a strong argument against compromising the degree of national control and the national instruments which had produced such results.

Politics

But this was only one of the many arguments which would be heard when it came to deciding how Norway ordered its relations with the EEC. Ultimately the matter would be determined by the balance of power between the major economic, social and political forces in the country at the time the decision had to be made. What these were, and their relative strength, had just been put to the test in a general election held in September 1969. Apart from being a guide to these questions, this election was itself to prove important for the outcome, because almost immediately afterwards the issue of Norwegian membership was re-opened for a third time. It had therefore determined which parties would be in office, and what the balance of parliamentary forces would be, when the Norwegians had to make up their minds.

Regarding the divisions within Norway the election was generally interpreted as showing that the modernisation of its economy had created a society in which, as elsewhere in Western Europe, the basic political division ran between socialists and non-socialists. It was true that the election had underlined the continuing importance of long-standing regional variations in Norwegian politics, notably the character of the southwest as a stronghold of distinct rural cultural and moral values.[39] But fundamentally the country's political structure appeared to be adapting to industrialisation and the accompanying social changes. The economic class division of modern industrial society around which European politics had revolved since the nineteenth century seemed during the 1960s to have become the major political dividing line in Norway too.

On one side of it was the Labour party, flanked to the left by the tiny Communist party (out of parliament since 1957)[40] and the rather larger Socialist People's party (SPP), formed by dissident neutralists expelled from the Labour party in 1960.[41] A coalition between Labour and the SPP, which won two seats in 1961 and again in 1965, had been ruled out by both because of their fundamental disagreement over foreign policy, although the 1961 to 1965 legislative period had demonstrated how an overall socialist majority in parliament could open the way for a minority Labour government relying on SPP support in many domestic questions and on the non-socialist parties in foreign policy. This possibility was excluded after the 1969 election because the SPP was no longer represented in parliament. But Labour had recovered well from its defeat four years earlier, winning seventy-four of the 150 seats, and seemed able to look forward to a return to office after the 1973 election, perhaps even earlier if the non-socialist coalition were to disintegrate.

On the other side were the four non-socialist parties — the Conservatives, Liberals, Christian People's party and agrarian Centre party — which had won a majority in 1965 and formed a coalition.[42] Popularly (and by Labour) they were known as the bourgeois parties. Applied to all four, the label was misleading, as a description of both the parties' voters and programmes. But it accurately expressed the general view of where they stood on the left-right axis of politics, and that what united them was their opposition to socialism. The 1969 election again gave them a parliamentary majority, and so confirmed their coalition in office for a further four years. This was its most important result, both at home and, as it proved, for Norway's relations with Europe. But there were other features of the result which made their victory look more like a political defeat. Labour had reaffirmed its position as by far the largest party. Their majority in parliament had been reduced from ten to two. The coalition's

24

political cohesion had been undermined by changes in the relative strengths of the four parties, partly at each other's expense. Nevertheless their continuation in office despite these internal difficulties, combined with Labour's recovery, seemed to confirm that the division between these two almost equally balanced forces would be the only significant one in Norwegian politics in the coming decade.

But this left-right view was too simple a description of Norwegian politics in 1970. In some respects, for example, there were deeper conflicts of ideology and interest between the coalition parties than between some of them and Labour; certainly the coalition was no monolithic bloc sub-divided only by out-dated party labels and personal ambitions. On the left as well there were important differences, not only between Labour and the flank parties but within the Labour party itself. Some of these differences within the coalition and on the left could be explained in conventional left-right terms: for example the differences between the Conservatives and radical Liberals over economic and social policy, or the left-wing socialists' dislike of Norway's NATO membership. But not all.

To come closer to political reality the left-right view had to be modified by that regional voting map which had re-emerged with greater clarity in 1969. Nor was that surprising in a country where nature and distances still produced such varied economic and social conditions. There was still a gulf between a northern fisherman and an Oslo industrial worker, or between a large farmer in the eastern valleys and a shipowner in one of Norway's major ports. It was partly a question of different economic interests. But it also reflected continuing differences between rural and urban society in a country where each had to a certain extent acquired distinctive linguistic, cultural and even moral characteristics which had frequently stood in opposition to each other during the previous 150 years. It was as much the continuing vitality of these non-economic differences as present economic conflicts, which was reflected in such striking regional voting variations as the Christian People's party's strength in the southwest and the Conservatives' in Oslo. For they had given rise to parties and loyalties with an independent identity and role in national politics, even while they remained closely linked to their economic origins.[43]

The parties most clearly based on the left-right axis were the Conservatives and the three left-wing parties, those on the older town-country axis the agrarian Centre party, the Christian People's party and the Conservatives. The fact that the Conservatives could be ranged squarely on each — but in alliance with the Centre and Christians on the first, while in opposition to them on the second — demonstrated how these two dominant axes in twentieth century Norwegian politics cut through each other and by so doing greatly complicated the pattern of conflicts within society and politics. In varying degrees all the modern parties were the product of this mixture of economic, regional, social and cultural divisions. Their mixed origins still stamped them and their relations with each other in 1970.

The largest party in the coalition was the Conservative party, with its main strength in the capital and surrounding Oslo fjord region. Predominantly urban, defending the virtues of free enterprise while accepting the welfare state and some state intervention, it was preeminently the party of business, industry and shipping. Originally it had been founded as the political organisation of the powerful civil servant class when, after governing Norway for the first half century of the union with Sweden, it found itself challenged by an alliance of farmers and the radical section of Norway's small urban bourgeoisie.[44] Subsequently the party had expanded to include the shipowners and businessmen needing a political vehicle for their struggles with radicals, agrarian interests and the growing working-class movement.[45] Its position in the cultural struggles which enflamed national politics around that time followed naturally from its economic and social character. The Conservatives were fundamentally out of sympathy and usually at odds with the rural cultural and reforming movements from the provinces. They were the defenders of *riksmål,* the Dano-Norwegian language of public and academic life and Oslo society against *landsmål* (literally country speech), the pure Norwegian language constructed on the basis of old provincial dialects which became at once the vehicle of cultural nationalism and of rural opposition to Oslo control. It was the liberal theology of the capital's university and Lutheran state church, and the latter's centralised, clerical control of religious matters, which was the target of the powerful lay Protestant fundamentalist movement whose bastions were in the rural areas of the southwest. The temperance movement closely associated with fundamentalism held as little appeal for the urban middle-class as did *landsmål* or the prayer house. The gulf opened up on the non-socialist side of politics by all these hotly disputed questions was just as deep as that between the Conservatives and socialists. It was so deep as to be seldom politically bridgeable, except in wartime or on a few particular policy issues,[46] until the early 1960s.

The Conservatives' hold on power had been weakened first by the farmers and urban radicals organised in the Liberal party, then by the growing Labour movement, and finally by the introduction of proportional representation in 1920.[47] Nevertheless they had withstood the multi-party system better than had the Liberals, because they defended well-defined economic interests which had no other party to turn to, and because Conservative voters of a thoroughly urban but non-radical disposition had a very limited choice. After the mid-

1930s, however, the avenue to political power had been blocked by Labour and by the Conservatives' own historical differences with the other non-socialist parties. Their problem in that respect was simple and permanent. Unlike Labour (which had never won less than 40 per cent of the votes in a national election after 1933) they were not large enough to govern alone as either a majority or a minority government. Coalition with Labour was ruled out. But the other three non-socialist parties — the so-called 'middle-parties' — disliked the Conservatives too, and none of them would have risked coalescing with it unless the other two were similarly compromised. What finally enabled the Conservatives to break out of this isolation and to move back into power was that the three middle-parties became equally frustrated with permanent opposition, there was an electoral reform in 1952 which favoured the smaller parties at Labour's expense,[48] and then in 1961 the election of two SPP representatives to parliament deprived Labour of its overall majority. In 1963 the four non-socialist parties formed a minority government, though it was very soon brought down by the combined votes of Labour and the SPP.[49] Then in 1965 a non-socialist majority at last provided the parliamentary basis for a stable coalition. For the Conservatives, with no alternative combination if it failed, this coalition was at once a historic political achivement and an alliance it would pay a high price to maintain. Even the losses it suffered in the 1969 election did not alter this fact. It would need very serious disagreements, or an issue of great importance to the party, to make the Conservatives put the coalition at risk or decide themselves to break it up.

The Liberals had been the Conservatives' great rivals in the nineteenth and early twentieth centuries. It was the Liberal party which had forced them out of power in 1884, governed the country for twenty-one of the next thirty-four years and alternated in government with them during the period of unstable minority governments between 1919 and 1935.[50] Originally the organisation through which the landowning farmers and radical bourgeoisie asserted their political rights and economic interests against the civil servants and succeeded in establishing parliamentary control of the executive in 1884, the Liberal party had thereafter continued to provide a political home for Norway's nationalist, provincial, radical and anti-establishment movements. Opponents of union with Sweden, large and small farmers, working-class reformers, rural decentralisers, landsmål speakers, Protestant fundamentalists, teetotallers: the Liberal party had accommodated them all, only periodically splitting as the internal strains of such a heterogeneous collection snapped the organisational bonds. That was at once the party's weakness and the story of its twentieth century decline. One by one the major interest groups broke away to form their own political organisations — first the working-class in the late nineteenth century, then the larger farmers alienated by the predominance of radical urban elements favouring small farmer policies, finally the fundamentalists and teetotallers alienated by a Liberal government's repeal of prohibition in 1926 — leaving the Liberals to continue seeking support from the same disparate sources, but with ever less success as time went by.[51] By the early 1960s they had been reduced to an uneasy alliance whose main pillars were secular urban radicals in the Oslo region, pragmatic moderates in the urban areas of the south and west, and fundamentalists, teetotallers and *landsmål* speakers in the rural areas of the southwest.[52] The great danger for the party was that an issue would arise on which a lowest common denominator could no longer be found to hold such odd political bedfellows together.

When it came to choosing political allies, the Liberals' problem followed naturally from the party's heterogeneous character: they suffered the pull of conflicting attractions, and in a coalition ran the risk of losing whatever distinctive character they still retained. All the possible combinations were dangerous. Any form of alliance with Labour — an idea which held definite attractions for some on the left of the party in 1969[53] — risked driving less radical Liberal voters over to the other two middle-parties and casting the Liberals in the role of a mere extension to Norway's political giant. In the so-called 'middle-alternative' (Liberals, Centre and Christians alone) they risked becoming indistinguishable from the other two or, if they tried to avoid this by taking an independent line, of alienating some of their voters by opposing policies of which they approved. A non-socialist coalition without the Conservatives was ruled out anyway because it could muster less than a third of the seats in parliament. The four-party alternative with the Conservatives could command a parliamentary base, but added to the risks of the middle-alternative the danger of alienating radical Liberals who preferred Labour to the Conservatives. That these were real dangers was shown in 1969, when after four years of coalition the party lost five of its eighteen seats, suffering particularly heavy losses to the Christians in the southwest coastal region.[54] Continuing in coalition seemed like condemning itself to a slow political death. Yet any alternative would probably only mean a swifter demise because breaking up the coalition would bring it general odium among non-socialist voters and leave it isolated in opposition. But it was a restless, dissatisfied party which began the coalition's new term of office, apparently bound to it for lack of any better option, yet with influential sections of the party and the Liberal media in Oslo increasingly looking for a means of breaking out.

One of the heaviest earlier blows to the party had been the establishment of the Agrarian party in 1920.[55] Among its primary objectives then as later were high farm prices, protection against imports, control over national agricultural policy and marketing, and decentralisation of power from Oslo to the local governments where the farmers' influence was greater. Nationalistic and protectionist, the Agrarian party was the political voice of the larger farmers and the forest owners against Oslo, modern industrial society, trade liberalisation and internationalism.[56] In the agricultural producer organisations it possessed something akin to what Labour had in the trade unions, namely closely allied interest organisations wielding influence from the highest national level right down to the individual voter's workplace. As on the socialist side, the leaders of the political and economic wings of the movement tended to move easily and naturally between the two. The Agrarians' strongholds were in the east inland and central regions where the larger farms and forests were situated. For the votes of the farm labourers, forest workers and smallholders, they had to compete with the Labour party, which had early established itself among those less well-off sections of the rural population as well as among the small fishermen and farmers of the peripheries.[57] The Agrarians had survived the post-war decline in agricultural numbers well, however, doubling their parliamentary seats to twenty in the two decades after 1949: the electoral reform in 1952 had helped, and although there were fewer farmers, there were proportionately more of the larger ones who would be more likely to vote Agrarian than Labour. The party had also tried to widen its appeal beyond the farm vote, changing its name to the Centre party in 1959 and thereby claiming for itself a place on the electorally fluid middle ground of Norwegian politics. That had not met with much success during the 1960s, but by 1970 new themes in the political debate such as scarcity of natural resources, pollution and over-centralisation were helping to lend its traditional rural programme a more modern, even progressive, appeal.

Unlike the Conservatives and Liberals, the Centre party had benefited electorally from a coalition whose prime minister, Per Borten, was a popular Centrist politician. Paradoxically however it was Centrists who had shown themselves most ready to put their party objectives before the coalition's survival.[58] The main reason for this was the agricultural organisations' influential position in the party's policy-making organs. Despite the new name, the *raison d'être* of the Centre party remained the promotion of agriculture's interests. To this had recently been added a second factor. Coalition with the Conservatives had always been suspect in certain sections of the party. It was positively disliked by many of the younger members who were becoming increasingly influential by the late 1960s. Propagating a radical populist version of old Agrarian themes, this pressure group within the Centre party looked to the day when the four-party coalition could be replaced by one between the Centre, Liberal and Christian parties alone. So like parts of the Liberal party, it entered the coalition's second term in 1969 with little enthusiasm. If it was not as yet actively working for the coalition's collapse, at least it was not averse to the prospect and might well start doing so if a political situation arose which offered a realistic opportunity of carrying the remainder of the party along with it.

The last of the coalition parties, the Christian People's party, was like the Centre party in wielding a greater political influence than mere parliamentary numbers would suggest. This was because those Christian values which it so rigorously defended were still respected ones far beyond the west and southwest regions where the party's main strength lay; other parties had to be cautious when opposing the Christian People's party. Originally organised in 1933 by former Liberal supporters in those two regions,[59] the heartland of fundamentalism and cultural opposition to the secular, urbanising and centralising forces in modern Norway, the Christians had entered national politics and parliament in 1945 with a programme of national reconstruction on the basis of Christian teaching. Such a Christian party was a common enough phenomenon in post-war Western Europe, but Norway's was unique in being and remaining not a broad inter-denominational coalition of more or less Christian politicians, but a vehicle for anti-clerical puritans and pietists in politics. Religion and social morals were their primary concerns, and issues like restricting the sale of alcohol, religious instruction in schools, family questions and, later, abortion, were the ones on which they took strong stands and initiatives. With an electoral base which resembled Labour's in consisting predominantly of lower income voters, the Christians approved in general of some state intervention and measures for greater economic and social equality. But on the whole the economic questions which were fundamental for the other parties were for them, although certainly not unimportant, secondary. Likewise in foreign affairs it was questions related to the developing countries which most engaged the concern of a party closely connected with the considerable missionary activity of Norway's lay Protestant churches.[60] The Christians had several strengths as a party. One was their solid regional base. Another was the tight network of missionary societies established throughout the country, not only for work abroad but also for preaching and social work at home; these provided the Christians with a grass-roots base similar to those the other parties possessed in their local political organisations.[61] A third and invaluable asset was the internal cohesion conferred by unquestioned acceptance of a set of simple, primary values. For the Christian People's party Christian values and teaching

30

were what agricultural interests were for the Centre party: a readily identifiable and supreme guide to action and an indissoluble political cementing agent.

Next to the Conservatives, the Christian People's party was the party most intent on preserving the coalition. The Christians had benefited from it electorally. They showed a keen appreciation of the opportunities which membership of the government offered for implementing their policies, along with considerable scepticism about the realism of the 'middle-alternative' so attractive to radicals in the Centre and Liberal parties. And, like the Conservatives, the alternative of a formal or even informal alliance with the Labour party was considered out of the question, in the Christians' case because of deep differences over questions of religious education and social morals. The Christians moreover were the party least likely to pose a threat to the coalition's continuation. It was true that their cultural policies had led to clashes with the radical wing of the Liberal party after 1965. But the Christians were not closely bound to the interests of a particular sector of the economy, as were the Conservatives and Centre party. Nor did they have an ideologically radical wing with real influence on party policy, as did the Liberals and, by 1970 at least, the Centre party. So they were unlikely to be found defending sectional economic interests with such uncompromising determination as to threaten the coalition's existence. Nor did any part of the party feel so politically constrained or offended by alliance with the Conservatives as to be predisposed to pull out of the coalition if a suitable opportunity or issue presented itself on which to do so.

The 1969 election had slightly altered the relative strengths of the four parties in parliament. The Conservatives were reduced by two seats to twenty-nine and the Liberals by five seats to thirteen; the Christians were up by one to fourteen and the Centre party by two to eighteen. But this was not reflected in any changes in the government. This had been put together in 1965 only after hard bargaining,[62] and its membership had scarcely changed at all since then,[63] mainly because this would require equally hard renegotiations between the four parties, which could well damage the coalition's stability and prestige. So Per Borten from the Centre party remained prime minister, and the division of posts between the parties stayed the same too, with the Conservatives keeping the ministries most involved in international affairs, including the foreign ministry itself. But this continuity could not disguise the decline in genuine unity which had been taking place over the previous year or so. Slowly but steadily the balance between solidarity and party advantage had been tilting towards the latter under the weight of policy and personality differences and then electoral rivalries. Disagreements had even begun to undermine its ability to pursue clear and consistent policies on some major issues. This weakness at the government level was all the more damaging because the coalition had only a very loose existence in parliament, where the parties had not only continued to act and vote separately but on occasion even to vote against proposals presented by a unanimous government. So what was lost in ministerial unity was unlikely to be made up for by parliamentary co-operation.[64]

The autonomy of the individual coalition parties was reflected in the prime minister's position. Per Borten had been chosen as prime minister by the four parties during the negotiations which followed the 1965 election. Even after his selection it was the parties which had gone on to negotiate the distribution of ministries. So only they could make changes, and when for example the Conservative and Liberal parties reshuffled their leading politicians between government and parliament in 1970 they scarcely consulted the prime minister, treating the matter as a purely internal party affair.[65] Borten's political writ hardly ran beyond the Centre party, and even within that was limited by the greater independence of parliamentary groups in a political system which excluded ministers from sitting in parliament. Within the government Borten was in practice no more than *primus inter pares*. He was a prime minister whose authority depended on continuing agreement between the parties regarding the main lines of government policy and on retaining his ministers' confidence in the future of a government under his leadership.

It was these which were to disappear within a year of the election. The question of EEC membership was to destroy the first, while Borten himself was to contribute in no small measure to the disappearance of the second by his increasingly ambiguous position on this major question. Some maintained that Borten's personality was the key factor here:[66] that it made ambiguity an almost natural position for him to adopt on such a controversial issue. But the weakness of his position *vis-à-vis* government colleagues and his own party probably played an important part too. For the pattern of public statements alternating between formal support for government policy and implied agreement with a diverging Centre party one, which became so familiar in 1970, was nothing new or confined to the EEC question. It had already characterised Borten's handling of other questions which had caused serious disagreements between the coalition parties, and was probably his way of trying to balance between a government and party on neither of which he could impose his authority.[67] But it was a method which depended on the existence of sufficient political will in all four parties to maintain the coalition despite its internal disagreements, and on their differences being bridgeable by compromises and verbal imprecisions. In the case of EEC membership that was not possible, and Borten's ambiguity not only ultimately failed to enable him to balance between the opposing views, but itself contributed to the outcome he probably least desired, namely the collapse of the coalition he headed.

The coalition was also weakened by the aftermath of the Conservative and Liberal parties' losses in the September 1969 election. The election result sharpened their dissatisfaction with Per Borten as prime minister. It increased the Liberals' restlessness. In both parties it led to leadership changes which ultimately weakened the government's standing and cohesion and strengthened the individual parties at its expense. Both parties' chairmen were replaced in the first half of 1970 by politicians who had been in the government since 1965, but who then transferred back to parliament in order to combine the leadership of their parties' parliamentary groups with the post of chairman.[68] Rightly or wrongly these moves were interpreted in some quarters as proof of their loss of confidence in the coalition's future: they were said to be transferring their political platforms back to parliament in the expectation that power would increasingly shift towards the parties and their parliamentary groups as the government's paralysis over relations with the EEC deepened.[69] This reading of the situation was reinforced by the sudden retirement of John Lyng, the long-serving Conservative foreign minister and generally acknowledged architect of the coalition, just one month before Norway's negotiations with the EEC opened in June 1970. With his departure the coalition also lost one of its strongest personalities and pillars. The presence in parliament of the new Conservative and Liberal chairmen, Kåre Willoch and Helge Seip, might have been an advantage for the coalition had it been united on policy. But as its seemingly irreconcilable differences over EEC membership became apparent the effect was the opposite. The sharpened confrontations in parliament between strongly and vocally led groups only worsened the atmosphere. That, in turn, made co-operation in government even more difficult.

Labour was the party which at the time seemed to have most to gain from all this. In 1970 Labour was the largest and best organised party in Norway. The long years in government after the mid-1930s had drawn into its ranks a substantial number of the country's best administrative and academic talents. But its electoral strength still lay in that alliance forged in the early twentieth century between the workers of town and country: between the industrial workers, the fishermen, small farmers and forestry workers. It was strongest in the industrial southeast and the north, in the urban areas and economic peripheries; weakest in the south and west, where the less marked economic inequalities and the continuing vitality of rural cultural and religious traditions had modified the impact of modern class conflicts. Appealing to town and country, and being so spread geographically and socially, Labour had had to have room for *riksmål* and *landsmål* speakers, for teetotallers and opponents of temperance, and for voters with strong religious beliefs or none; on the whole these old Norwegian conflicts had assumed much less importance on the socialist side of politics than on the non-socialist side. It was also Labour which had given the primary producer organisations their powerful position,[70] but which at the same time had set as its objective the modernisation and industrialisation of the economy. Labour, in short, had succeeded in spanning the country and many of its numerous economic and social divisions. In normal times this was its strength. It was to be a weakness when an issue arose, such as EEC membership, which set all these various sources of support pulling strongly in opposite directions.[71]

Labour's defeat in 1965 had been variously attributed to the electorate's wish for a change after nearly thirty years of Labour government, a changing social structure, the reformed electoral system, and the way this had helped the Socialist People's party to make inroads into traditional Labour strongholds in the northern and industrial constituencies while splitting the socialist vote elsewhere.[72] The party's recovery in 1969 appeared to confound the predictions of long-term decline, especially as half the first-time voters had chosen Labour.[73] Up in the northern fishing communities too the party had recovered all its 1965 losses to the SPP.[74] With over 46 per cent of the vote, a squabbling coalition and its left-wing rival out of parliament, Labour seemed able to look forward to a period of strong opposition followed by a return to office.

The Socialist People's party, which had gained 6 per cent of the vote in 1965 only to lose nearly half of it again in 1969, had been a political thorn in Labour's left flank ever since its establishment. It not only competed for the same voters, but for Labour's left-wing was a permanent reminder of doctrinal purity and a source of recurrent *crises de conscience*.[75] Basically the SPP was a two-pillar alliance between urban left-wing pacifists and neutralists and a variable percentage of fishermen, workers and radicals in the peripheries, especially the north.[76] Its success up there was hardly surprising: relatively poor and disadvantaged for so long, it was the north which had returned the first Labour representatives to parliament in 1903[77] and its northernmost constituency of Finnmark still in 1969 gave the Communists 4 per cent of the vote compared to a national average of 1 per cent.[78] When Labour was in office some of the fishermen, smallholders and workers dissatisfied with the government in particular or just conditions in general had shown themselves ready to vote for another left-wing party if it presented itself. But in 1969, after four

34

years out of office, voting Labour had itself become once more a way of complaining about low fish prices, bad catches or foreign trawlers spoiling the nets. The SPP, however, although weakened and demoralised after its defeat,[79] was still there as an alternative for them and a permanent threat to Labour.

These northern fishermen and Oslo socialists had one thing in common which they shared with Centrist farmers, with Christian People's party voters for whom radical socialism was anathema, and even with some of the sophisticated economic planners in the capital's central administration. They stood on the same side of one more of the numerous divisions within this small population of less than four million. This one cut right across the predominant left-right axis of politics, and many Norwegians were to find their place on one side or the other of it only hesitatingly and with difficulty.[80] But within almost exactly three years of the 1969 election the large majority were to have done so, creating two almost equal blocks on either side of it. What separated them was their response to the type of international co-operation and modern industrial economy and society developing in the EEC, and their position on the question of how far and in what way Norway should participate in it. On one side would be those who regarded the EEC, and especially the prospect of joining it, as a threat to a way of life and doing things which they wished to preserve or establish. Some of these would see their economic interests directly threatened, others their cultural and moral values, others their social and political objectives within Norway itself. The groups on the other side of this division were to be equally various. But what united them would be that with differing degrees of enthusiasm they welcomed, accepted or simply considered unavoidable Norway's accommodation to the modern Europe being created to the south. It was not too difficult to predict roughly where this line would run and to which side of it the main economic interests and political parties would tend. What was foreseen by few as the new decade opened was the depth of this division, the way it was to be capable of dissolving long-standing political loyalties, and the way in which for nearly three years it was to dominate political life.

Foreign Policy[81]

The decision about joining the EEC was one which spanned the normal boundary line between domestic and foreign policy in a way that was obvious for all to grasp. It was foreign policy in that it concerned the country's relations with other European states. But it would also affect their own daily lives more directly (if not necessarily more profoundly) than other aspects of Norway's foreign relations, such as its NATO membership. The fisherman or farmer could see that it would alter where decisions were taken that bore directly on his job and standard of living: decisions about fish prices, milk prices, and subsidy levels. It would affect who took these decisions: whether it remained his own producer organisations bargaining directly with the government, or became instead the government in distant Oslo bargaining with other governments in even more distant Brussels. He knew that what was involved here was not just the future organisation of relations between the states of Western Europe, but the distribution of power inside Norway itself: the power of various groups in relation to each other and over their own affairs.

So what was at stake in the long run was the shape and direction of Norwegian society. Without the protection against imports and large subsidies, the small dairy farmer, for example, did not see how he could remain competitive. It might be true that the development of Norway's economy and society would be more or less the same whether they joined the EEC or not. Their economy was too open and too dependent on Western Europe for them to avoid being fundamentally influenced by these external international developments. But still there was a difference between 'more' and 'less'. And it was this difference which many thought so important.

The way in which this question of relations with the EEC reached right into the domestic sphere and became entangled with internal politics was what distinguished it from most other foreign policy questions. It also partly explains the bitter and deep disagreements unknown in Norway over any other issue of external relations since independence. It was why in the end it had to be decided by the balance of economic and social forces within the country. That in turn — because some of the major divisions over the EEC did not conform to the normal left-right pattern of politics — was why the main dividing line over the EEC did not coincide with the other major aspect of Norway's foreign relations, its security policy.

On this the division ran between the far left and the rest, as it generally did in post-war Western Europe.[82] Membership of the Atlantic alliance, the foundation of Norway's foreign policy since 1949, was supported by all the large parties and according to public opinion polls by a big majority of the electorate too.[83] In this case parties and people could see very clearly that their security was at stake as it was not, at least not so directly and obviously, in the decision about entering the EEC. NATO was concerned with the inviolability of Norway's frontiers, not how they arranged their affairs inside them. It did not interfere in agricultural policy or fishing limits, with the regulations governing capital flows, or with the level of taxes on alcohol. So Centre party farmers were among the staunchest NATO supporters, as were Christian People's party voters. Even left-wing members of the Labour party, if with inner reservations and some distaste, had gone along with a security policy based on the American guarantee.

It was recent history which had been decisive for all these groups when the Labour government took Norway into the Atlantic alliance in 1949, thereby finally breaking that post-1905 tradition of neutrality and non-involvement in European great power politics to which it had briefly tried to return in 1945. The German invasion and occupation had taught them that neutrality was no defence against aggression by a large power. Only peacetime guarantees of external assistance, not international law or Norway's own small military forces, would deter a potential aggressor. It had also demonstrated the value and vulnerability of the country's strategic position and coastline, and had accustomed Norwegians to working in alliance with the Western powers. These lessons, but especially the experience of sudden attack and occupation, were what had made the Norwegians reject a Swedish solution when the Cold War turned the Soviet Union from a wartime liberator into a very present threat on its northern frontier.

In the twenty years since 1949 the Atlantic alliance had given Norway the security it sought and provided the stable primary framework for its foreign policy. The country's self-imposed ban on the siting of NATO bases and nuclear weapons on its territory in peacetime had been designed primarily to reassure the Soviet Union. It had not prevented Norway from otherwise participating fully in all alliance activities, especially the system of political consultations, to which it attached such importance as a source of information and a means of influencing the policies of its larger allies. As in other Western European countries there were differences of emphasis on some alliance questions involving other members (decolonisation, for example, and United States policy in Vietnam and towards Greece). But the broad consensus in support of NATO membership had helped to ensure that foreign policy was not on the whole a major issue between the large parties or among the public at large.

The same pattern of widespread consensus, differences of emphasis within it, and a basically different line from the small left-wing, was repeated in the case of the Nordic region. In 1949 Norway had rejected the idea of a neutral Scandinavian defence pact with Sweden and Denmark in favour of the Atlantic alliance, and this parting of the ways over security policy had set the limits for their subsequent relations. Norway, Iceland and Denmark belonged to NATO, Sweden was non-aligned, Finland had its special relationship with the Soviet Union. This had not prevented close economic co-operation (such as the creation of a common labour market) or the establishment of inter-parliamentary institutions (the Nordic Council in 1952) or even very close and increasingly formalised foreign policy consultations between their governments. But no government in Oslo — or in Copenhagen, Helsinki or Stockholm for that matter — would have allowed regional co-operation to affect its chosen security policy or (except in Sweden's case) its primary relationship with countries outside the region. The differences within this Norwegian consensus about Nordic policy concerned the extent and type of economic co-operation compatible with NATO membership and the way such co-operation would affect the interests of various sectors of the Norwegian economy. But they were manageable because of this agreement on the fundamental lines of policy, and because despite its greater economic importance by 1969 and the ties of shared culture, language and history, the Nordic area was of essentially secondary importance within the overall framework of Norwegian foreign policy.

For those who wanted to break away from the Atlantic alliance or whose commitment to it was less than wholehearted, the Nordic area had quite a different importance. For the former — crypto-neutralists in the Labour party, the SPP and Communists — it offered an alternative foreign policy framework and a means of freeing Norway from the Atlantic one by means of ever closer co-operation with neutral Sweden and Finland. For the halfhearted Atlanticists it represented a counter-weight to an over-close identification and co-operation with the Western powers on questions and in areas beyond the alliance's strictly military functions and North Atlantic scope. Like the belief in distinctive Nordic political and cultural values, this was a view of the place of Nordic co-operation in Norwegian foreign policy which had always found support in some Labour party circles. But by the later 1960s it was also gaining ground in other parties such as the Liberal party's radical wing and in all the youth organisations except the Conservative party's.

Yet another version of the 'Nordic alternative' had been appearing during the 1960s though. This was Nordic co-operation as an alternative and barrier to joining the EEC. Foreshadowing the alliances of 1970-72, it was supported both by those whose ultimate aim was a new security policy and by Atlanticists who envisaged little more than a continuation of the limited post-1949 co-operation which left Norway's NATO membership untouched. For both groups Nordic co-operation had a political value less for itself than for what could be achieved or avoided by means of it. 'Nordic co-operation' had become in some circles a euphemism for 'keep Norway out of the EEC' or 'take Norway out of NATO'. Hence the heavy political overtones which projects for extending Nordic economic co-operation had always had since the second world war, and never more so than by the late 1960s.

For those who wanted Norway to leave or limit its participation in NATO, United Nations membership and relations with developing countries had the same element of being a means to an end, not just an end in themselves: they offered alternative foreign policy priorities and a means of eventually loosening or counter-balancing Norway's ties with the Atlantic alliance. The pattern seen in the Nordic region was repeated here. Again it was a case of the neutralists, communists, and those who went along with NATO membership without liking it, attaching a much higher priority and altogether different significance to an aspect of Norway's external relations that the majority also thought important, but definitely secondary. In public statements Norwegian foreign ministers and diplomats might emphasise the high priority they attached to the United Nations, but it was NATO's ministerial council which they regarded as the central forum for their country's diplomacy. Similarly, Norwegian governments had given diplomatic and financial support to decolonisation movements throughout the 1950s and 1960s. But they had done so without at any time calling into question Norway's political as well as economic integration into the industrialised Western world: into not only its trading system and economic organisations, but its network of political institutions and contacts and its security system.

Indeed Norway's whole post-war history had been one of increasing integration into these. And it was from this perspective that many Norwegians regarded the question of joining an enlarged EEC. For them the EEC was but one more example, if a very important one, of this process of Western integration, and Norwegian membership would be but one further stage in Norway's fuller participation in it. Entering the EEC would be a continuation of the country's post-war foreign policy, not a new departure.[84] Moreover it would be a continuation which over the last eight years had been set in motion through an application for membership negotiations by two different governments, together representing all Norway's major parties, and which had twice been approved with large majorities by parliament. Some might not like it; more might be unenthusiastic. But that the process should be reversed after receiving such endorsement seemed to many unthinkable, and probably to most very unlikely.

2. Norway and the EEC

Yet three years later this widespread view that Norway was set on a course for EEC membership if only the external obstacles were removed was proved wrong.[1] Norway did not join with the other applicants, and the process of integration was checked. Partly this was the result of events during the years of negotiations and campaigning which led up to the referendum in September 1972. But it was also because the expectation of what would happen if ever the EEC opened the way to enlargement was based on a misreading of the situation in Norway by the time the 1970s opened.

It was known from public opinion polls that EEC membership had never received the support of more than about a quarter of the electorate.[2] There had always been a large percentage who were undecided, and the remainder were divided as between an association or free trade agreement, or no agreement at all. Public opinion was important because the Labour government which was in office when the question first arose in 1961 had promised to hold a referendum before parliament took its final decision, and the non-socialist coalition which succeeded it had reaffirmed this commitment. Although the constitution did not provide for referenda, they had been held before on four other major political questions: the dissolution of the union with Sweden and the choice between a monarchy and a republic in 1905, prohibition of the sale of spirits in 1919, and the repeal of prohibition seven years later. The proposal that one should be held on the highly controversial decision to enter the EEC was difficult to reject once it had been publicly launched,[3] and once the government and political parties had made the concession it was politically impossible to retract. Whether members of parliament would feel bound by the result when the time came would depend perhaps on the character of the campaign and the size of the majority one way or the other. Most politicians seemed to accept that, although the referendum would formally be only a consultative one, the result would in practice be binding on them and therefore decide the matter.

Yet the prospect of one after nearly a decade of adverse public opinion polls was not regarded as a serious argument against expecting

Norway to join the EEC if Britain entered and acceptable terms could be negotiated. Underlying this sanguine attitude seemed to be two assumptions. The first was that membership would receive fairly solid backing from most of those groups which normally had the greatest influence on the electorate in such questions: the politicians, press, administration, and large economic organisations.[4] Some opposition existed in these circles, notably in the primary sector and political parties close to it. But it was considered a minority view lacking a convincing alternative — a reading of the situation apparently confirmed by the 1967 parliamentary vote in favour of applying for membership negotiations, because on that occasion many of those who had opposed it in 1962 had reversed their position. The second assumption was that the electorate was on the whole easily influenced: that if most of the leading politicians and interest organisations declared membership to be necessary and the terms acceptable, then the voters would follow this advice and produce a referendum result which coincided with the view of the majority in parliament. Again this seemed to have been confirmed in 1967, by the way in which public opinion had swung in a more favourable direction in line with the trend of voting in parliament.[5]

The second assumption — that the voters' choice would depend on the influence brought to bear on them — was not necessarily proved wrong in September 1972. Some described the 'no' as a victory for the independence of mind of the 'man in the street'.[6] It seems more probable, however, that what it really reflected was the greater success of those who campaigned to persuade people to vote that way, because the first assumption — of a fairly solidly united establishment — was definitely wrong by 1969, if it had ever been justified. It was true that there was a large majority for membership in parliament and the administration, but even there the minority opposed to it was far from negligible. In not a few of the economic, social and cultural organisations outside but close to the normal centres of political power, it was even larger. In that respect, as in several others, the situation had been changing since the conventional view crystallised in 1967.

1945-61

When Norway joined Britain in EFTA instead of the continental Europeans in the EEC at the end of the 1950s, it was simply continuing along well-established lines of policy towards Europe. One of these was to keep in step with Britain: to avoid coming into conflict with

British policy in security matters or endangering Norway's considerable economic interests in British markets. This principle of Norwegian foreign policy went back to the nineteenth century when the British navy controlled the sea-lanes vital to the country's shipping and trade, took a substantial part of Norway's timber exports, and in effect played the role of guarantor of Norwegian neutrality.[7] By the 1950s Britain no longer dominated the seas and Norway relied principally on the United States for its security. But Britain was still Norway's largest export market, while the recent wartime alliance had strengthened the ties of sentiment and the old habit of looking to Britain for a lead. The vital post-war security relationship with the United States, moreover, had had the effect of intensifying Norway's traditional westward orientation. More than ever the Norwegians looked westwards, particularly in security and political questions, rather than southwards towards the continent. Indeed after the second world war they regarded any close co-operation with Western Europe that did not also include Britain and the United States as a potential threat to their much more important relationship with the two Anglo-Saxon naval powers, which controlled the Atlantic and were alone in a position to afford Norway effective protection.

Keeping in line with Britain in European questions after 1945 was made easier by the two countries having very similar views on the form which Western European co-operation should take.[8] Both favoured traditional inter-governmental arrangements and rejected the supra-national proposals originating from the continental countries which were later to establish the EEC. In the Norwegians' case this was partly a reflection of their general attitude towards the countries in question. Links with continental Europe, especially with the culturally alien Latin countries, were traditionally weak. Anti-German feeling was strong as a result of the war. The Norwegians were also sceptical about the viability of democratic institutions in some of the countries to the south. But it was two other factors which were chiefly responsible for their reluctance to surrender any sovereignty to a Western European organisation. The first was their fear of endangering the all-important Anglo-Saxon connection. The other was simply the Norwegians' wish to retain the fullest possible control over their own domestic affairs, which they had just regained after five years of German occupation;[9] the Labour government in particular wanted a free hand in its planning for economic recovery and social reform. The most effective way of maintaining that control seemed to them to be the establishment of strict limits on the powers of any international organisation of which Norway was a member. Indeed the Norwegian constitution expressly forbade the transfer to international organisations of powers invested by it in Norwegian institutions.[10] It was a defensive, legalistic approach to international co-operation. But it was the traditional Norwegian answer to the problem of preserving as much as possible of a small country's genuine independence.

Before the second world war they had tried to do this by limiting their involvement in international politics generally, and especially in European politics.[11] Neutrality had expressed not only a small nation's fear of being a pawn in great power politics, but the hope that by demonstratively keeping out of them, they would be left at peace and in control of their own affairs within their national frontiers. As a policy for achieving these two objectives, the doctrine of limited involvement had manifestly failed in April 1940. The invasion and occupation had convinced many Norwegians that the best way of remaining in control at home was to co-operate with others abroad, and especially with large powers which could provide the protection they so obviously needed. So after the war a policy of participation had replaced non-involvement as regards military alliances and international affairs generally.[12] But there had remained the clear limitation on the form of co-operation and on the powers which could be surrendered for the sake of it.

Until the end of the 1950s this created no problems. The international organisations Norway joined, notably the United Nations, NATO, the Organisation for European Economic Co-operation (OEEC), EFTA, and the Nordic Council, permitted them to enjoy the advantages of close co-operation with other countries while retaining the constitutional ban on any derogation from the powers of their national authorities. In these organisations the forms of national sovereignty were maintained. The commitments entered into involved some limitation on their freedom of action, but in return they gained a voice in international decisions and agreements which would have affected them anyway. Participation was seen as giving them a greater degree of real, if indirect, control over their own affairs. The only serious challenge to this traditional type of international co-operation came from the six continental countries which in 1957 established the EEC. In that organisation powers belonging to national parliaments and administrations were to be progressively transferred to EEC institutions, majority voting was intended eventually to replace unanimity, and in the commission there was a body specifically designed to act as the motor and guardian of supra-nationality. However as long as Britain remained outside to lead EFTA, the rival trading group, the EEC's existence did not worry the Norwegians too much. Britain's policy meant that they faced no conflicts between their preference for avoiding supra-national arrangements if possible, their Atlantic orientation, and their tradition of following Britain's lead in European affairs. Indeed as the 1950s drew to a close, these main strands of Norwegian policy appeared to be as much in harmony as they had been throughout the preceding fifteen years.

Despite this some Norwegians had been asking since the early 1950s how long they could continue to be so inflexible about where the line was drawn for their participation in international co-opera-tion.[13] Did it always have to be at the point at which co-operation required a transfer of powers from domestic to international bodies? Or ought it instead to be decided from case to case in the light of the Norwegian interests involved and the net gain or loss in terms of genuine control over their own affairs? The second course would involve a political judgement instead of a legal one and thus be more appropriate, they argued, to a world in which in some areas the boundary between national and international decision-making was becoming increasingly blurred. It would also ensure that legal obstacles did not prevent Norway from participating in new forms of internation-al co-operation which its economic or political interests would be best served by joining.

The first signs of thinking about constitutional reform, in 1952, came against the background of the moves being made at that time towards Western European integration and received the encourage-ment of the foreign minister, Halvard Lange.[14] The immediate impetus was the prospect of an American supported European Defence Com-munity; there was some concern that a Norwegian refusal to participate in it could damage Norway's relations with the United States and weaken its position in NATO. The idea of a constitutional amend-ment, which would make possible a transfer of powers to such a European organisation if necessary, was thus a step mooted not out of enthusiasm for European co-operation as such, but in order to safeguard a vital Norwegian interest, in this case the Atlantic security relationship. As such it was typical of the Norwegians' basic approach to European co-operation, and the EEC in particular, over the next twenty years. When the proposed defence community foundered on French opposition, the spur to reform disappeared and the subject lapsed.

It did not drop out of sight entirely however. Labour parliamen-tarians were sympathetic towards the idea, especially those active in European organisations like the Council of Europe,[15] while the prag-matic argument of loosening the constitutional constraint on defending Norwegian interests carried weight with those responsible for con-ducting the country's foreign policy.[16] The subject was raised again in 1956, and although parliament rejected reform on that occasion, sup-port for the idea gradually increased over the next four years as the Conservatives and some Liberals and Christians parted company with the Centre party and came to favour the idea. By 1960 the necessity of an eventual amendment to the constitution seemed to be accepted by all but a minority of parliamentarians, and the principle point at issue was now the exact terms on which specific powers could be transferred to an international organisation, in particular the size of the majority which would be required to do so.[17] But the urgency which would have caused the government to push for reform and bring the matter to a decision was absent. There was no pressing issue to force the pace, and the one which would have done so — the question of joining the EEC — was not a subject of serious political discussion. The Norwegians themselves had no wish to join the EEC, and with Britain outside it there was no pressure on them to think about doing so.

The first application 1961-63

The situation changed when Britain applied to join the EEC in July 1961 and was immediately followed by Denmark. If their applications were successful some three-quarters of Norway's exports would be going to the enlarged EEC, with Britain, the Norwegians' largest export market, behind its common external tariff.[18] EFTA would disappear or lose much of its importance. The long-term political consequences seemed as serious. For if the EEC succeeded in developing the system of close political co-operation then under discussion among its members, the paths of Britain and Norway might diverge not only economically but in foreign affairs too.

The British application forced the Norwegians to think seriously about EEC membership for the first time. The main lines of their post-war policy towards Europe had diverged, and they had to decide which would receive priority. It was true that parliamentarians had slowly been accustoming themselves to the idea of a closer form of international co-operation than was permitted under the constitution as it stood. But outside the small circle of people closely concerned with foreign affairs, most of the country's politicians and political parties, and certainly the great majority of voters, were quite unprepared for the decisions they now had to make. Many, probably most, knew very little about the EEC. The idea of joining it was new and unexpected, and required them to re-think their relations with continental Europe and with the Atlantic world to which they felt much closer.

It was April 1962, nine months after the British application, before the Labour government had requested and received from parliament a mandate to apply to the EEC for negotiations about full membership. This long gap between the two applications was not, however, due to any serious doubts in the government about the necessity of doing so, but rather to the time required for the political and constitutional preparations.[19] Faced by the sudden reversal of British policy, the government in Oslo saw no alternative but to follow suit. Membership was made conditional on the terms, of course, and especially on adequate safeguards for the primary sector. There was also to be a consultative referendum after the completion of negotiations and before parliament's final vote on the matter. But there seemed few in the government or central administration who doubted that if Britain joined Norway would have to do so as well.

British policy was thus the decisive factor in 1961-62.[20] It still acted as an irresistible magnet for most Norwegian politicians, who regarded it as practically unthinkable to diverge from Britain on such a major issue: if Britain joined then Norway must, and if Britain's negotiations failed then Norway would also stay outside. The economic arguments seemed overwhelming to the government and to many on the opposition benches. The exporters claimed that trade would suffer heavily if they stayed outside an enlarged EEC. Shipping urged that they join in order to be in a position to influence any future EEC shipping policy in a non-protectionist way. The foreign policy and security arguments pointed in the same direction. The predominant view was that Norway's long-term security would be undermined if it isolated itself from an organisation which included all the major Western European NATO member states and seemed set on deepening its political as well as economic integration. The prospect of entering along with Britain also eased some of the Norwegians' major worries about the EEC. It was assumed that Britain could be relied on to resist any unwelcome development of supra-national institutions as well as buttress the forces of democracy within the continental member states. Even more important, the Norwegians were confident that an EEC which included Britain would be firmly turned towards the Atlantic, thereby ruling out any danger of their new continental commitments weakening Norway's ties with the United States.

This permanent concern about their relationship with the United States was another important element in the Labour government's thinking in 1961-62, just as it had been a decade earlier when Halvard Lange encouraged the idea of constitutional reform. They suddenly woke up to the fact that the Americans were very much in favour of European unification and the EEC. The Kennedy administration was encouraging it as the pre-requisite for a strong Atlantic alliance. If the EEC was thus marked out to be the European pillar of an 'Atlantic partnership', then the Norwegians risked being pushed onto the sidelines of Atlantic co-operation if they stayed outside when it was enlarged. So by early 1962 joining the EEC seemed to have become a necessary means to Norway's primary foreign policy objective of maintaining the United States' commitment to defend their country and Norway's place in Western security co-operation.

Some of the other earlier reasons for ruling out EEC membership had also lost much of their weight by the early 1960s. Anti-German feeling had not disappeared (as the debate about the first application showed), but after several years of co-operation in the OEEC (after 1961 OECD) and NATO it was at least no longer the potent force and constraint on government policy that it had been earlier. After a decade of liberalising trade within the OEEC and EFTA, Norwegian manufacturing industry felt rather more confident about facing competition from the EEC countries. The government and economic planners too were more confident about their ability to control the domestic economy even with a considerable degree of free trade and more liberal capital movements. In short the experience of international co-operation and competition in the previous decade had gone some way towards removing that defensiveness which, with one outstanding exception, namely the shipping community, had characterised the Norwegians' attitude towards international involvements ever since independence.

Having reached its decision that Norway must apply for membership, the government had to get it accepted by its own party and parliament. In doing this it had several advantages which the Labour government in office ten years later was not to enjoy. The suddenness with which the question had arisen and the widespread unfamiliarity with it meant that, initially at least, there were not only many voters, but also many politicians and party activists who had no very firm position on it. Inside the Labour party in particular there was probably a greater willingness to accept the leadership's view of the matter than there was to be in 1972. The prime minister and Labour party chairman, Einar Gerhardsen, who had headed successive governments for most of the post-war period, enjoyed an authority and firm control over his party's policy and organisation which his successor as chairman after 1965, Trygve Bratteli, with his very different personality and conception of party leadership, was not even to attempt to emulate. It helped too that the young Norwegians of 1961 very quickly discovered their European idealism in response to the prospect of entering the EEC. The early 1960s was the period when the idea of European unification made its greatest appeal to politically interested young people in Western Europe, and Norway now proved to be no exception. Labour's youth organisation declared itself in favour of membership, and so did the other two major party youth groups, the Conservatives and Liberals.[21]

But Labour was split on the question and so were the party's voters.

It very soon became clear that the conflicts and alliances over the EEC were going to differ from the normal pattern.[22] The government's staunchest allies, for example, were the Conservatives. Labour's main opponent in domestic politics, the Conservatives were united with it now in according highest priority to the interests of shipping and the major export industries and to maintaining Norway's ties with Britain and its place in the Atlantic alliance. The economic philosophy behind the Treaty of Rome was close to their own. The economic interests they represented were, with a few exceptions,[23] overwhelmingly in favour of membership. The security policies and general political complexions of the EEC states were more congenial to the Conservatives than those of the Nordic countries, the attraction of co-operation with which always exerted a pull away from Western Europe for some in the Labour party. So the Conservatives were united in supporting an application for membership and were the only party apart from the Centrists and the two small left-wing ones which suffered no serious splits over the question. Those Liberals and Christians who supported membership did so for much the same reasons as the government and Conservatives: the interests of trade and shipping, the pull of British policy, and anxiety lest staying out should gradually cut Norway off from the mainstream of Atlantic co-operation. But while it was Christian People's party voters in urban areas who tended to be more open to such arguments, the pattern was more complicated in the Liberal party. There, apart from a section of the radical urban wing which temporarily swung right over to advocating a federal Europe, the main source of support for membership came from Liberal voters in the towns and rural areas of the south and west,[24] where they had become accustomed through decades of participation in local government to adopting a more pragmatic, less ideological position than their fellow Liberals in the Labour and Conservative-dominated east.[25] This pro-market alliance between most of the Labour party, the Conservatives, and parts of the Liberal and Christian parties had on its side the bulk of the press and the economic organisations representing the two sides of industry, the employers' federation of Norwegian industries and the confederation of trade unions. It was an unusual line up in Norwegian politics, but it appeared a very strong one.

The combination opposing it was equally unusual in the 1960s, but with clearly traceable antecedents in earlier Norwegian history. It also demonstrated how the lines drawn over the EEC differed from those over security policy. The pro-NATO middle-parties were all represented, allied now with the neutralist SPP and pro-Soviet communists under the banner of 'national sovereignty'. The whole of the Centre party was there, in keeping with its nationalistic, protectionist outlook and its consistent opposition to new forms of international co-operation. As the political vehicle of the farmers whose interest organisations strongly opposed EEC membership, the Centrists argued against a step which would mean the end of import controls and a national agricultural policy. Most of the Oslo-dominated Liberals in the east, traditional defenders of national values and national independence, rejected it as a threat to Norway's freedom of action in international affairs and in economic and social policy at home. As a platform to advocate their views they had the country's second largest newspaper, *Dagbladet*. The anti-market Christians were led by those fundamentalist, rural opponents of centralisation and secular values in the south and west. In opposing membership they were continuing the struggle they had been waging against these trends within Norway itself for the past century. Inside the EEC, they feared government would become even more distant, bureaucratic and centralising, the threat to the cultural and moral values they sought to uphold even greater. Fundamentalists, farmers, city radicals: looking at this middle-party anti-market alliance some Norwegians recognised in it the revival of an earlier powerful combination. It was the same alliance of economic interests and ideology which had challenged and defeated the central government and bureaucracy in Oslo in the 1880s and then gone on to generate that assertion of nationalism which led to the break up of the union with Sweden in 1905.[26] The question was whether it would prove as powerful in modern industrial Norway of the 1960s as it had done eighty years before.

The anti-marketeers on the left came from the Labour party as well as the SPP and Communist party. Labour supporters rejected their government's policy on grounds that ranged from the national, economic and cultural arguments of the middle-parties to the specifically socialist ones which were also to be heard in the other applicant countries. They disliked the predominantly conservative governments and free enterprise economies of the countries to which Norway would become so closely bound. They disliked the liberal capitalist principles of the Treaty of Rome. They feared that being in the EEC would deprive the Norwegian government and parliament of that control over the economy necessary to pursue socialist policies and reforms at home. General foreign policy considerations also lay behind their opposition to membership, unlike many of the middle-party anti-marketeers who drew a sharp distinction between the EEC and the Atlantic alliance, emphasising their support for the second but disputing that that now required them to agree to join the first. The left socialists made a clear connection between foreign policy and EEC membership (as did most pro-marketeers). On the left of the Labour party the decision to join the Atlantic alliance in 1949 had always been regarded an an unfortunate departure from Norway's pre-war neutrality. Those who took this view were consequently extremely reluctant now to travel even further along that road by integrating Norway into an organisation which they considered little more than the European wing of NATO. A similar combination of ideological and foreign policy considerations explained the SPP's attitude. For a party whose ultimate aim was a non-aligned, socialist Norway, the EEC was a double anathema.

Although by spring 1962 the supporters and opponents of membership were almost equally balanced in the electorate,[27] the former predominated in parliament. In March the dilatory debates about constitutional reform were finally brought to an end when an amendment was passed enabling parliament to transfer to an international organisation the right to exercise powers constitutionally vested in Norwegian authorities. A three-quarters majority would be needed to do so, and the powers transferred had to be restricted to a 'functionally limited area'.[28] The vote on the amendment preceded and almost exactly anticipated that in April on the government's recommendation that Norway apply for EEC membership. In the second vote, 113 of parliament's 150 members supported the government's proposal: sixty-three of Labour's seventy-four members, the Conservative party, twelve of the fourteen Liberals, and eight of the fifteen Christians. In a separate vote on a proposal that Norway limit its link with the EEC to an association agreement, thirty-eight voted for this solution: the Centre party, eleven Labour members, two Liberals and nine Christians. Only the two SPP members wanted to restrict negotiations to a free trade agreement.[29] The anti-marketeers had been defeated, and in May the government sent Norway's application to Brussels. But although they had failed to prevent this step, the anti-marketeers had demonstrated that their numbers in parliament might well reach the one-quarter needed to stop the later passage of a treaty to take Norway into the EEC.

They had also demonstrated their strength in the country and their ability to mobilise the voters to their cause. When the question first arose in the autumn of 1961 the public opinion polls revealed a hesitant, undecided electorate, in which many had no opinion (indeed nearly a third claimed not even to have heard of the EEC);[30] but those in favour of some sort of agreement with the EEC outnumbered those opposed to any agreement at all. Six months later opinions were much more formed and polarised, with a sharp increase in opposition to membership, especially among middle-party voters.[31] Although in part a natural consequence of the debate in progress at national level, this development in public opinion also owed something to the activity of the national cross-party organisation established early on to co-ordinate the campaign against EEC membership.[32] All these features — the anti-marketeers' greater strength outside than inside parliament, the cross-party campaign organisation, and its success in winning over or hardening opinion against entry into the EEC — were features of the first round of the EEC debate which were noteworthy in view of what was to happen later. There were others. The debate and passions aroused by this question had been highly charged and bitter. The promise of a referendum, far from calming the atmosphere, only served as a greater spur to each side to win over public opinion, even before the negotiations had properly begun. The discussions about political co-operation taking place at that time in the EEC, although they came to nothing, added considerably to the anti-marketeers' arsenal of arguments against membership.[33] The anti-marketeers had succeeded in overcoming their very deep disagreements over domestic and foreign policy, especially security policy, in order to achieve their common objective.

On this first occasion, however, the issue was decided not by the Norwegians but the French. France's veto on British entry in January 1963 put an end to the negotiations about Norwegian membership. With that the question disappeared as quickly as it had arisen, and ceased to disturb the normal working of the political system.

The second application 1966-67

When next it reappeared there had been changes in both the domestic political situation and the EEC itself which combined to produce a rather different debate and outcome.

The non-socialist parties had been in office for just over eighteen months when Britain renewed its application for membership in May 1967 and thereby faced them with the necessity of deciding whether or not to follow the British lead yet again. It was a policy decision which seemed capable of splitting the coalition wide open. Five of its fifteen ministers had advocated an association agreement in 1962, including the prime minister, Per Borten, and the Christian People's party chairman, Kjell Bondevik.[34] Two of them, the Centrist, Dagfinn Vårvik, and the Liberal, Helge Seip, had done so from their positions as the editors of the Centre party's main newspaper *Nationen* and the Oslo-based Liberal *Dagbladet*. The six Conservative ministers, on the other hand, were determined supporters of EEC membership, and they included the foreign minister, John Lyng.[35] On balance there appeared to be a majority for membership in the government, even if the position of some ministers was unclear. In parliament the majority was much larger. The Conservative and Labour parties, the two largest with well over half the seats between them, maintained their previous policies on the question. There was also a majority for membership among the coalition parties. But in parliament, as in the government, the issue cut right through the coalition's ranks, threatening to place its parties and even different groups within some parties, on either side of the dividing line.

In view of the majorities for membership in the government and parliament, and the Conservatives' uncompromising position on the matter, it was obvious that the coalition would only survive the second appearance of the EEC question if the minority which had voted against membership the first time now abandoned its opposition to it. No serious difficulties about doing so were encountered in the Liberal party. But in both the Centre and Christian parties the anti-marketeers put up a stronger resistance and it took several months — from November 1966 when the British government announced its intention of renewing Britain's application until it did so in the following May — for these two parties to resolve their internal differences and agree on a course of action.[36] When they did so, it was to give their support to a unanimous government recommendation to parliament that Norway apply for negotiations on the basis of membership. Like its Labour predecessor, the government made entry conditional on British membership and on satisfactory safeguards for the primary sector. It too promised a consultative referendum before parliament made its final decision.

Both at the time and during the following two or three years this unanimity was interpreted as signalling the conversion of most of the middle-parties' anti-marketeers to membership, or at least their acquiescence in a step which they at last recognised as politically inevitable. In reality the unanimity was a product of the particular circumstances of 1966-67, not of any decisive change of heart among those who had opposed membership in 1962.

The background to their willingness to support a renewed application for membership negotiations was France's obvious reluctance to admit Britain to the EEC this time either. Because of this the Norwegians were generally much more sceptical about Britain's chances of success than the British government itself appeared to be. So the question of their own entry was very much a hypothetical one as seen from Oslo, and one about which it seemed highly probable they would not in the event have to reach a decision because the way would be barred on the EEC's side.[37] The real, and pressing, question which those previously opposed to membership had to answer was not whether they were now prepared to join the EEC but whether they were prepared to break up the coalition over a question

52

which might well never arise. And this, as their decision showed, they were not ready to do.[38]

What they did was agree to a government recommendation which, contrary to the interpretation widely placed on it, did not in itself necessarily indicate a change of position on their part regarding the principle of membership. The recommendation was that the country apply for membership negotiations 'as the best means of clarifying the basis for Norway's relations with the EEC'.[39] That, as it stood, was not a commitment to the objective of joining the EEC, only to negotiate on the basis of article 237 of the Treaty of Rome. It established a clear distinction between the decision to seek such negotiations and any subsequent one about the type of agreement Norway ultimately chose to conclude. The Labour government had also made such a distinction, of course, but it had made it quite clear when doing so that its aim was to enter the EEC if Britain did.[40] The wording of the application submitted in 1967 also in fact went further than the government's original recommendation, by stating that Norway's objective was membership and expressing the hope that any difficulties raised by Norway's special problems could be overcome during the negotiations.[41] But this, like the pro-market government report to parliament on the subject, was the work of the foreign ministry, overwhelmingly in favour of membership and with a Conservative minister at its head. It did not affect the view of those middle-party ministers and members of parliament who had voted for negotiations primarily in order to hold the coalition together, that their vote on the application in no way bound them as regards the position they would later take in any vote for or against joining the EEC.

The hope of many of them, of course, was that it would never come to a second vote. Their first line of defence was French policy, which was widely expected to prevent negotiations beginning at all. But if that failed and France agreed to serious enlargement negotiations after all, there would still be opportunities to raise obstacles to entry on the Norwegian side. The first would come when drawing up the negotiating mandate, and in particular when defining the safeguards required for the primary sector. It would be possible to raise demands that the EEC would be almost certain to reject. If it proved impossible to impose such an anti-market mandate on the government and the negotiations ran their course to a successful conclusion, there would still be two more opportunities for those who had by then definitely decided to work against membership. There would be the referendum. Then the treaty of accession would have to win a three-quarters majority in parliament. Before that stage had been reached the coalition would probably have collapsed under the strain of its internal disagreements. But at least the anti-marketeers and sceptics in its ranks had their defences well-prepared when they agreed to the application in 1967.

That did not necessarily mean that all those politicians who were uncertain about what their final position would be (and they probably outnumbered firm anti-marketeers) were merely engaging in a tactical manoeuvre to keep the coalition in office when they voted for membership negotiations in July 1967. In 1967 the EEC looked rather different from what it had been four years before — and from what it was to look like four years later. French policy under President de Gaulle had slowed down the pace of economic integration, prevented the introduction of majority voting, and made earlier hopes of close political co-operation appear quite unrealistic. If the EEC remained simply a customs union with an agricultural policy, then the sovereignty argument against membership would carry less conviction, while the economic disadvantages of staying outside an enlarged EEC would weigh more heavily than would have been the case if entry required a substantial transfer of national powers to Brussels. If Sweden joined, the economic argument would be even stronger. That would place the largest, most dynamic, and by 1967 practically duty-free market for Norwegian manufactures behind the EEC's common external tariff. The very fact that non-aligned Sweden could even consider membership was also regarded by many Norwegians as a reassuring commentary on the EEC's prospects of ever achieving a degree of economic and political integration which might threaten the independence of its member states.

When parliament debated the government's recommendation in July 1967 only thirteen voted against it, compared with the thirty-seven mustered against the Labour government in 1962.[42] Four Centrists and three Christians maintained their opposition, and they were joined from the socialist side by four Labour and the two SPP members. In 1962 the anti-marketeers had very nearly reached the one-quarter required to block the passage of a treaty of accession. Five years later they seemed a politically insignificant group. The voting figures were in fact misleading insofar as they concealed the significant number of middle-party members who had expressed serious doubts and reservations during the course of the debate, but then gone on to support the government in the final vote.[43] They also concealed the calculations about French policy which were an essential element in the situation. But it was the 136 to thirteen majority for negotiations which persuaded many observers, even parliamentarians, that the Norwegian political establishment was at last practically united about the country's European policy: the coalition parties had agreed to submit an application to the EEC for membership negotiations, and the only alternative government, a Labour one, was committed to the same policy. Other circumstances surrounding the second appli-

54

cation strengthened this view. 1967 marked the high point of public support for membership in the polls, with figures which offered hopes of a fairly easy victory in any referendum on the subject.[44] By contrast to 1962 the issue had aroused little public debate and only feeble extra-parliamentary opposition.[45] The non-socialists had been leaderless. The left-wing socialists, even if they had not already been fully engaged in a campaign to end Norway's NATO membership, were therefore deprived of that alliance with the middle-parties which alone could make them a really influential force in Norwegian politics.

So although negotiations with the EEC did not even reach the opening preliminaries this time — as anticipated, France placed another veto on British membership at the end of the year — this second application seemed to mark a turning point in the clarification of Norwegian policy. The application remained in Brussels along with those of the other three countries seeking membership. And it was the events of 1967 which during the next two years were generally taken as a guide to what would happen if it were ever to be followed up by an offer of negotiations from the EEC.

Yet in some respects it was 1962 which would have been a better guide to what happened after France agreed to enlargement negotiations at the Hague summit conference in December 1969. In 1962 most Norwegians had expected negotiations to open quickly and be concluded quite rapidly; faced, it seemed, by the prospect of finding themselves inside the EEC before very long, the debate had been intense and uncompromising. In 1967 there was widespread scepticism about negotiations getting under way at all, and this gave a theoretical character to the whole elaborate process of drawing up the government's recommendation, debating it in parliament, and submitting an application to the EEC. In 1970 the situation was to be more like that of 1962 than 1967. Secondly, in 1962 the EEC had seemed to be moving steadily towards ever closer economic and political integration, and it had therefore been possible to argue plausibly that membership would eventually lead to a substantial transfer of power from Norwegian to EEC institutions. In 1967 the EEC's development was blocked by French policy. After the Hague summit, however, economic integration and political co-operation were back again on the EEC's agenda, this time even including plans for a so-called 'union'. Lastly, in 1962 the Centre party, enjoying the freedom of opposition, had voted unanimously against membership negotiations. In 1967 the constraints of coalition had overcome the reluctance of most Centrists to follow the majority line. In 1970 the party was still in coalition, but one that by then was politically weaker than it had been three years earlier and in which solidarity was already waning.

Apart from this loosening of the bonds holding the coalition together and with it the middle-parties' anti-marketeers in check, there were several developments between the second application and the Hague summit which strengthened the potential opposition to EEC membership.

Events in the EEC further alienated the farmers and fishermen, from whom the core of economic opposition to entry had always come. In 1967 the farmers' opposition had been muted owing to the political situation at home and the reassuring evidence that French policy would keep Norway out anyway. The agricultural organisations had nevertheless made it clear that the only condition on which they could possibly go along with membership was that the common agricultural policy was not applied in Norway — a condition which the EEC was hardly likely to accept. Their argument for this had been much the same as five years before. Applying the common agricultural policy would mean dismantling much of the Norwegian subsidy system and at the same time forcing them to compete on equal terms in an unprotected home market against EEC imports; given Norwegian agriculture's natural disadvantages, they maintained that this would lead to a sharp drop in farm incomes and a depopulation of the countryside.[46] In the period after the second application their determination to maintain an independent national agricultural policy was hardened by the publication in early 1969 of a commission report on agriculture, the so-called Mansholt report. This proposed a drastic rationalisation of EEC agriculture, including a halving of the labour force by 1980 and a reduction in the number of small farms of the kind that predominated in Norway. Similar proposals appeared at the same time in France, where the cost of the common agricultural policy, its encouragement of over-production, and the need to draw labour off the land for the country's industry seemed to be leading to a re-thinking of farm policy.[47] For Norway's farmers the result of all this was merely to confirm their predictions of what awaited them in the EEC. In particular, the commission's plan appeared to provide conclusive proof that the EEC's aim would be to close down Norway's small farms, not help them to survive with special conditions and exemptions such as the pro-marketeers maintained it would be possible to obtain.[48]

The fishermen's interests seemed threatened by another commission proposal. Their position on membership was more ambivalent than the farmers' because their interests pulled in different directions. On the one hand, the coastal fishermen with their small vessels and small capital resources feared the competition of an enlarged EEC's trawler fleet, not only in the rich fishing banks off Norway's northern coast but on land too if the foreign fishermen were given the right to land

and sell fish in Norway. On the other hand, as exporters the Norwegians were themselves interested in obtaining free access to the EEC markets for their fresh and processed fish products. This difficult balance of interests had been evident both in 1962 and 1967. In 1967, attracted by the EEC markets and anxious about continued access to the British one, they had agreed to membership negotiations as a means of establishing whether their twelve-mile limit and the powers of their producer organisations could be retained inside the EEC.[49] Uncertainty about this was due to the fact that at that time the Six had not agreed on a common fisheries policy, although the commission had put forward proposals for one in 1966. These proposals foresaw a strict application of the Treaty of Rome's principles of non-discrimination and free competition, with member states' fishing grounds opened to the vessels of other member states. Soon after the second French veto on enlargement, a step towards translating them into EEC policy was taken when in May 1968 the commission published three draft directives for fisheries policy based on its earlier proposals.[50] The effect of this in Norway was to increase the probability of an alliance between the coastal fishermen and farmers against any agreement with the EEC which allowed the introduction of EEC policies to their sectors of the economy. After the publication of these proposals there were only two ways in which the pro-marketeers would be able to prevent such a primary producer front against membership. One would be to stop the commission's recommendations being accepted by the council of ministers. The other, should that prove impossible, would be to stop the commission's recommendations being accepted by the same thing as an exclusive fishing limit and then (not the least difficult part) convince the fishermen that it did. Doing this, and obtaining an agreement which the farmers could accept, were clearly going to be the most crucial yet complicated aspects of any Norwegian entry negotiations.

Not only was the primary sector more united in its opposition by 1970, its political allies were potentially more numerous. Even in 1967 doubts and reservations about EEC membership had been more widespread in the middle-parties and sections of the Labour party than the parliamentary voting figures revealed. In the next two years they received a powerful stimulus from a development that was not confined to Norway, although the form it took there was naturally conditioned by the country's political culture and party system. This was the way in which social criticism and ideology came to the forefront of Western European politics again in the late 1960s. A wave of unrest and dissatisfaction with the existing order swept over the Western world. In France the intellectual and political upheaval sparked off the chain of events which led to President de Gaulle's resignation in

April 1969. In West Germany it had the universities in turmoil and helped to bring the coalition of social democrats and liberals to office five months after the French president's departure. The challenge was not only to the institutions, but to central economic and social objectives of the post-war period. Economic growth, efficiency, mobility and technological innovation seemed less important to their critics than the goals of equality and social reform. Not the achievements but the shortcomings and problems of Western industrial society moved into the centre of political debate.

In Norway the immediate effect of this was not as dramatic as in some countries on the continent. But its longer term impact was probably as profound — not least because of its interaction after 1970 with the debate about Norway's relations with the EEC. By the time of the Hague summit conference the influence of the new political climate was already making itself felt in several ways which were important for the outcome of that debate. As elsewhere in Western Europe the socialist left was radicalised. In the Liberal party the old tradition of social radicalism received a powerful boost, especially in the eastern urban wing. The strong strain of populism in Norway's political culture was also revived, most strikingly in the Centre and Liberal parties. Dislike of modern capitalism, big business, centralisation and state bureaucracies was still deeply rooted in parties whose original *raison d'être* had been to fight them and their threat to the rural economy and the small man. Now, shorn of much of its neo-marxist terminology, the popular, vaguely left-wing critique of industrial society which had become current throughout Western Europe produced a more modern brand of Norwegian populism which proved to have a strong appeal for the young and especially for radically inclined middle-party supporters.

As far as relations with the EEC were concerned, the effect of this was to widen the range of arguments against membership and produce a much more receptive audience for criticism of the EEC on social as well as economic and political grounds. The left had always emphasised social arguments, but in 1962 they had played only a subordinate role in the middle-party opposition and in 1967 these parties had scarcely mentioned them.[51] Two years later, by contrast, the stimulus to economic growth, industrialisation and rationalisation which joining the EEC was expected to produce had become a persuasive argument against entry in circles beyond the primary sector and Centre party. So too had the Treaty of Rome's objective of eliminating economic barriers, which anti-marketeers claimed would increase the trend to centralisation and regional inequalities as well as the pressures on people to abandon their traditional ways of life — a telling point at a time when regional policy had come to occupy a prominent and controversial role in domestic politics. A closer co-ordination and steering of the European economy was now rejected not only because of its threat to national independence, but because it would lead to powerful bureaucracies and less local democracy. These social arguments had the appeal of reflecting themes current in the wider European debate. They also enabled the sectional interests of the farmers and fishermen to assume a wider social relevance. No longer were their interests regarded merely from the perspective of regional policy: their future was seen as being an important aspect of the fundamental question of what sort of society the Norwegians wanted to live in. With the modern populists, and their debates about social values and objectives, the political system acquired new tensions. But the alliance against EEC membership gained an important new component. For, combining as they did the economic conservatism of the primary producers and the ideological radicalism of the left-wing socialists, the populists were able to fill the role of a much needed ideological bridge between these two wings of the anti-market alliance.

Apart from the academic community, it was particularly to educated and politically conscious young people that the new ideas of the late 1960s appealed. In the 1969 election about half of those voting for the first time had chosen the Labour party. But the outlook of these new Labour voters, as of those who voted Liberal or Centre, was generally more radical and ideological than that of older party members and voters. It was seen in domestic politics. And it was seen in foreign affairs, where the Vietnam war was providing their introduction to American foreign policy, and their feelings of solidarity were usually reserved for the developing countries, not for the American-led Western world with which the older generation still identified so closely. Their view of Europe also differed from that of their elders who had run the country's foreign policy since the second world war. They saw Britain as it was by the end of the 1960s, without the memories and sentiments of older Norwegians. They saw the EEC as it had become by then and not as its founders had hoped it would develop: an organisation concerned with prosaic economic matters, part of the industrialised world with all its problems, and run by professional politicians and civil servants. It was hardly an organisation capable of inspiring in the young of 1970 the enthusiasm it had generated in young Norwegians a decade earlier, even if their enthusiasm and idealism had not already long been transferred to other causes. More important for Norway's relations with the EEC, however, was the fact that the general social and political outlook of many of these young people was such that it would take little to turn this lack of enthusiasm into active opposition to joining the EEC. With new voters making up 12 per cent of the electorate in

1969, this could have a major impact on the outcome of a referendum.

Younger Norwegians were not the only ones for whom British policy was no longer the pre-eminent consideration it had still been just a few years before, when the first application was made. Those who attached primary importance to the social issues which had recently come so much more to the fore again in Norwegian politics were correspondingly less impressed by arguments for EEC membership based on the traditional principles of protecting Norwegian interests in British markets and keeping close to Britain in European affairs. More generally, the persistent economic problems from which Britain had suffered in the 1960s, and its declining international status, had reduced its influence in Oslo.[52] It was less significant for Norway's defence, and as a market it was relatively less important even if still the largest single one. Successive British governments, moreover, had demonstrated throughout the decade that Norwegian interests ranked fairly low on their list of priorities. EFTA, the cornerstone of Norwegian foreign trade by the late 1960s, they had treated as a *pis aller* to be abandoned as soon as France stopped blocking the way into the EEC. Within EFTA Britain had breached the free trade rules with import controls and aided its aluminium industry in ways which aroused vigorous Norwegian protests.[53] Altogether it had scarcely been an encouragement to continue the old habit of looking to Britain for a lead, even if the Norwegians had not in the meantime become more prosperous, more industrialised, more self-confident and therefore more inclined anyway to take an independent view of their interests and European developments.

Finally there had been two other developments outside Norway which were to strengthen opposition to joining the EEC when the question came up again in 1970. The first was the renewed impetus which events in the late 1960s gave to political co-operation and a closer co-ordination of economic and monetary policy between members of the EEC. Several strands came together to produce the Hague summit's decision to establish a system of formalised foreign policy co-operation.[54] The obstacle of President de Gaulle had been removed in the previous April. The apparent prospect of US troop withdrawals and a US-Soviet strategic arms limitation agreement affecting European interests combined to make a concerted European approach appear more urgent, while both the West German government and its European allies wanted the new *Ostpolitik* to be balanced by closer ties between themselves. The French government was also intent on ending the foreign policy consultations between Britain and the other five EEC members which had developed in the Western European Union after the second French veto: it wanted them brought within an EEC context where French views would be represented. The background to the Hague summit's decision to establish an economic and monetary union was the severe disturbances in the international exchange markets since 1967, and in particular the French and German parity changes in the autumn of 1969. These posed a serious threat to the common agricultural market in which prices were fixed in a common unit of account.[55] Precisely what arrangements these decisions in principle about political co-operation and economic and monetary union would lead to was unclear: they had been passed on to the EEC's foreign ministers and council of ministers to translate into concrete plans acceptable to all concerned. But what mattered in Norway was less the details than the very fact that foreign policy co-operation was back in the forefront of EEC planning and that the Six had declared their aim of establishing a 'union'. The first had always been regarded as a potentially serious obstacle to membership by many who were ready to join an EEC restricted to economic co-operation on the Gaullist model. The second aroused Norwegian fears of being submerged in a large continental federation, striking a particularly raw national nerve because of the deep-seated Norwegian suspicion of 'unions' in which the country's independence had been sunk for over five hundred years. To quite a number of Norwegians it seemed that at the Hague the EEC had simultaneously opened the door to them and announced its intention of transforming the EEC into an organisation which Norway could not agree to join.

The other development had taken place outside Europe, and while not in itself creating opposition to EEC membership it added to the arguments which could be used against it.[56] The number of sovereign states had increased rapidly in the 1960s as former colonies gained their independence. Many of these new states could be described as small like Norway, whether measured in terms of size, population or economic resources. So by 1970 being small had become a common phenomenon, a characteristic of most states because by then there were many more small ones than large ones. These newly independent states, moreover, whatever the actual extent of their economic or political dependence on the outside world, were as jealous of the forms of national sovereignty as ever the Norwegians themselves had been. In particular they insisted on their sovereign status being respected in the structure and voting procedures of international organisations. Norway's anti-marketeers could use this to support the argument that the type of supra-national organisation foreseen by the Treaty of Rome was not suited to the world of the 1970s. The ideology of integration popular in the 1950s, they argued, had been the product of a world in which there were relatively few states and a preponderance of the larger ones. But now there were so many small ones that these had a right to demand forms of international co-operation which would not undermine their independence, at the regional level as well as in wider international organisations. In Western Europe that meant that it was not the EEC but EFTA which provided the model for the future: not integration but co-operation between sovereign states had to be the guiding principle for Norway's relations with Western Europe.

Whatever changes had taken place during the late 1960s however — in the Norwegian political climate, in Britain's standing and influence, in the prospects for agriculture and fisheries inside the EEC, in the EEC's own plans for its future development — Norway's application for membership negotiations was still in Brussels. The objective of joining an enlarged EEC was now taken almost for granted by the large majority of politicians, civil servants, businessmen, and others with influence on Norwegian policy and public opinion. What was more, many of these were also under the impression that the former opponents of membership had dropped their opposition in 1967. For after July 1967 the precise wording of the government's recommendation — that Norway seek membership negotiations 'as the best means of clarifying Norway's relations with the EEC' — tended to be ignored or forgotten, as did the conditions and reservations with which a number of those who voted for the second application had done so. In some cases this was undoubtedly deliberate: people were to get accustomed to the idea that there was an overwhelming consensus about the necessity of joining the EEC. In other cases it was because the distinction between agreeing to negotiate and conceding the desirability of membership had not been clearly grasped. Others simply considered it so unrealistic to imagine that a Norwegian government could enter into negotiations without in fact committing itself to join (subject to a referendum) if the EEC offered reasonable terms, that they regarded the distinction as having served the purely domestic political function of mollifying the opposition within the middle-parties.

Not all the pro-marketeers took so sanguine a view of this supposed consensus (even if they insisted on its existence in public). Many Conservatives in particular were under no illusion that the government's unanimity in 1967 indicated a fundamental change of outlook among all those of their coalition colleagues who had voted against a membership application in 1962 but in favour of it the second time. Most Conservatives were well aware that 1967 had been only a consolidation of the first step towards their goal, and they remained very much on their guard against any backsliding from the official position established. Nor did the anti-marketeers or those still harbouring serious doubts fail to keep clear, at least to themselves, the distinction set up in 1967.[57] But they knew that submitting the application had been a potentially dangerous step. For if negotiations once got underway they might be concluded so quickly that there would be little opportunity to organise an effective opposition. It might also prove politically impossible for the government to pull out of the process once it had become too deeply involved (as most pro-marketeers hoped and expected that it would). In that event the decision to negotiate would have pre-empted the formally separate one about the principle of membership.

But there might still be time for them to recover the ground lost in 1967. In the year or so after the second veto, entry appeared safely blocked by President de Gaulle whose term of office did not expire until 1972. As for how to recover it without engaging in that direct confrontation from which they had drawn back in 1967 and could still very well lose, the most effective way would be to erect obstacles to joining the EEC that would make it extremely difficult to do so even if French policy were to change. A chance to do this seemed to present itself very soon after the president's veto. It came in the form of inter-Nordic negotiations aimed at establishing closer economic co-operation between their countries. Although many anti-marketeers did not immediately recognise in them the opportunity they were seeking, they had certainly done so by the time the Hague summit conference made the need for obstacles acute. Most pro-marketeers knew this, which was why the Norwegian debate about Nordic economic co-operation between 1968 and 1970 ultimately became one about the country's relations with the EEC, and a prelude to the real EEC debate which followed.

3. Nordek: Prelude to the EEC debate

Although Norway's application remained in Brussels after November 1967, the prospect of it ever leading to negotiations seemed less than good during much of the next two years. Until spring 1969 President de Gaulle blocked the way, and even when he resigned his successor, President Pompidou, was a man closely identified with de Gaulle's European policies and dependent on the large Gaullist majority in the national assembly. The EEC itself seemed to be stagnating in deep disagreements between France and the other five members over this issue of enlargement, and even its survival in the same form was regarded as doubtful by some prominent Norwegian politicians.[1] The Soames affair in early 1969 had seemed to reveal the fluidity of French thinking on this point, as well as marking a new nadir in Anglo-French relations.[2] It was not until later that year — with President Pompidou looking less tied to his predecessor's policy and the Gaullist majority's views on Europe, and with a new coalition in office in West Germany — that it began to seem that the way to an enlargement of the EEC might at last be opening up. Even then memories of 1962 and 1967 created a fair degree of scepticism in Oslo, as in London, about the real aims of French policy and the chances of any entry negotiations succeeding.[3]

The Norwegians themselves could do little more than watch and wait on events and on the negotiations between the larger states of Western Europe. For pro-marketeers it was a period in which they could only keep reiterating that Norway's application was still in Brussels, watch for any signs of change in the EEC, and try if possible to strengthen their negotiating position in case such a change occurred. At the same time they had to ensure that the EEC option was not closed on Norway's side: that nothing was done which might prevent Norway entering the EEC if the opportunity did present itself at some time in the future. That meant avoiding international agreements which could prove incompatible with it. Doing so was not without problems, however, as long as the prospect of EEC enlargement looked so unpromising. It was not easy, for example, to be certain about what would or would not be incompatible with membership when the EEC's own future was so uncertain — as was shown by the pro-marketeers' own disagreements on this point. In trying to avoid such commitments, moreover, they were vulnerable to the argument that Norway could not remain passive, shunning other immediately advantageous arrangements in the hope of the EEC one day opening a door that could well stay closed for ever.[4]

The negotiations and treaty[5]

This was the case when in February 1968 the Danes proposed that the Nordic countries examine the possiblities for intensifying their regional economic co-operation in view of the fact that EEC membership seemed to be ruled out for any of them in the foreseeable future. The Danes argued that although this could not be a substitute for each of them eventually reaching the type of agreement it wanted with the EEC (in Denmark's case membership), it would strengthen them economically in the waiting period and improve their eventual bargaining position in Brussels. The main features of the co-operation they envisaged were a customs union, freer agricultural trade, and joint institutions to co-ordinate economic policy. With the three Scandinavian countries outside the EEC, Finnish participation also appeared politically possible.[6]

In Norway the coalition government's immediate response was cautious, even sceptical.[7] This was entirely in keeping with the four parties' previous record in Nordic economic co-operation. In the 1950s all of them for various and sometimes different reasons had opposed the idea of a Nordic customs union when most of the governing Labour party had been in favour of it.[8] One reason for their reserve in 1968 was the radical character of the original Danish proposals: the organisation for economic co-operation (Nordek) which the Danes wished to see established included, for example, a supra-national element similar to the EEC commission in its institutional arrangements. Another reason was economic. Industry feared for its competitive position in a customs union with Sweden; agriculture faced three countries producing surpluses and suspected the Danes of aiming to establish a replica of the EEC's hated common agricultural policy in the Nordic area.[9] In addition quite a few Atlanticists were uneasy about an organisation which would include two neutrals, one of which had a special relationship with the Soviet Union.[10] The Conservatives were wary of too close an involvement in an organisation which was likely to be dominated by Sweden, not only because of the long-standing Norwegian fear of control by Swedish industry and finance,[11] but also because of the socialists' seemingly unbreakable hold on government in that country. Another important reason for caution among pro-marketeers, though, again especially Conservatives, was the effect which the existence of such a Nordic organisation could have on Norway's chances of entering the EEC. Time and again during the next two years they were to show their concern about this aspect by the way they emphasised that the government was obliged to carry out the mandate given it by parliament in July 1967, and that this ruled out any regional commitments incompatible with EEC membership.[12]

The government agreed to enter into the negotiations only after the original Danish proposals had been modified and safeguards relating both to general foreign policy and the EEC option had been included in the mandate for the four-nation committee which was to conduct the negotiations. These safeguards, couched in the form of principles, were also later included in the preamble to the Nordek treaty. The first principle was that the closer co-operation envisaged was not to affect their foreign and security policies — a principle which all four governments, not just the Norwegian, were anxious to underline. The same applied to the second principle, which was that Nordek was to take such a form as would facilitate their entry into an enlarged European trading area or their co-operation with it.[13] The pro-market-eers attached considerable importance to this limitation on Nordek and kept it very much to the forefront of the debate during the next two years. Nor was it initially unwelcome to the anti-marketeers. Most of them did want at least a free trade agreement with the EEC. In the early stages moreover they had doubts about Nordek on economic grounds, and it would have offered an escape clause if they wished to avoid concluding a treaty for that reason.

The practical effect of the second principle was seen in several of the treaty's clauses by the time it was ready for signing in February 1970. Thus provision was made for revising it if one or more of the signatories opened membership negotiations with the EEC.[14] The customs union's external tariff levels were set as close to those of the EEC as GATT rules would permit. In the latter phase of the negotiations, against a background of changing French policy and the Hague summit conference, it was also agreed that during the first stage of the customs union (from 1972 to 1974) no alterations would be made in national tariff levels which required a move away from those of the EEC.[15] The whole treaty was designed moreover to be as flexible as possible, very much with this uncertainty about the wider European situation in mind. There were some very specific commitments, concerning in particular the customs union's tariff levels and transitional periods, the financial transfers to ease structural adaptations and stabilise primary sector prices, and the limited increase in agricultural trade with which the Danes had finally to be satisfied.

But otherwise the treaty was essentially a framework to be filled in later with more or less ambitious policies depending on the international situation and on each government's view of its interests when the time came.[16] The negotiators had concentrated primarily on drawing up the principles on which their co-operation would be based, the inter-governmental institutions which would negotiate the joint policies and co-ordinate their implementation, and a time-table for establishing the customs union and reaching agreement on long-term policies for other sectors. Decisions in Nordek had to be unanimous, and the treaty provided for relatively easy withdrawal from specific commitments, even from the treaty itself, should any country consider this necessary.[17]

Thus in its final form Nordek hardly looked like the threat to Norway's freedom of action which some pro-marketeers maintained it would become. And there were other pro-marketeers, no less strongly in favour of joining an enlarged EEC, who argued that Nordek would not be an obstacle to doing so: that the safeguards in the negotiating mandate and treaty preamble excluded this possibility, and that therefore objections to the project on that ground must be a cover for other motives. Other motives than just a concern to keep open the EEC option certainly did explain some of the reservations. But there were also genuine differences of opinion about what would be compatible with EEC membership, just as there were about what kind of Nordic arrangements would help or hinder them in reaching this goal — opinions which could never be tested afterwards because the treaty remained unsigned.

Although the negotiations had begun in 1968, it was February 1970 before they were concluded. Difficulties in reconciling the four countries' economic interests, together with delays due to extraneous events like national elections, had held up the final stages until late 1969. In the meantime the situation inside the EEC had altered, and in December the Hague summit cleared the way for negotiations about Danish, Norwegian, and perhaps even Swedish membership. So the final phase of the Nordek negotiations coincided with these three countries' preparations to take up where they had left off in 1967. Just as it had been events in the EEC which led to the idea of Nordek in the first place, so now it was developments there which caused the project to fail. For it was not only the three Scandinavian governments which, when it came to a choice, gave priority to their economic and political relations with states outside the Nordic region. So did the Finns. After a period of uncertainty following the Hague summit they appear to have concluded that entering a customs union with three states which might soon be joining the EEC was inadvisable on foreign policy grounds, and early in April they postponed indefinitely signing the treaty.[18] The Swedes were unwilling to go ahead without the Finns, and a purely Scandinavian agreement would have required extensive renegotiations.[19] All three governments were by then anyway engrossed in preparing for the forthcoming negotiations in Brussels.

So Nordek was abandoned: to become at once a monument to the limits of Nordic co-operation, and the embodiment for Norway's anti-marketeers of a Nordic alternative sacrificed to the aim of EEC membership but still attainable in the future if only that goal was in turn rejected.

'Both . . .and'

The government had entered the Nordek negotiations not least for domestic reasons. Nordic co-operation was thought to be popular with the voters by the late 1960s, and the Danish prime minister had launched his proposal in the full glare of a Nordic Council plenary session. It was also a favourite Labour party cause, so the coalition could expect attacks from that quarter in a pre-election year if it refused even to examine the idea.[20] This view of Nordek as a popular project went on to condition the whole subsequent debate. Because of it few politicians openly questioned the value of the project as such. Even the Conservatives, whose lack of enthusiasm was obvious from start to finish, confined themselves on the whole to criticising particular features and pointing to specific disadvantages for Norway.[21]

Once embarked on the negotiations the government's official line became that while the possibility of membership negotiations with the EEC had to be kept open and receive priority, there was no necessary conflict between doing this and concluding a Nordic agreement in the meantime. It was a case of 'both . . . and' not 'either . . . or'.[22] 'Both . . . and' quickly became a standard formula in debates about European and Nordic policy, a shorthand expression for the truism that Norway belonged both to Western Europe and the Nordic area, and therefore had to look after its interests both in the one and in the other. In particular they needed trade agreements with both. This would be especially important if Norway joined the EEC while Sweden stayed outside, because then they would require a guarantee of continued duty-free access to the Swedish market.[23] It was noticeable that the Conservatives used the formula less frequently than did for example the Labour party. But even the sceptical Conservatives did not openly dissent from it. Again they restricted themselves to a more indirect approach, in this case insisting on an exact definition of what each element of the 'both . . . and' formula meant. For in its very vagueness lay not only its political convenience but, as some pro-marketeers saw it, its danger.

In one respect vagueness was unavoidable. Uncertainty about French policy and the EEC's future made it impossible to be dogmatic about exactly what sort of agreement Norway would eventually be able to obtain from the Six: the Norwegians could say what they wanted, but in practice they would be limited by what the EEC offered. But 'both . . . and' could also be used to conceal the sometimes very different objectives of those using this neat consensus formula. For some it expanded to 'both EEC membership and the Nordek treaty', for others to the vaguer 'both a European agreement and a Nordic one'. For some it meant 'both EEC membership and a compatible Nordic agreement', for others 'both Nordek and a compatible agreement with the EEC'. But as long as it was not expanded and each element not clearly defined, different groups could use the same phrase while pursuing diametrically opposed aims. It also left unclear what forms of co-operation could be combined with each other. Would membership of a Nordic customs union be compatible with belonging to the EEC's customs union? And even if that was technically possible — and some used the Benelux example to argue that it was[24] — could a customs union containing two neutrals be combined politically with one embedded in the Atlantic alliance?

The formula's lack of precision made it ideal for those opposed to EEC membership, who under its cover could encourage what they hoped would develop into an alternative to it. It was ideal too for those whose minds were not yet made up about the EEC, or who were in the process of changing them. 'Both . . . and' even had a compensating advantage for those pro-marketeers who recognised its utility for their opponents. By repeatedly expanding it to 'both EEC membership and . . .' they were able to underline that a Nordic treaty would not be a substitute, and to do so moreover during a period when Nordek was capturing the headlines and the EEC receiving little publicity or only such as drew attention to its unattractive condition. There were still other pro-marketeers for whom, far from being a mere catchphrase, 'both . . . and' exactly expressed their calculation that Norway probably had to have an agreement with both or end up with neither: that achieving Nordek, in other words, would be an important step forward in the process of taking Norway into the EEC.[25]

So there was never a simple inverse relationship between support for EEC membership and for Nordek: it was some pro-marketeers who were most enthusiastic about Nordek. But the inverse relationship was an important feature of the debate too. It was the one which came to predominate within the coalition, where the dividing line which gradually clarified over this question foreshadowed that which opened up immediately afterwards over the EEC.

The coalition and Nordek

Disagreements about Nordek were not confined to the coalition. The Conservative and Labour parties, the two parties most strongly in favour of EEC membership, were far apart as regards the enthusiasm they displayed for this Nordic project. But whereas in their case this was not due to differences over the EEC, it gradually became clear that such differences were an important factor on the coalition side, especially in the later stages. For those not wedded to the conventional view that the debate about European policy had been finally settled in 1967, the evidence mounted that the vote on the second application had not removed but merely covered over the non-socialist parties' deep divisions over it. Some of the declared opponents of membership were seen to be still seeking ways of preventing it.[26] Coalition politicians who were thought to have accepted the majority view in 1967 were now found to be at best neutral.[27] New sources of opposition appeared too, usually not announcing their position explicitly at this stage — indeed in some cases only defining it to themselves as a consequence of the two-year Nordek debate — but revealing their attitude to the EEC through their comments on Nordek.[28] Implicit in their praise for Nordek's institutions, for example, was a criticism of the EEC's very different ones. From their enthusiasm for what they described as the unique social and cultural values of the Nordic peoples could be read a clear preference for maintaining a distance from the rather different societies and cultures of continental Europe. Those coalition pro-marketeers who knew how illusory was the four parties' official consensus on European policy could read the signs all too easily — which partly explained their barely concealed relief when the whole plan ultimately collapsed.[29]

But the differences within the coalition over Nordek never approximated those which were to arise over the EEC after 1970. For one thing Nordek did not compare with the EEC in either the scope or binding nature of its commitments. Nor did any important economic group feel so threatened as to mobilise for total opposition by the time the treaty was ready. Industry was generally unhappy about the customs union,[30] but after December 1969 could hope that it would never be implemented in the form foreseen. Another important factor was that until well into 1969 French policy, by blocking an enlargement of the EEC, had the effect of disguising those differences directly related to Nordek's implications for any future membership negotiations. It was only as the way into the EEC started to open up that these became ever clearer and more openly expressed. But then, almost immediately, the Nordek debate as such was abruptly terminated by Finland's withdrawal, and it became but one aspect of the much wider controversy over Norway's relations with the EEC.

Initially moreover the coalition's main opponents in the EEC issue, the Conservative and Centre parties, both saw Nordek as a danger to the economic interests they represented. Denmark wanted a common agricultural market, while the Swedes were insisting on a full industrial customs union as the condition for their participation and in particular for the large financial transfers they would be making to the others. In Oslo this created an alliance between the political representatives of agriculture and industry which lasted as long as each sector felt threatened and French policy allowed their basic disagreement over the EEC to remain latent.[31] It ended when these two elements holding the alliance together disappeared almost simultaneously in the course of 1969. The reversal of policy in Paris revived their conflict over the EEC. And while the Swedes stood firm on their demand, the Danes yielded, having to be content with a system of Nordic preferences and the promise of an eventual agreement on long-term principles for agricultural policy.[32] The Centre party, its anxieties about Nordek largely removed[33] but its fears about the EEC fast reviving, swung round to become an enthusiastic supporter of Nordic co-operation. The Conservatives remained sceptical about Nordek on economic grounds and increasingly wary about the effect it could have on the EEC negotiations which now seemed a possibility after all.[34]

By the end of 1969, then, the coalition contained within itself several divergent views about Nordek. The first, and fundamental, division ran between pro-marketeers and anti-marketeers. For the supporters of EEC membership, irrespective of whether they were in favour of Nordek or reserved about it, this Nordic project was strictly subordinate to the aim of entering an enlarged EEC. For the anti-marketeers, on the other hand, Nordek had already come to seem a possible alternative and barrier to the EEC. Not all the coalition's members could be placed neatly on one side or other of this line: a fair number of Christians and Liberals, perhaps even a few pragmatists in the Centre party, had still not decided where they would stand on the EEC when the time came. Then there was a second division which ran between the pro-marketeers themselves. Some thought the existence of Nordek would be an advantage in any later membership negotiations in Brussels, others a disadvantage. In most cases their disagreement on this point could be explained only by reference to general political outlook, economic or party interest, or long-standing attitudes towards Nordic co-operation. Its effect however was to confuse the lines of conflict over European policy within the coalition and disguise the fact that it was the first division, between pro- and anti-marketeers, which was the really important one.

The Conservatives were the main exponents of the argument that Nordek could become an obstacle to entering the EEC.[35] They started from the view that it would not be possible in practice to belong to the two customs unions simultaneously, or that at least it would be so difficult to arrange as to be a major complicating factor in any negotiations in Brussels. They considered the often-quoted Benelux example to be inapplicable, partly because it had existed prior to the EEC's establishment, but mainly because none of its members had been prevented from joining the EEC on general foreign policy grounds. In Nordek's case, Finland's position would certainly prevent it seeking EEC membership, while Sweden's neutrality might well ultimately do so too, or even make Swedish membership unacceptable to the EEC. So a Nordic customs union could not be fitted into the EEC in the way the Benelux had been. And if Norway's economy had in the meantime become so integrated with those of the two neutrals that breaking up or out of Nordek came to be considered too high an economic price to pay for EEC membership, then the EEC option would have been effectively blocked for Norway too. Even if it were not an economically insuperable obstacle, preserving Nordek might by then have become a persuasive argument within Norway itself for staying outside the EEC. Nordek would in that case have become the anti-marketeers' already functioning alternative, enabling them more easily to persuade the voters that there was no real economic need to join the EEC at all.

The Conservatives rejected the view that Nordek would strengthen its members' negotiating position in Brussels and therefore the prospect of bringing home good entry terms — one of the main arguments of those pro-marketeers in favour of Nordek. The four countries would not be able to negotiate as a bloc, the Conservatives argued, because of their diverging economic and political interests and the different types of agreement they would consequently have to seek with the EEC.[36] Indeed Nordek might be counter-productive, in that it could create the impression in the EEC that they were now less interested in broader European arrangements.[37] So it would be far preferable to continue with the limited, pragmatic sort of arrangements for individual sectors of their economies which had characterised post-war Nordic co-operation until now. They had proved a highly successful form of co-operation and could much more easily be adapted to changes in their relations with the EEC.

Those coalition pro-marketeers in the Christian and Liberal parties who disagreed with this view of Nordek did so for a variety of reasons. Most of them seemed to place more confidence in the safeguards and flexibility built into the treaty — probably because past experience had convinced them that neither Denmark nor Sweden would ever let a Nordic arrangement stand in the way of protecting their much more important interests in the EEC's markets, through membership in Denmark's case, membership or a free trade agreement in Sweden's. So if the EEC did open the door to enlargement neither Denmark nor Sweden were likely to try to prevent Norway entering it. Indeed on past form the Danes would be in Brussels long before the Norwegians.[38] These pro-marketeers therefore saw no reason why Nordek should become an obstacle to entering the EEC. Whether it would positively help them to secure membership on acceptable terms was another matter. Some thought it would probably make little difference, but as it would not be a handicap either saw no reason why Norway should forfeit the tangible economic benefits of Nordek, however limited.[39] If the EEC option never materialised, then Nordek would be better than nothing.[40] Others, on the other hand, thought Nordek would be an advantage in any entry negotiations and supported it partly for that reason.[41] They argued that having the additional weight of such an economic organisation behind them would improve Norway's bargaining position, even if it proved impossible for the four to act as a bloc. By the same token it would help Sweden and Finland to obtain favourable agreements, and that in turn should lessen opposition to membership in Norway itself. They probably also hoped that Nordek would draw the two neutrals closer to Western Europe,[42] which again would ease the way into the EEC for Norway and Denmark. This last argument for Nordek was seldom voiced in public for obvious reasons, but it was essentially the same calculation that in Helsinki contributed to the decision to pull out of the project.

Others went further than merely seeing some advantages in having a Nordic agreement prior to negotiating with the Six, and regarded it as very important for the achievement of EEC membership itself. These were the pro-marketeers who had not forgotten what happened in 1962 when it seemed there was a good chance of Norway's application succeeding, and who even after 1967 did not underestimate the real extent of the opposition. Their calculation was that a Nordek treaty sufficiently flexible to be combined with membership would be an important aid in overcoming that opposition and winning a referendum. To do that they would have to obtain terms which the primary sector could accept, demonstrate that membership would not lead to new economic and political barriers in the Nordic region, and deprive the opposition of a plausible alternative. In Nordek they saw a means of helping to do all three. They believed it would strengthen Norway's bargaining position in Brussels, and thus help them to get good terms for agriculture and fisheries. It would lay the spectre of trade barriers between Norway and the countries which stayed outside.[43] And it would be the end of the anti-marketeers' 'Nordic alternative' because it would have been achieved already, and after suitable adjustments could be retained after Norway and Denmark, perhaps Sweden too, had joined the EEC.

The coalition anti-marketeers were well aware of these calculations and that there was a risk of Nordek becoming a bridge into the EEC instead of an insurmountable barrier. That was why by 1969 they were insisting that Nordek be regarded as an end in itself, not merely a transitional, adaptable arrangement, a stage on the way into the EEC. But few went so far yet as to say openly that they hoped it would prevent the government ever successfully carrying out parliament's mandate of July 1967. There was still little inclination even in the Centre party to provoke an open conflict over the question. It would endanger the coalition. The anti-marketeers still could not hope to win a parliamentary majority for their view. And until well into 1969 such a direct confrontation seemed unnecessary anyway because there seemed a good chance that they would win by default: it looked as though the choice of EEC membership would not be offered to Norway, and even if it was at some time in the future, Norway's economy would probably by then have become so bound up with those of Sweden and Finland that membership would appear either unnecessary or impossible.

Still, what the anti-marketeers and those who were neutral or reserved had to say about Nordek revealed a lot about their thinking on the issues raised by EEC membership just as the debate was about to begin again. Here were heard some of the arguments that would feature prominently in the coming referendum campaign, and from the same groups and politicians — Centrists, Christians and left Liberals — who would form the backbone of the non-socialist opposition. The feature of Nordek to which they attached most importance was that it in no way infringed Norway's national sovereignty.[44] It was a purely inter-governmental organisation like EFTA,[45] with no provision for majority voting or for a supra-national body of civil servants enjoying the right of initiative in policy-making such as were found in the EEC. National parliaments would retain undiminished control over their governments and over national policy. For a number of coalition politicians this was evidently a vital question of principle, and not just for the Centre party, which had consistently taken a restrictive line on this point and so obviously had the national control of agricultural policy in mind. Prominent Christian People's party politicians who were not as yet identified with the anti-market cause emphasised it in their speeches,[46] and so did those left Liberals who were now increasingly talking again about the need to extend democratic control over government and retain the freedom to introduce social reforms in Norway itself. A second feature they all stressed was that because Nordek respected its members' sovereignty, Nordic co-operation, however close, would not threaten the Norwegians' control over their own economy. In particular they would retain control over the areas to which these groups attached especial importance, namely the primary sector, capital movements and the right of business establishment. The Norwegians themselves would determine the level and selling price of the increased imports of Nordic agricultural produce. The fishermen's exclusive fishing limit would remain closed to foreign vessels. The powers of the primary sector's producer organisations would be unaffected. The regulations governing capital movements would be eased only in step with the general development of Nordic economic co-operation, which would mean in practice as the Norwegians themselves saw fit.[47] And the same applied to the right of business establishment. The treaty even contained a comprehensive list of permanent exceptions to foreigners' rights to own property and natural resources in Norway.[48]

It was also pointed out that in Nordek Norway would be co-operating with countries which did not differ too greatly in size or economic strength from itself. Sweden's industrial and financial strength would probably give it some advantages in Nordek bargaining and would certainly pose a challenge to Norwegian manufacturers in their home market. But that would hardly compare with the disparities of size and resources to be found in the EEC, where the small members had to defend their independence and interests against major powers like West Germany and France. When it came to close economic co-operation, it was an organisation such as Nordek that offered a small country like Norway the best chance of combining the maximum autonomy with the advantages of scale and pooled resources.[49]

Moreover Nordek, it was argued, would bring together four countries with similar social systems and values which differed considerably in some respects from those found elsewhere in Western Europe. This, and its implications for Norway's future social development, was an argument for Nordek (and against the EEC) which the Liberals were the first to stress on the coalition's side, though it was quickly taken up by Centre party speakers too. What distinguished the Nordic countries, according to this line of argument, was their egalitarian and democratic character, which in turn was due to the fact that they were small nations of small, scattered communities in which the individual could enjoy a greater independence and influence on local and public affairs than was possible in large states. At a time when the bureaucratic and impersonal character of big political units was being recognised as one of the major problems of modern society, these particular features of the Nordic countries should be accorded their proper value and preserved. Smallness was not a disadvantage, but one of their main assets, which would enable them to tackle more successfully the problems of decentralising power and subjecting it to democratic control at all levels of government. Nordek's value was that it offered them an international organisation which, by preserving its members' national sovereignty, would allow them to keep the social and political advantages of smallness while gaining some of the economic advantages of size. In a world of large economic units moreover Nordek would provide a bulwark behind which the Nordic countries could continue to develop their societies on the principles of democracy, decentralisation and equality. Viewed from this perspective Nordek possessed an importance which went far beyond the economic benefits it was expected to bring — an importance which meant that it should not be sacrificed for the sake of EEC membership.[50] Indeed as the EEC was regarded as being everything that Nordek was praised for not being — large, bureaucratic, dominated by big countries with less egalitarian and democratic traditions and social systems — the whole logic of this argument, as of the others for Nordek, pointed to a rejection of EEC membership.

Socialists and Nordek

Socialist views on the EEC were to be gleaned from the Nordek debate only through the various arguments they used in support of the project. For in keeping with their previous positions on Nordic co-operation, both the Labour party and Socialist People's party were in favour of it, and this applied, with one notable exception, to all Labour's pro-marketeers.

The official Labour party line was very similar to the coalition's, namely that there existed no necessary conflict between Nordek and a later entry into the EEC.[51] But from the outset Labour welcomed Nordek with considerably more enthusiasm. It had supported the idea of a customs union in the 1950s for economic, political and ideological reasons which now, more than a decade later, it considered no less persuasive. By the late 1960s moreover its spokesmen had another argument for such a step. This was that the free trade introduced within EFTA had reached the stage where it required a greater co-ordination of national economic policies and an extension of state planning on a regional scale. Only this would ensure that the national authorities retained control over the developments set in motion by freer trade, and that the Nordic countries reaped the full benefits of the economic integration which was taking place between them.[52] A customs union would build on free trade to make the most efficient use of the four countries' resources, while the financial, industrial and technological co-operation foreseen in the Nordek treaty would enable them to combine their resources to the same end. The result would be to put all of them in a better position to withstand the increasingly harsh competition from outside the region.[53]

As to how Nordek would affect Norway's chances of eventually entering an enlarged EEC, Labour's answer to this was to draw a sharp distinction between the Nordic and wider Western European areas. Nordek was a necessary response to specific Nordic problems which would have to be tackled however the four countries' relations with the EEC developed. But its existence would not lessen each country's simultaneous need to protect its interests within Western Europe. The two areas were separate, with different problems and different tasks, and participation in close co-operation within one would not exclude participation in the other — as long, that is, as the forms of co-operation were kept compatible with each other. The proviso, of course, begged the question which the Conservatives had posed and expressed their doubts about: would Nordek in practice prove compatible with EEC membership? Labour's answer to this was the same as that given by some coalition pro-marketeers. Its spokesmen pointed to the principle laid down in the treaty preamble that Nordek was to facilitate the four countries' entry into an enlarged European market or their co-operation with it.[54] To the objection that this principle was a mere formal safeguard, they too pointed to the reality of Danish and Swedish self-interest, which they were convinced could be relied on to ensure that it was never allowed to become a mere formality. Nordek would not become an obstacle to membership for the countries which wanted to join the EEC, because Denmark and Sweden would not let it stand in their way, nor would the Norwegian Labour and Conservative parties.

On the contrary, most Labour spokesmen seemed to agree with those coalition pro-marketeers who argued that Nordek would be an advantage when negotiating with the EEC. Like them, they thought Nordek would strengthen Norway's bargaining position in Brussels.[55] By guaranteeing continued industrial free trade within the region, it would remove the spectre of new tariff barriers between Norway and Sweden.[56] It might even ease Sweden's way into the EEC, thereby dealing a heavy blow to any anti-market campaign in Norway. Exactly how membership of the two customs unions was to be reconciled in practice was left vague. But as Nordek had been designed to be adaptable in this respect, the general assumption was that any problems of fitting the two together would be overcome relatively easily.

The discordant voice in this Labour consensus was none other than Halvard Lange, foreign minister from 1946 until the party left office in 1965, and the party's outstanding post-war figure in international affairs. On two points Lange took a line very similar to the Conservatives'. He doubted whether Nordek would improve its members' negotiating positions *vis-à-vis* the EEC. The issues would be too numerous and complicated, the four countries' interests too different, even conflicting, for them even to co-operate very closely in Brussels, let alone negotiate as a bloc. More fundamentally, he questioned whether membership of these two customs unions could be combined. Like the Conservatives, he argued that the countries' different foreign and security policies would set a limit to the degree of economic integration compatible with later entry to the EEC for Norway and Denmark.[57] Lange was an Atlanticist who regarded European questions from that perspective. By 1969 moreover some of the views with which he was identified were out of step with the more left-wing tone of some party pronouncements on foreign policy (if not with the real priorities of Labour's leaders, which remained unchanged). Although alone in voicing such doubts about Nordek however, Lange's views were noteworthy as a possible pointer to similar but unexpressed doubts among other Labour Atlanticists and pro-marketeers — doubts concealed behind the solid front of party consensus.[58]

If that was so then they might have been reinforced by the way in which their own anti-marketeers openly supported Nordek as an alternative to EEC membership.[59] Like their allies on the coalition side, the socialist anti-marketeers recognised the danger of Nordek turning into a bridge into the EEC instead of a barrier. But like them they hoped that if Norway's economy was tied so tightly to those of Sweden and Finland, the point would be reached at which membership would be ruled out. They too were ready to take the risk in order, while there was time, to build up a functioning regional alternative to which they could point in any future struggle for public opinion. For those socialists who were neutralists too — the SPP, some on Labour's left — Nordek also offered a hope of eventually detaching Norway from the Atlantic alliance by means of economic integration with the Nordic neutrals and by helping to win the vital first step of preventing Norwegian entry into the EEC. The SPP was more reserved in its support for Nordek than were the anti-marketeers in the Labour and coalition parties.[60] It disliked Sweden's big international companies and the powerful family groups which still played so large a role in Swedish finance and industry. But faced by the risk of Norway one day entering the EEC and the possibility of perhaps averting that by joining Nordek now, the Socialist People's party had no doubts about choosing a customs union with the capitalist but at least non-aligned Sweden.

As the French presidential election campaign brought the first clear evidence that French government thinking on EEC enlargement might be changing, the arguments linking Nordek and Norwegian entry into the EEC became more explicit. The pro-marketeers who saw Nordek as a possible hindrance to membership began calling for a more cautious approach to the Nordic negotiations. Some wanted to await clarification about French policy before making any treaty commitments.[61] At least, they said, the Norwegians must now discuss Nordek with the wider European context much more prominently to the fore and ensure that nothing in the treaty could complicate Norway's position if negotiations began with the EEC.[62] By contrast, from the anti-marketeers and pro-marketeers who supported Nordek came calls for more speed and urgency in the Nordic negotiations.[63] The former were anxious to get their Nordic barriers as strong as possible in the shape of a signed and ratified treaty, the latter to strengthen their bridge to Brussels as the way began to open up.

When at last the treaty was ready for signature in February 1970, the same calls were coming even more insistently from each side. The Conservatives thought the work of revising the Nordek treaty should already be underway.[64] Labour, Centre and Liberal party spokesmen wanted the signing and ratifications to take place as soon as possible.[65] But that was not where the real dividing line over European policy ran, as most observers were coming to recognise. For the pro-marketeers who were urging a rapid conclusion of the treaty were unwilling to remove the main obstacle to doing so, namely the three Scandinavian countries' plans to open negotiations with the EEC, which had put Finland's accession to Nordek in jeopardy. The real division ran between those who gave priority to negotiations with the EEC whatever the consequences for Nordek and those who gave priority to Nordek, either because they already opposed EEC membership or because they were moving towards that position. But the latter were in a weak position from which to press their views. The government's hands were bound by the 1967 vote and the application in Brussels. And there was no majority in parliament for reversing that policy and withdrawing the application.

The government in Oslo, like those in Copenhagen and Stockholm, began its preparations to take up where President de Gaulle's veto had stopped them in 1967. Finland withdrew from Nordek. Those pro-marketeers who had seen in Nordek a means of helping them to take Norway into the EEC lost the advantages they would have gained from it if their calculations were correct. The anti-marketeers lost the Nordek treaty but retained the Nordic alternative for use in the campaign about EEC membership which was about to begin. Nordek was dead, the Finns left the other three in no doubt about that. But perhaps, after all, it was to prove more useful to Norway's anti-marketeers in that form, as something which could be offered, however unrealistically, in place of joining the EEC, than if Nordek had been established in 1970 as they wanted.

4. The opening of negotiations and fall of the coalition

Two months after the Finns withdrew from Nordek, negotiations began between the EEC and the four countries applying for membership, Britain, Denmark, Eire and Norway. Eight months later, in March 1971, the government in Oslo fell, the fundamental cause being differences over this question. And although by then substantive negotiations had scarcely started and the referendum was a year and a half away, the ground had already been laid for the electorate's 'no' to membership in September 1972.

'Negotiations bind' versus 'wait and see'

Although Nordek had demonstrated the coalition's serious divisions over relations with the EEC, the government was again able to unite on a report to parliament at the beginning of June. At that stage neither its own preparations nor the contacts with Brussels had reached the point where it was required to go beyond a repetition of those formulas of 1967 which could accommodate a variety of conflicting interpretations. It asked parliament to reaffirm its support for the 1967 application for membership negotiations 'as the best means of clarifying the basis for Norway's relations with the EEC', and made entry conditional on obtaining terms which would 'protect special Norwegian interests in a satisfactory manner',[1] particularly 'permanent special arrangements' for agriculture.[2] The majority by which parliament did so on 25 June — 132 to seventeen — was almost as large as in 1967.[3] Those voting against — seven Centrists, three Christians, seven Labour party members — were four more than in 1967. But they still numbered less than half the thirty-eight needed to prevent ratification of a treaty of accession.

As in 1967 the two factors producing this apparently overwhelming support for negotiations were the reluctance of the anti-marketeers in the coalition to push their opposition to an open confrontation and uncertainty about whether Britain's negotiations would succeed. The chances of Britain entering the EEC on this third attempt were rated better than they had been three years before. But the possibility of failure remained open until the late spring of 1971[4] — until after the coalition government had left office. This influenced the calculations of most of the politicians in Oslo. In particular, for those non-socialists who hoped to keep the coalition together while pursuing their European objective, it was a strong argument for not pressing their differences to breaking point until the outcome of Britain's negotiations was certain. If they failed, there would be no question of Norway entering the EEC, and this threat to the coalition would therefore be removed. If they succeeded, then the time would have come for the Norwegians to settle their own differences.

In one important respect, however, the situation was very different from 1967. Negotiations were going to begin this time. Those opposed to membership or with real doubts about it faced the prospect of Norway being drawn inextricably into a web of commitments by the very fact of beginning the process at all.[5] 'The negotiating table would bind' them,[6] they feared, or at least the ministers sitting at it. They could not know how fast the negotiations would go or how much time they would have to organise their opposition. Once negotiations had started, would there be a point at which they could find a pretext and parliamentary majority for stopping them? What if the EEC granted the Norwegians' request for special terms for the primary sector? Would they be able to win a referendum then? In this situation, any steps in the direction of membership could well be irreversible. The EEC, for example, had made it a condition of opening negotiations that the applicants accepted at the outset the Treaty of Rome and its political objectives, all subsequent EEC decisions, the guidelines laid down for the EEC's future development, and the principle that the applicants' problems be solved by transitional arrangements, not permanent exceptions from EEC rules.[7] Accepting this condition would itself be a first step into the EEC, because it would undermine later objections on any of these grounds. It would also seem to mean accepting the common agricultural policy as it stood and any EEC fisheries policy agreed on before Norway joined, as well as the results of the planning for foreign policy co-operation and economic and monetary union set in motion at the Hague summit. The prospect was of gradually sliding into the EEC through a process of accumulating concessions, commitments and agreements which it would be very difficult to stop, and which could easily acquire an appearance of irreversibility to politicians and voters alike.

This of course was what the supporters of membership were hoping. That negotiations were at last beginning was their major tactical advantage. It seemed not unreasonable to assume that before long they would reach a point of no return, politically and psychologically, and then produce entry terms which would win a referendum. However, precisely because negotiations were beginning, the pro-marketeers found themselves having to underline the distinction between negotiating and a later decision about joining the EEC.[8] This was necessary both with an eye to Norway's bargaining position in Brussels and in order to avoid any doubts at home about their determination to defend Norwegian interests. But doing this served as a constant reminder that there was still a real choice in the matter: that entering into negotiations was not setting them on an irreversible course into the EEC. As long as negotiations continued it was an obstacle to campaigning for their views as openly and actively as their opponents were very soon to start doing. The risk here was that if the anti-marketeers occupied the field alone for too long, public opinion might have become so hardened against membership by the time the negotiations had finished that even good terms would not enable them to recover the lost ground in time to win the referendum.

Aware of this danger, the pro-marketeers tried to turn to their advantage the distinction between negotiating and deciding in the light of the outcome whether or not to join the EEC. The application, they argued, certainly implied a wish to join if acceptable terms could be obtained. But the only commitment at this stage was to negotiate: parliament had taken no decision on the principle of membership and would not until the terms were known. So the responsible course for politicians and voters alike, they said, was to await the conclusion of negotiations before adopting hard and fast positions or organising campaigns either for or against membership. They should all 'wait and see' what the negotiations produced.[9] It was an argument designed to gain them a breathing-space at home while they obtained terms in Brussels with which they could then defeat their opponents. The latter naturally understood this,[10] which was why they ignored the attempted imposition of a truce, which 'wait and see' really amounted to.

The coalition

By the time parliament debated the EEC in June 1970, four groups had crystallised within the coalition.[11] One — the Conservatives, along with some members of the Liberal and Christian People's parties — wanted both to hold the coalition together and take Norway into an enlarged EEC. A much smaller second group openly gave priority to keeping Norway out of the EEC, some even if this meant breaking up the coalition, others partly because it probably would do so; in parliament this group was represented by the seven Centrists and three Christians who at the end of the debate voted to withdraw the 1967 application. The third, made up of the rest of the Centre party, did not want to join the EEC but like the pro-marketeers of the first group hoped to achieve their aim without destroying the coalition, or at least without incurring the responsibility for doing so. The last group included most Christians and Liberals. They were mainly concerned at this stage to resolve the serious splits that had emerged within their own parties. They therefore played a less prominent part in the manoeuvrings and public exchanges of this period than did the Conservatives and Centre party.

For the Conservatives both their aims were high priorities. Only the coalition could save them from permanent opposition; EEC membership was important to the economic interests they represented and on general foreign policy grounds. That was their dilemma, faced by a Centre party and sections of the Liberal and Christian parties which were beginning to look almost as determined to prevent membership as they themselves were to achieve it. But until well into 1970 they seemed to think that there was a reasonable chance of combining their two objectives. Negotiations had started. Unless broken off by Brussels or Oslo they should acquire their own momentum, bit by bit binding the ministers engaged in them and the parliamentarians who had voted for them. Initially the Conservatives appeared optimistic about the possibility of obtaining terms which would satisfy the primary producers, or at least detach the fishermen from the farmers.[12] They were also counting on the self-interest of their coalition partners to help them. Ending the coalition would put the other parties back into opposition too, and the Conservatives could hope that their partners' desire to hold onto office would inhibit them from pushing opposition to extremes. Then there was Per Borten, who presumably wanted to remain prime minister, but could do so only if he continued the negotiations — the only policy for which there was a majority in parliament. While negotiations lasted his influence would be another check on the Centre party, and if he then recommended the result, the Conservatives were confident that the electorate would return a 'yes' to membership. If some non-socialists, even a majority of the Centre party, opposed it in the final vote in parliament, even that need not in itself bring down the coalition. It was, after all, an established principle that the parliamentary groups could enjoy such a degree of independence without it necessarily ending their co-operation in government. Nor would non-socialist defections seriously threaten the ratification process as long as Labour's members stayed in line. And the Conservatives saw no reason to doubt that Labour's organisation would deliver the votes, both in parliament and at the referendum. For once, the strength and discipline of their major political opponent should be working to the Conservatives' advantage.

Because of their wish to hold the coalition together, the Conservatives were more circumspect about pressing their views on the EEC than they might otherwise have been. All their public statements made it clear that they wanted Norway to join the EEC and regarded the application as practically a commitment to do so if the Six gave them terms which safeguarded the primary sector's legitimate interests.[13] But for much of 1970 they held back from openly applying pressure to those who appeared doubtful or neutral, no doubt hoping that as long as the negotiations were allowed to continue to a conclusion the final terms would satisfy most of them. All these calculations, however, were based on the assumption that EEC membership was an issue not essentially different from others about which the coalition parties had disagreed before. The minority, in other words, would carry on a shorter or longer argument in government, and perhaps even vote against the government's recommendation in parliament to mark their dissent; but then they would adapt themselves to the new situation, preferring to remain in power rather than let Labour in. But this was a fundamentally mistaken assessment of the situation, and the Conservatives' error on this point was the single most important reason why their calculations were so soon upset. The question of whether or not to join the EEC was not like any other for those opposed to it. It was different in being considered of such vital importance that in the last resort many of them would push their opposition to breaking point. And as the Conservatives discovered, the anti-marketeers were now more self-confident and determined than they had been in 1967. Neither 'wait and see' arguments nor tactful handling were going to pacify them.

It was the anti-marketeers' disagreements about tactics which confused the picture in 1970 and prolonged the coalition's life into 1971. The minority who insisted on declaring their opposition openly and immediately did so from a mixture of principle and tactics. Their basic reasons for rejecting membership — the threat to national independence and to the powers of particular groups in Norway, their fear of submersion in a large multi-national organisation, the very nature of the EEC and its long-term objectives — were not such as could be negotiated about. They did not want to enter the EEC on any terms and therefore refused to vote for an application to negotiate about them.[14] But they also recognised the danger of allowing negotiations to begin: once started, how and when were they to be stopped? So in June they joined with the socialist anti-marketeers in parliament to propose that Norway withdraw its application, revive Nordek, and then participate in a joint Nordic approach to the EEC for talks about the economic consequences of British membership for their four countries.[15]

Most of the Centre party, on the other hand, preferred a more indirect form of opposition at this stage, while uncertainty still surrounded French intentions and Britain's negotiations. An open reversal of the party's 1967 position would lead inevitably to a confrontation with the Conservatives, and, as public opinion polls showed a large majority of the Centre party voters still in favour of the coalition,[16] it could be difficult to justify breaking it up on mere possibilities which might never materialise. So the majority decided to vote for negotiations but combine their consent with reservations and conditions which, if adopted, would rule out a successful conclusion to them.[17] The Centre party wanted an initial phase of preparatory talks, entered into without that prior acceptance of the EEC's political aims which the Six had made a condition for negotiations. The object of these talks would be to clarify whether the EEC's long-term goals, particularly those implied by its plans for political co-operation, were compatible with the Centre party's objectives for Norway and the constitutional limitations on the type of powers which parliament could transfer to international organisations. During these talks the government was to remain in close contact with parliament, which would be free to call for a new government report once the talks had brought more information on these points. It was this report which would provide the Centre party with its opportunity to call for a halt to the negotiations.[18] Next, the Centre party set up conditions for the entry terms which were obviously incompatible with membership. The 'permanent special arrangements' for agriculture were defined as the retention of Norway's national agricultural policy. Regional arrangements for the naturally disadvantaged areas were unacceptable: the common agricultural policy was not to apply to any part of Norway. The fishing limit was to remain permanently closed to foreign vessels, and again it was the whole coast which was to be excluded from any EEC plans for non-discriminatory access, not just the north with its coastal fishing industry and regional problems. The EEC's objective of freeing barriers to economic activity was not explicitly rejected. But again exceptions were required which would prevent it being put into effect in Norway. In particular there was to be no weakening of national control over capital movements, business establishment or the exploitation of the country's natural resources.[19]

The party recognised the risk of being drawn into a process which it could be difficult to stop. But in June it still preferred to run that risk rather than face the immediate political consequences of openly opposing membership negotiations. It was on this point though that the balance of opinion in the party began to shift during the second half of the year. Could Per Borten, who had argued for postponing any confrontation and relying on indirect methods of preventing membership as long as possible, be relied on to block entry into the EEC if it looked like costing him the premiership? Could the Centre party's ministers be counted on to do so, for that matter, if it meant losing their posts? Could those outside parliament be sure that the parliamentary group would act to stop the slide into the EEC before the point of no return had been reached? And who was to judge where that point was: Per Borten, the parliamentary group, the national conference which was not due to meet until April 1971? As 1970 drew to a close the differences over these questions intensified. More and more of those who opposed membership seemed to be moving towards the minority's position of wanting a clear anti-EEC front and an end to the dangerous process of negotiations and concessions in Brussels.[20] As they did so the political basis of the coalition was steadily whittled away. For by then its continuation had become largely dependent on this balance of tactical opinion within the Centre party.

The Christians and Liberals occupied a key place in the calculations of both the Conservative and Centre parties. Each hoped to draw them over to its side, leaving the other isolated with a choice between abandoning its position on the EEC or incurring the responsibility for breaking up the coalition. If the Christians and Liberals came out in favour of membership, the Centre party would be left in an uncomfortable alliance with the left socialists and communists. If they decided to oppose it, the Conservatives would be left defending it along with Labour. All the Liberal members of parliament and a majority of the Christians had confirmed their support for negotiations in the June vote. But in fact both parties were now seen to be much more seriously divided over the issue, in parliament and in the country, than most observers, or even their own leaders, had realised until it resurfaced after the Hague summit. By early 1971 it had become an entirely open question what their final positions would be.

The leaders of the Christian People's party were apparently taken by surprise at the extent of anti-market feeling among ordinary party members and voters. The parliamentarians seemed to have got seriously out of touch with their constituents' views on the question. To make matters worse, they saw the coalition being gradually torn apart between its Conservative and Centre party poles as the year wore on, with each seeking Christian support against the other on a question the Christians themselves were so divided over. The reaction of most of the party's leaders was to maintain a cautious, neutral stance; even those already identified with one side or the other usually expressed themselves with notable moderation.[21] They seemed to be waiting on events — in the government, in Brussels, especially in the party — and were obviously anxious to avoid hard and fast positions until the situation was clearer. In the coalition they avoided being drawn into the acrimonious public exchanges which became increasingly frequent after the middle of 1970. In parliament reserved neutrality was the impression given by the party chairman's conditions for giving his support to negotiations. There would have to be a careful examination, he said, of the effects on agriculture and fisheries, regional policy and the legislation regulating alcohol sales, and satisfactory solutions found to the problems created by EEC membership. He thought the EEC's plans for political co-operation and economic and monetary union could pose a serious threat to national sovereignty and parliamentary control. Again he wanted a thorough study of these points before any final decisions were taken.[22] Altogether the problems of entering the EEC seemed to loom larger than any benefits. The Christian People's party also wanted the government to examine alternatives to membership while negotiations were proceeding — a proposal the Conservative foreign minister rejected on the grounds that such an investigation would only come in question if the membership negotiations ran into serious difficulties, and then only be possible when the EEC's negotiations with the other EFTA countries had revealed the terms it was prepared to offer to non-applicants.[23] When the coalition fell in March 1971 the party's leaders were still balancing cautiously between the two sides. But the impression was that they were moving closer to an anti-market position in response to the mounting and active opposition to membership among their rank and file.[24] And in the conditions set up in the previous June they already had a platform from which to break with the negotiations should they decide to do so, or to reject entry later should they run their full course.

The Liberals' supporters were more evenly divided than the Christians.[25] But, like the Christians, the Liberal party as such looked less likely to back membership by early 1971 than it had done a year before. The re-emergence of the question had coincided with the change of chairmen which followed the 1969 election. The former chairman, Gunnar Garbo, had been identified with the party's radical wing and the Nordek debate had shown him to be moving closer to the anti-market camp even before the Hague summit. His successor, Helge Seip, was closer to the party's centre on domestic policy and by the late 1960s an outspoken advocate of EEC membership. The chairmanship contest had been a setback for the radicals and thus for the party's anti-marketeers, who had stayed in line with party policy when parliament debated the EEC soon afterwards. By the end of the year however — the change of leadership having done nothing to halt the party's decline in the polls[26] — they were beginning to recover some of the ground lost in the spring, and their influence was clearly visible in the party's sharpening position on the EEC. The chairman of the committee set up to examine the question, Hans Hammond Rossbach, was a prominent younger member of parliament who would soon be playing an active part in the anti-market campaign. They were helped by the party's conditions for voting for negotiations. These stressed the importance of regarding the question from an overall social perspective, and in particular the way in which membership would affect the party's aims of strengthening local democracy and achieving greater social and economic equality.[27] These conditions would reduce the importance of the entry terms compared with political judgements about the nature of the EEC and its probable future development: it would allow Liberals to vote 'no' if they wished, however good the final entry terms were. In January these conditions were further sharpened, reflecting the obvious increase in anti-market feeling within the party by then. More emphasis was placed on the consequences for democracy and national control, and like the Christians the Liberals wanted an investigation of the alternatives to membership while negotiations were taking place.[28]

The Liberals however differed from the Christians in the way they were soon pressing their views with an apparent unconcern about exacerbating the party's internal conflicts. The character of the Liberal party and the personalities involved partly explained this. But so did the fact that by then important sections of the party were ready to end the coalition. As a consequence this powerful constraint on the Christians was absent. Seip had made himself a vocal defender of the coalition.[29] But, like his position on the EEC, the new chairman's view represented only one within the party. *Dagbladet,* the Oslo daily newspaper close to the Liberals, had already announced that it believed the coalition should give way to a minority Labour government as the best way of reviving the Liberals' fortunes and establishing clear fronts over the EEC.[30] What was more, the paper was actively working towards this end by publishing a series of exposures, interviews and stories calculated to highlight the coalition's disagreements over the EEC and worsen relations between its members. The radicals and young Liberals wanted a break too.[31] The idea of playing an independent balancing role between socialists and non-socialists had been gaining ground for some time.[32] Now the EEC debate gave additional attraction to a course which would also free the party for participation in an anti-EEC front. Pro-market Liberals were dissatisfied with the coalition too. On the whole however they still regarded it as preferable to opposition. Their discontent was directed more at the way the coalition was being led. It was calls for a change of leadership, not an end to the coalition, which were being heard more frequently from that quarter by 1971. And by that was meant a change of prime minister.[33]

Per Borten's balancing act at the head of the government had become increasingly precarious as 1970 wore on. As prime minister he had twice recommended membership negotiations and was personally identified with the government's official policy. Continuing with it moreover was the only way of keeping the coalition in office, for the present at least. But his own Centre party was now leading the opposition to membership in the coalition and in parliament. Borten had been influential in persuading most of them to vote for negotiations in June.[34] The party as a whole however seemed determined to frustrate those negotiations before they had got very far, and to wreck the coalition if it looked like taking Norway into the EEC. Borten's own position on membership remained unclear, even to most of his ministers and party colleagues.[35] One obvious reason for this was that to have committed himself openly to either side would have made his position impossible. But there were many who thought it was also because Borten remained fundamentally flexible and pragmatic, following no very firm guiding principle beyond keeping the government going, waiting on events, and hoping that somehow or other the matter would resolve itself.[36] In 1970 he had at least some grounds for hoping that it would. Britain's negotiations might fail; Norway's might break down over agriculture and fisheries; or the EEC might grant Norway's requests for the primary sector, which in turn might modify the Centre party's attitude; or the Christians and Liberals might join the Centre party in opposition to membership and the Conservatives find that when it came to the point they preferred being in office at home to being in the EEC.

But whatever Borten's private calculations and views, there was no doubt about the effect of his efforts to hold the Centre party to negotiations and span the widening gap between them and the pro-marketeers. It was to win the coalition a little longer life, but at the price of increasing its tensions to breaking point and then himself providing the issue on which they were released and it collapsed. Borten kept his party from openly disavowing government policy, but only by agreeing to tactics which eroded the coalition's morale and political credibility and the trust between its members. Borten himself, in a number of public statements and speeches, sought by implication to dissociate himself from government policy, presumably in order to appease the mounting dissatisfaction in his party. But that had the same effect as the Centre party's tactics, as well as the serious consequence of offending by its disloyalty not only pro-marketeers but also ministers who stood nearer to the Centrists on the EEC itself.

The first and outstanding example of this was in June, when Borten used a press conference to criticise the recently retired Conservative foreign minister, John Lyng, for a letter sent to the EEC two months earlier.[37] The ostensible cause for offence was that in the Norwegian version the minister had expressed Norway's positive attitude towards the EEC's aim of 'political unification' (though the original French text had used the more acceptable term 'co-operation').[38] This attack on the former Conservative chairman — which opened a gulf between Borten and that party and was severely criticised from other quarters too[39] — was generally interpreted as an attempt to reassure his own party by creating the impression that the Conservatives, who still controlled the foreign ministry, were using it, almost behind his back, to go further in committing Norway than was compatible with official policy. The incident coincided with reported disagreements between Borten and the Conservatives over who should lead Norway's negotiating delegation in Brussels, and to which ministry he should report, the foreign ministry or the prime minister's office (as had been the case for the Nordek negotiations).[40] Eventually a regular diplomat was appointed and the foreign ministry's responsibility confirmed.[41] But at the same time a small government committee was established to provide overall direction, and this included two prominent earlier opponents of membership, Borten himself and the Christian, Kjell Bondevik.[42]

The so-called 'letter affair' was followed by speeches and interviews in which Borten seemed intent on creating the impression that he at least had considerable doubts about joining the EEC. He described the economic arguments for membership as being weaker now than they had been in the mid-1960s. He thought public attitudes had changed too, especially younger peoples', and politicians would have to take account of that.[43] He feared that the individual's opportunities for influencing decisions affecting his own life would be reduced inside the EEC. Indeed he gave it as his view that the real division over this question was between those who gave highest priority to the individual — as did he and his party — and those for whom purely economic criteria were more important.[44] He thought that in the formulation of Norwegian policy not enough weight had yet been given to the question of how membership would affect such fundamental objectives as greater equality and more decentralisation and participation; this would have to be rectified when the final decision came to be taken.[45] The whole tone of his statements was one of sceptical neutrality. It was increasingly difficult to reconcile with the negotiations on which his government had embarked.

Most observers regarded it, however, as merely another example of the Centrists' strategy of pursuing one policy in government and another outside it. In government its ministers went along with the negotiations. Outside it they expressed grave doubts about them in interviews and speeches,[46] while in parliament the Centrists played the role of opposition on European policy. As yet the party was not calling for a withdrawal of the application, even though its condition of an opening phase of non-binding preparatory negotiations had been ignored.[47] But by late 1970 its spokesmen were preparing to do so by emphasising what they described as new features in the situation, which according to them undermined several of the key assumptions on which parliament had confirmed the application in the summer. Outstanding among these was the publication of the EEC's Werner plan for establishing an economic and monetary union by the end of the decade, with a first three year stage beginning in 1971, in which there would be a progressive harmonisation of members' economic policies. This the Centrists described as such a serious threat to national sovereignty that it required a thorough re-examination of what membership would involve, especially the constitutional issues raised by such a degree of integration.[48] Next there was the EEC's common fisheries policy, agreed in principle at the end of June and reaffirmed in October. It was a policy which most Norwegians considered unacceptable as it stood, but the Centrists went much further, claiming that it proved there was no place in the EEC for a small country like Norway or for its coastal fishermen.[49] Then in November came a clear indication that Sweden would not be seeking membership, and again the Centrists argued that an important assumption underlying Norway's application had been removed.[50] By then they were also using the recent oil discoveries in the North Sea to claim that the economic argument for membership had been overthrown and the retention of national control over Norwegian resources made more vital than ever.[51] It all amounted to a rejection of membership without explicitly saying so.

Statements and counter-statements from the coalition's pro-marketeers and anti-marketeers multiplied in the press as the year wore on.[52] Some were in response to *Dagbladet's* revelations, which became a regular feature of the last months of the coalition's life and finally sparked off the crisis which ended it. Especially damaging to the coalition were its reports of private Centre party policy debates, which showed the true extent of its opposition to membership and the tactical considerations behind its agreement to negotiations in the summer.[53] One object of these particular leaks seemed to be to force the Centre party into open opposition in order to establish clear fronts on the issue, and thereby halt that slide into the EEC which ever more anti-marketeers feared would be the result of the party hesitating too long out of a desire to preserve the coalition. If that was so, then they achieved their aim. The leaks forced the coalition's pro-marketeers to take up the challenge to agreed policy which had been revealed. That in turn forced the Centre party to confirm or deny the truth of the leaks, or else harden the impression of duplicity if they would do neither. Gradually but steadily the last shreds of mutual confidence were worn away and the government's standing destroyed.

By the autumn the press was speculating about how and when the coalition would fall. The belief hardened that its only hope of surviving was the failure of Britain's negotiations. Even newspapers which had supported the coalition since the early 1960s began to question whether it should, let alone could, continue in view of the widening gap between its members over European policy. The idea of a minority Labour government was floated. Some pro-marketeers advocated it because they were coming to see in it their best hope of taking Norway into the EEC, some anti-marketeers because they thought that ending the coalition was necessary in order to free the middle-parties to campaign against membership. Even newspapers which still hoped the coalition could be saved argued that this would require a change of leadership.[54] Per Borten, that is, would have to go. Criticism of him mounted in the press and from the coalition benches in parliament, where it was said that his comments on European policy were damaging the government at home and the credibility of Norwegian policy abroad. But on its side the Centre party made it plain that its condition for staying in the coalition was that Per Borten remained prime minister. If any of the other three parties forced his resignation, the Centre party would leave with him. The coalition had to continue as it was, or not at all.[55]

By the beginning of 1971 the exchanges had become sharper and more personal, the irreconcilable differences over European policy more glaring. The level of mutual irritation continued to rise as each new leak or interview or speech was followed by rebuttals, replies and more press comment. But none of the coalition parties' leaders seemed ready to bring their differences to a head, while the Centre party's solid front behind Borten had led to a stalemate as regards reforming the government. Most of its politicians were still waiting for some clarification in Britain's negotiations and hoping to hold the coalition together somehow. None wanted to assume the responsibility for the final break if it nevertheless came. The situation seemed deadlocked.

The negotiations

The disagreements which were bringing about the coalition's disintegration in Oslo were reflected in the negotiations in Brussels. While it was in office these got no further than the preliminaries of the formal opening session on 30 June, two ministerial level negotiating sessions in September and December, meetings of experts and the exchange of preparatory information. The pace was determined by Britain's negotiations. The entry of the three smaller applicants was conditional on their success, and the EEC's absorption in them left it little time for the other three.[56] So until early June 1971, when the main problems between Britain and the Six were settled in principle, the EEC was not ready for substantive negotiations. This probably helped the government to survive longer than it would have done had the pace been faster. For it was able to postpone decisions on the negotiating mandates for agriculture and fisheries, which were still not formally settled when it fell, despite discussions having by then gone on for nearly a year.

The Norwegian statement at the opening meeting on 30 June was obviously influenced by the reservations with which the Centrists and Christians had agreed to negotiate at all.[57] The EEC's condition for opening negotiations was that the applicants accepted the Treaty of Rome, its political objectives, all subsequent decisions, and the guidelines drawn up for the EEC's further development. Yet the statement confined itself to describing the Treaty of Rome and later decisions based on it as 'a suitable basis for wider European co-operation'. It did not expressly accept the political objectives. Approval was restricted to 'the treaty's objective', which could be interpreted as including the political aspects but could also (as subsequent Centre party comments demonstrated)[58] be understood as excluding them. Its only reference to the sensitive questions of political co-operation and economic and monetary union was to express an interest in participating in international monetary co-operation and to agree to the subject of political co-operation being discussed in another context.

Most of the statement was a detailed description of the special problems which Norway would face inside the EEC because of its geographical position, natural disadvantages and economic structure. At the centre were the problems of agriculture and fisheries. It was explained that these two sectors provided the basis for settlement in large areas of the country. So it was vital that they were able to retain their present structure and level of production after entry. However as Norwegian food prices were higher than those in the EEC and Norwegian producers also received price subsidies not allowed under the common agricultural policy, applying that policy without any modifications would result in an estimated fall of between 40 and 50 per cent in agricultural incomes. To avoid this and the serious impact it would have on production and regional settlement, Norway would require permanent special arrangements: permanent because the country's disadvantages in this sector were the result of geography and climate, and could therefore not be solved by transitional measures. As Norwegian production would be of merely marginal significance in an enlarged EEC, being non-exporting and contributing only 0.5 per cent to total production, it was argued that the EEC would be able to grant such permanent exceptions from its rules without any noticeable effect on its agricultural sector or its common policy. As for Norway's fishing industry, its problems were also described as being the result of natural and therefore permanent conditions. It was a predominantly coastal industry, especially in the north where the difficulty of providing an economic basis for settlement was greatest. This made the question of fishing limits of vital importance to Norway. The EEC's common fisheries policy would have to take account of this, and the Norwegians said they hoped to be allowed to put their views on the subject as soon as the negotiations had opened.

Capital movements and business establishment were the other two questions singled out as being of particular importance. Again, any Norwegian government would have included them, as all had taken a restrictive line on them in international negotiations. But their prominence in this opening statement no doubt owed something to the emphasis the coalition's anti-marketeers were placing on them. The EEC was told that Norway required foreign capital and had traditionally imported large amounts. But being a small economy with small industrial and business units by international standards, the form and size of such capital imports could profoundly affect the country's economic and social structure and the government's ability to manage the economy. That was why, for example, the laws regulating the exploitation of Norway's natural resources had occupied such a central place in economic policy. Here, as in the primary sector, the EEC's regulations and plans would create special problems which would have to be taken up in the forthcoming negotiations.

It was a reserved statement, betraying none of that enthusiasm for the broader political perspectives of European co-operation which characterised pro-marketeers' speeches at home and would undoubtedly have featured in a Conservative or Labour party opening declaration.[59] But like so many coalition pronouncements on European policy it was addressed to two very different audiences: in this case to the Six in Brussels and to the watchful opposition within the coalition's own ranks. It had two aims. The first, which was to be a general Norwegian objective throughout the next eighteen months, was to portray their country as a special case requiring and deserving special terms; in this the statement largely achieved its purpose. The second, a purely coalition concern, was to cover and accommodate its own internal disagreements. Here it succeeded only partially. The statement managed to reconcile the coalition's differences temporarily, but it scarcely concealed them.

Their reconciliation was to prove more difficult as the negotiations continued. At the September meeting the Six asked for that full and formal acceptance of their conditions for negotiations which Norway had failed to give in June. This the foreign minister now gave. He attached two reservations: Norway would still be asking for permanent special arrangements for agriculture, and it would want to take up for further negotiations any EEC decisions on fisheries policy which failed to satisfy its requirements.[60] But the main point — for the anti-marketeers at home as well as the EEC[61] — was that Norway had met the EEC's demand that, in principle at least, it accepted all the decisions taken on the basis of the EEC's treaties and that applicants' problems in adjusting to them were to be solved through transitional arrangements. Similarly, the government's official comment on the Davignon report on political co-operation was couched in cautious tones and emphasised the pragmatic, limited nature of the proposed foreign policy consultations; they went no further, the government said, than the consultations in which Norway already took part in other organisations. But at the same time the government also accepted the EEC's invitation to participate in the twice yearly foreign ministers' meetings even before the outcome of the entry negotiations was known.[62]

Those opposed to membership regarded both these steps as dangerous concessions. The Centre party had objected to Norway accepting the EEC's political objectives until after the completion of a preparatory negotiating stage. Now the foreign minister had done so, and also accepted the guidelines for the EEC's development laid down at the Hague summit. As for the EEC's plans for political co-operation contained in the Davignon report, when recommending negotiations in the summer the majority in the foreign relations committee had reserved its position on these; it had said that if they went beyond normal inter-governmental consultations, a separate parliamentary decision would be required to approve Norwegian participation.[63] Now the government and pro-marketeers argued that the co-operation foreseen in the report was well within these limits.[64] The anti-marketeers, on the other hand, maintained that the perspectives the report opened up went far beyond them and that, taken in conjunction with the Werner report on economic and monetary union, they raised serious constitutional issues which would have to be examined before the negotiations went much further — and which might well require them to be broken off as incompatible with the constitution.[65] Despite these objections, however, the government had now committed Norway to joining in the new Davignon system, which although formally outside the scope of the EEC's institutions was in fact a significant extension of the EEC's character and activities. It was beginning to seem as though after only three months the negotiating table was indeed binding the government, including its Centrist ministers and prime minister, and that the process of concessions and commitments which would take Norway into the EEC was well under way.

But in fact the negotiations had already produced an invaluable piece of propaganda for the anti-marketeers, which more than made up for these concessions. On the day they began, the EEC finally settled the principles of its common fisheries policy, and these included non-discriminatory access to member states' fishing limits. Exclusive belts would be reserved for coastal fishermen in certain areas, but only for a five-year transitional period and only up to three miles. For the Six this decision was simultaneously part of the completion of its agricultural policy and of its preparations for negotiating as a community.[66] Its timing, however, could hardly have been more unfortunate from the Norwegian pro-marketeers' point of view. They had argued that it would be possible for Norway to influence the EEC's fisheries policy once negotiations had started, partly because the EEC would scarcely be able to ignore the views of Western Europe's largest fishing nation, partly because it was a fundamental principle that no member's vital interests (applicant member's in this case) would be ignored in framing common policies.[67] The next eighteen months were to prove them right on both points. But the EEC was not willing to let an applicant influence decisions which were a completion of existing policies and part of the very difficult internal adjustment of interests required to face the applicants as a single negotiating team. In domestic political terms the pro-marketeers had miscalculated in arguing that it would be possible to do so, for the result now was only to increase the propaganda value to their opponents of the EEC's striking demonstration that it was not. Even after 30 June, however, the government, and especially its pro-market ministers, continued to urge the EEC to take Norway's views into account before making its final decisions, the deadline for which was 1 November. Again the EEC refused. And again the effect was to strengthen the impression that the Six were deliberately ignoring Norwegian interests. At the September meeting the foreign minister obtained an assurance that the Six would recognise Norway's interests in this sector 'at the appropriate time'.[68] But that did not stop them going on to confirm their previous decision regarding non-discriminatory access a month later.

The pro-marketeers knew what the impact of this would be on public opinion. They conceded that the EEC had been fully entitled to act as it did. But they made no secret of their view that by doing so these six continental countries had displayed a total lack of understanding for the political importance of the fishing industry in Norway.[69] They tried to play down the significance of the decision and its timing. They pointed out for example that the unfortunate coincidence of dates had been due to delays in resolving the Six's own disagreements; that the Six had been bound by the Hague summit agreements to complete this part of their agricultural policy before negotiations opened; that they had needed a joint negotiating position;[70] and that this policy should be regarded as no more than a starting point for the revised one which would emerge from the forthcoming negotiations with the three biggest fishing countries in Western Europe.[71] But even those who wanted Norway in an enlarged EEC had to agree that unless the new policy was changed, or at least modified in Norway's case, it would present an almost insurmountable obstacle to Norwegian entry.[72]

None of their explanations removed the popular impression that right at the outset Norway had been snubbed, its interests not merely ignored but blatantly attacked before it was in a position to defend them. Again and again the anti-marketeers were to come back to this during the coming two years. This, they said, had shown how the other members would treat the Norwegians if they joined the EEC. They would have no influence, even on decisions of such importance to them; the large states would simply over-rule them. As for this policy being only a starting point, it was precisely because the Six were intent on gaining entry to Norway's rich protected fishing banks for their trawler fleets that they had fixed the principle of non-discriminatory access before the Norwegians were able to veto it.[73] Per Borten's comments seemed to show that the prime minister himself agreed with this interpretation. Having waited all these years to agree on a fisheries policy, he said, the Six had settled on one diametrically opposed to what the Norwegians were asking for, and had chosen the very day Norway's negotiations opened to do it; the effect had been like a 'cold shower'.[74] The effect had also been to harden the fishing industry's opposition to membership. After 30 June 1970 those who wanted Norway in the EEC faced a wall of hostility and suspicion in the fishermen's organisations, which could probably have been overcome only by an entirely new common policy based on exclusive national limits, or by an explicit treaty guarantee that the 1970 policy would never apply to Norway. Their demand was simple and unalterable: the permanent retention of their exclusive twelve-mile fishing limit around the whole coast.[75] The Centre party supported them, of course, and all the anti-marketeers now made this one of the touchstones of whatever terms were eventually brought home from Brussels.[76] Nevertheless, however good they might be, the pro-market cause had been dealt a serious blow even before the negotiations had properly begun.

The agricultural organisations had already presented their demands. These were the same as in 1967. There was to be no weakening of import controls, no regional arrangements confined to disadvantaged areas, no change in the powers of the producer organisations, no change in the system of price subsidies, nothing that could lead to an alteration in the existing pattern and level of production. In short, the common agricultural policy was not to apply to Norway, which was to maintain its national agricultural policy even within the EEC.[77] These demands were known as the 'protection policy', because the retention of import controls was an essential feature of them. As they would obviously be unacceptable to the EEC, they really amounted to little more than a scarcely veiled rejection of membership. The alternative proposal for those permanent special arrangements Norway was requesting was the so-called 'compensation policy'.[78] Under this Norway would apply the common agricultural policy, including the price levels set in Brussels, and remove its quantitative controls on imports from EEC countries. But Norwegian farmers would receive monetary compensation amounting to the difference between EEC prices and a higher hypothetical internal price level set in negotiations between the state and agricultural organisations. So the producers would not lose financially by the lower price levels and freeing of imports. Most important, the compensation policy would open the way for membership by acceptance of the EEC's agricultural policy. So its advocates were those who supported membership or who at least were not yet ready to foreclose the option or bring the coalition's disagreements to a head.

When the government left office at the beginning of March it had still not presented to parliament its long awaited recommendation

on the agricultural section of the negotiating mandate.[79] The next ministerial level meeting in Brussels was set for 15 March, yet this key
issue appeared to be unresolved. The coalition seemed to have reached an *impasse* in the negotiations just at it had in the question of
its own leadership.

Labour and Europe

It was not only the coalition which had so far failed to state its position
on the crucial issue of the agricultural mandate. So had the Labour
party. It was implicit in the party's position on the EEC that it
would only support a proposal compatible with membership, and this
ruled out one based on the retention of import controls. But its
leaders had neither publicly rejected the protection policy nor openly
lent their support to the compensation policy which the agricultural
organisations disliked.[80] Labour was benefiting from the coalition's
difficulties over the EEC, and they obviously had no intention of
helping it out of them or diverting anti-market wrath onto themselves
by taking a stand when, because they were in opposition, they could
avoid doing so. This approach, cautious and largely determined by
domestic political considerations, was characteristic of their whole
handling of the EEC question before the party came back into office
in March 1971

Labour's 1969 programme committed the party to membership
negotiations in order to clarify the terms Norway could obtain, with
the clearly implied aim of joining the EEC if Britain did and if
satisfactory terms could be obtained for certain specific Norwegian
interests such as the primary sector.[81] Its leaders were practically
unanimous in wanting Norway in an enlarged EEC, and for much
the same reasons as in 1962 and 1967. Britain might be less important now politically and as a market, but the economic consequences
of simultaneously losing much of the benefits of EFTA and being
excluded from an EEC which included Britain and Denmark, perhaps even Sweden, were still considered an unanswerable argument
for following Britain once again. General foreign policy considerations
were equally important and pointed in the same direction. It was
still believed that staying outside an enlarged EEC would undermine
Norway's position in the Atlantic world and in the organisations of
Western co-operation, while joining would consolidate it. Other
arguments, such as European solidarity and working from inside to
create a socialist EEC, weighed more or less heavily with individual
Labour politicians and different sections of the party. But for the
generation which had risen to the top of the party in the 1940s and
1950s and still led it in 1970, it was the economic and foreign

policy arguments which counted. It was these which made it almost unthinkable for them that Norway should choose to stay outside an EEC which included most of its European NATO allies and was the largest market for its exports and its shipping services.

But Labour had other, equally important, objectives at home. Like the coalition parties, its leaders hoped to avoid the necessity of choosing between them and their European aims. One was the permanent concern to maintain unity in a party which spanned such diverse social and economic groups, with its left wing touching the SPP and its right firmly in the centre of Norwegian politics. That meant managing the EEC issue in a way which minimised the risks of internal conflicts. So did the second domestic objective, returning to power. The good 1969 election result had made this a realistic prospect for 1973, and the party was on the offensive. The public opinion polls showed its support rising — from 46.5 per cent in September 1969 to 50 per cent in December 1970[82] — and it was already campaigning hard for the mid-term local elections in September 1971. But the polls also showed that only a minority of the electorate supported EEC membership,[83] while the SPP had taken an anti-market stand which could be a danger if Labour's left-wing became seriously disaffected. This, combined with the uncertainty about Britain's negotiations, argued for a cautious handling of the question, and it was that which its leaders adopted. The correctness of their strategy appeared confirmed by the apparent paradox that the party's popularity was increasing, despite the unpopularity of its policy on the main issue of the day.

Behind their belief that they could successfully combine taking Norway into the EEC, keeping the party united, and returning to office was the assumption that in the end they would win the referendum and have a three-quarters majority in parliament for the treaty of accession. There was the electors' known propensity to be guided by the established political leaders. The June 1970 vote had confirmed that these, as represented in parliament at least, were still, as in 1967, set on the course of membership negotiations, albeit with varying degrees of enthusiasm and conviction. Labour's leaders knew they could rely on the Conservatives (just as the Conservatives thought they could count on Labour to deliver the votes). The Liberal party had a fair number of doubters, but its chairman was a pro-marketeer and the party seemed to have fallen in behind him. The Christians were divided, but at least half their parliamentary group was expected to vote for membership. So even if the whole Centre party were to vote against it, the anti-market minority would not muster the one-quarter needed to block ratification. And then the character and recent history of the Labour party itself seemed to rule out large scale defections from the official line. The leadership had won party backing for the main lines of its foreign policy ever since the war, most notably for the controversial decisions to take Norway into NATO in 1949 and seek EEC membership in 1962. Loyalty and respect for majority decisions were cardinal party principles, while the strict ban on the formation of separate groups within the party made it difficult to organise an effective opposition.[84] Labour moreover was a party with a highly developed sense of power after so many years in possession of it. It hardly seemed likely to sacrifice the imminent prospect of regaining office by tearing itself apart over this question of EEC membership — if only it was carefully handled.

All this, in turn, assumed that the question of joining the EEC was not so important a matter that opposition would be pushed to extremes or voters desert the party over that alone. It was the same assumption — based on the experience of 1967, not 1962 — which the Conservatives were making, and again it proved to be the original mistake which paved the way to defeat in September 1972. From it derived the Labour leaders' erroneous expectation that the party's anti-marketeers would obey the call for a truce until the negotiations were completed and then submit to majority decisions and the ban on group activity. From it too stemmed the equally mistaken impression that they could take Norway into the EEC without paying any significant price in terms of internal party conflict. Not a few of Labour's leaders would probably have been unwilling to pay such a price if they had been aware of its necessity.[85] But most of them apparently thought there was no need to make such a difficult choice and give clear priority to one or the other at an early stage. They thought they could achieve their European objective with arguments and tactics tailored to their domestic ones.

So the word went out that the party debate was to be 'objective and calm'.[86] They left no doubt about it being party policy to enter the EEC if acceptable terms could be negotiated: conference decisions, by which they must all abide, were not neutral on that point.[87] But at this stage all views would be given a fair hearing. Accordingly the party's national newspaper printed the speeches of Labour's anti-marketeers in the June parliamentary debate alongside those of Labour's members who defended the official line;[88] it also organised and printed round-table discussions between party leaders and prominent Labour anti-marketeers.[89] Party members and voters were asked to maintain an open, unprejudiced attitude.[90] They were to 'wait and see' the results of the negotiations, and until then avoid adopting rigid positions.[91] Not only did objectivity require this approach to so complex and important a question, they were told: so did the party's electoral interests. The leadership wanted the EEC question kept out of domestic politics as far as possible, and especially the local election campaign, lest it dampen party workers' enthusiasm and cost Labour votes.[92] Keep calm, wait and see, and stay united for the party's sake was the instruction from the top as the negotiations in Brussels began.[93]

The leadership's choice of arguments in favour of membership reflected this overriding concern to avoid party strife. The foreign and security policy considerations which weighed so heavily with them were heard, but not prominently; when used, it was more often with the emphasis on Western European unification as a basis for east-west detente or for helping the developing countries than as a necessary step to consolidate Norway's place in the west or protect Norway's own security interests. Economic arguments were more to the fore.[94] But the most prominent argument in this period was a socialist one, addressed specifically to the Labour party. This portrayed the Treaty of Rome as being merely a neutral framework, the economic and social policies with which it was filled out depending on the balance of political forces within the EEC at any particular time. The objectives enshrined in the treaty necessarily reflected the problems and outlook of the decade in which it was drawn up, and that was why it emphasised efficiency and economic growth rather than equality and the redistribution of wealth. Socialists, it was said, should not read out of them the EEC's objectives for the 1970s and 1980s, because these were changing as the problems facing its members changed. The EEC was not a socialist organisation (partly because socialists had left its shaping to conservative and capitalist forces), but it could be turned into one if the socialist parties joined forces with that aim in view. This, declared the leadership, was the historic challenge now presented to the Norwegian Labour party. Creating this socialist Europe moreover was becoming a pre-condition for achieving the party's objectives at home, because these increasingly required international action. How else, they asked, could they gain control over the multinational organisations or the violent exchange rate fluctuations of recent years, over pollution or the inflation which was threatening working people's living standards? Labour's ability to implement its programme at home would be affected by decisions taken in the EEC anyway, whether they belonged to it or not. So far better to have a voice in these decisions and ensure they were in accordance with socialist objectives. Seen from this perspective European policy was a natural and necessary extension of domestic policy, ideological conflicts at the European level an extension of those in Norway itself. There was no contradiction between socialism and EEC membership.[95]

This line of argument was partly intended to counter the objection that Conservative support for membership proved the EEC was a capitalist organisation in which it would be impossible to create a socialist society in Norway.[96] Not so, insisted the party's leaders: joining the EEC would be a continuation of the domestic struggle against the Conservatives at another level; the Conservatives might be working for the same end, but for very different reasons and with different aims.[97] One consequence of arguing like this before party audiences, however, was to rule out open co-operation with the Conservatives to achieve their common objective. So Norway's two largest parties went into the campaign separately and continued to fight it separately for the next two years, Labour moreover publicly distancing itself from the Conservatives with arguments calculated to cause the maximum confusion in the voters' minds about what the EEC was and why Norway should join it. It was partly because of this Labour concern not to be seen working closely with the Conservatives that the pro-marketeers never established a cross-party national campaign organisation comparable in effectiveness and political weight to that of their opponents.

This would not have been so serious for the outcome had the socialist argument for membership achieved its desired effect within the Labour party itself. But the evidence was that it did not. The public opinion polls pointed to Labour voters being unimpressed,[98] and those on the left found numerous counter-arguments. Norway, they said, was too small to influence the EEC's development; it was much more likely to be contaminated itself by the strong conservative forces in Western Europe. They regarded the continental and British social democratic parties as either too weak or not genuinely socialist. Only if the Nordic countries acted as a group inside the EEC might they perhaps exert some influence, but this was ruled out because Finland could not join and Sweden seemed to have decided not to.[99]

The conciliatory treatment of the party's anti-marketeers did not have the hoped for result either. These very soon demonstrated that they had no intention of waiting to see what the negotiations produced. Like those non-socialists who had voted against negotiations, they argued that as they were against membership on principle the terms were irrelevant.[100] They also accused their leaders of inconsistency. All the latters' statements on the EEC, they said, were a more or less open advocacy of membership, yet those who opposed it were expected to remain passive until the negotiations were over. The 'wait and see' line seemed to have little to do with objectivity and everything to do with tactics. The anti-marketeers were to do nothing while their leaders carried on an 'information programme' inside the party in preparation for the day when negotiations were successfully concluded and they could at last begin campaigning in earnest. By then party opinion was to have been sufficiently moulded to deliver the majority votes for membership with which the leaders could call for the minority's submission in accordance with party regulations. The only way to prevent this happening was by not waiting, but beginning to campaign immediately. This the anti-marketeers therefore proceeded to do. In the young socialists' national organisation they had a party base throughout the country. Sections of some trade unions were also opposed to membership. As yet they did not organise openly because that would have been a direct challenge to the ban on group activity, and they were also cautious about establishing links with organisations outside the party like the People's Movement, lest it open them to the charge of disloyalty.[101] But they criticised the composition of the party committee responsible for information work about the EEC and succeeded in having representatives of their own views appointed to it. And they began a secret signature-collecting campaign aimed at establishing their strength in the party, so that when at last they did emerge into the open they would be too large a minority to silence or ignore. That would be at the next biennial national conference in May 1971, when they would try to get the 1969 conference decisions on European policy changed or least modified.[102]

By the time Labour returned to office in March 1971 the internal opposition was already too large to be disciplined, let alone suppressed. The party's transfer from the opposition benches to government posed a threat to the anti-marketeers insofar as the leaders' appeals to loyalty and party unity could be expected to carry greater force with members when they came from their own government. But by then Labour's anti-marketeers were in a better position to resist pressure from above than they would have been just eight months before, and were therefore much better prepared for the campaign ahead.

The People's Movement and public opinion

There were plenty of other anti-marketeers who also ignored the call for a waiting period. Having failed to prevent the negotiations starting, their aim after June was to get them broken off before the middle-parties' leaders were too compromised to break free or the negotiations could be concluded with terms good enough to win a referendum. But they knew they might well fail to achieve this. It was therefore important to begin campaigning early in case they had to fight a referendum after all. They had to make the most of the period while their opponents were still handicapped by their own 'wait and see' line. The polls showed that some 40 per cent of the voters had no firm opinion on the subject as yet.[103] This was both an opportunity and a danger. The opportunity was that such people were open to influence from both sides. The danger was that on the pro-market side stood many of the politicians such voters normally listened to. The anti-marketeers' task, however, would be easier for being primarily a defensive one. Because the polls also showed that of those who had taken a position, more were against membership than were for it.[104] Their job would be not so much to change existing attitudes as to harden them.

To do this some form of organisation was required. None of the large parties represented in parliament could be used in 1970. The middle-parties were still in government: the Centre party not yet prised away from its policy of indirect opposition, the Christian and Liberal parties divided and still officially committed to waiting for the outcome of the negotiations. With the exception of the Conservatives all the parties' youth sections had come out against membership and set up the alternative aim of intensifying Nordic co-operation.[105] But although they would be important for the campaign itself, they hardly provided the organisational base or broad enough appeal to win over a majority of ordinary voters. By August 1970 the agricultural organisations had begun a public information campaign; but again they were working on too narrow a base. At the end of that month however a national campaign organisation was established — the People's Movement against Norwegian membership of the Common Market — financed mainly by the same organisations and directed by the same man, Arne Haugestad, who had been responsible for their information work.[106] The aim was to make the People's Movement's appeal as broad and national as possible, and this required a formal separation from the primary producer organisations. But they were well represented on its directing body, as were the anti-market left wingers. The official objective of the People's Movement was to work against entry into the EEC and supply people with the information which it accused the government and state administration of failing to provide. It too set up Nordic co-operation as an alternative to EEC membership and a joint Nordic application for free trade negotiations as the solution to any economic problems which British membership might create.[107]

The campaign launched by the People's Movement in the autumn followed closely the single issue campaigns which had been a notable feature of the 1960s and in which Haugestad himself had made his name. Like those movements — notably the campaigns against nuclear weapons and the Vietnam war, but also other smaller ones — it was cross-party and extra-parliamentary, relying on concentrated, simple propaganda, direct contact with the voters, and mobilising people influential in their local communities or professions but not normally active in politics. Its concentration on the one aim of preventing EEC membership was exactly suited to an issue which cut across normal party lines, united people with very different views on other domestic and foreign policy questions, and proved capable of arousing intense emotions and personal engagement. There were several reasons for the success of the People's Movement, apart from skilful leadership and a strategy suited to the issue. It had the financial and political backing of important interest groups.[108] It was able to organise and campaign well ahead of the pro-marketeers. The latter never established an organisation capable of matching it. The question on which it was campaigning proved to be one which could indeed mobilise the active support it needed from sections of society outside the narrow professional political establishment: from the highly qualified and often well-known professional people who supplied the expertise required to counter official arguments and reports, down to the many thousands of volunteers throughout the country who distributed the campaign leaflets, collected the signatures, and carried the campaign message. The message itself could be expressed in a relatively sophisticated manner, as in the detailed case for rejecting membership which the People's Movement published in reply to the government's report to parliament after the conclusion of negotiations in 1972.[109] More often though it was put over in the stark form suited to mass consumption.[110] All the fish would be taken by foreign trawlers. Norwegian agriculture would be ruined. Small industries would be forced out of business or bought up by foreign capital. The north would be depopulated. The country would be invaded by foreign workers, catholic ideas, continental drinking habits, and foreigners buying up their mountain huts, lakes and forests. Membership would spell disaster from which there would be no escape because the decision would be irrevocable.

Here the EEC's fisheries policy was invaluable. Just as useful though was the word 'union' with which the EEC was describing its proposed harmonisation of members' economic and financial policies. For in Norway that word was laden with all the historical and emotional overtones acquired through centuries of foreign domination within 'unions': the union with Denmark from the fourteenth century until 1813, followed after a few months of independence in which they gave themselves a constitution by the monarchical union with Sweden until 1905. The EEC could not have chosen a term more likely to arouse instinctive feelings of suspicion, defensiveness and national independence. Its 'union plans' very quickly moved to the centre of the People's Movement's campaign, providing definitive proof that all the anti-marketeers' particular predictions would be borne out.[111] Some leading pro-marketeers at least had no illusions about how effective this might prove to be. As one with considerable experience of his country's relations with the outside world put it: suspicion of the unknown, of any departure from established ways, was a natural and common phenomenon and not peculiar to Norway; but it was especially strong among a people like the Norwegians who had lived relatively isolated from the rest of Europe for so much of their history. It would be easier to confirm Norwegians in this natural reaction than to convince them of the need for change and for that much closer involvement with other countries which EEC menbership would entail.[112]

This judgement appeared to be confirmed in February 1971, five months after the People's Movement began its campaign. Throughout 1970 the public opinion polls had continued to record the pattern which had prevailed since 1962. Support for EEC membership hovered just above the 20 per cent mark, about 40 per cent were undecided, and the remainder preferred some other type of agreement or none at all.[113] At that stage the question seemed to have made only a slight impact on the public at large.[114] This was shown by the high percentage of respondents who described themselves as undecided or uninterested;[115] and also by the way the Labour party rose steadily in the monthly party polls despite officially favouring membership. That apparent contradiction owed something probably to the leadership's cautious handling of the question. But part of the explanation seemed to be that the EEC issue had not yet started influencing voters' attitudes towards the parties. Of the two most markedly anti-market parties, the Centre party had been doing relatively better in the polls than its coalition partners, while the SPP had marginally improved its position.[116] But this was not necessarily directly related to their positions on the EEC. The Centre party's performance, for example, may have been due to voters' reactions to the coalition's internal disagreements rather than the party's anti-market statements. As the coming crisis was to show, Per Borten remained a popular figure with much of the public whatever the views of his coalition colleagues.

In February, however, there was a sudden change in the EEC polls. The percentage supporting membership was suddenly halved. Only 12 per cent now wanted membership, nearly 50 per cent were undecided.[117] It took another few months for the voters to connect their views on the EEC and their party preferences. But then the Labour party, back in office and openly identified with the negotiations, began falling faster than it had risen in 1970. The discrepancy between the two sets of polls ended and both pointed clearly in the same direction: towards at least an initial success for the anti-marketeers and a harder battle for public opinion than those wanting Norway in the EEC had anticipated.

The end of the coalition

On 2 March 1971 the government resigned. On 10 March, after unsuccessful negotiations to continue it with Kjell Bondevik of the Christian People's party as prime minister in Borten's place, the Labour party formed a minority government. A government crisis had been expected some time in 1971. Pressures were mounting for a resolution of its differences over the EEC, party conferences were due in the spring, Per Borten was under increasing criticism from both pro-marketeers and anti-marketeers, and the press leaks and speculation were keeping attention focused on the coalition's difficulties. But the crisis broke earlier and more suddenly than anticipated, taking all involved by surprise and setting off three weeks of political confusion which ended the coalition in a way that itself became an obstacle to future attempts to revive it.

The immediate cause was Per Borten's handling of the latest leak in *Dagbladet*.[118] It developed into a crisis for several reasons. The general level of tension and his colleagues' dissatisfaction with Borten were both already high. The leak concerned the main cause of the coalition's disagreements, the negotiations in Brussels. Certain politicians — Borten himself, but also, for example, Helge Seip, by appearing to support the idea of a police investigation of the leak — behaved in a way which exacerbated the situation, but was understandable in the general atmosphere that had been building up for some time. For some of those involved it provided an opportunity moreover which they seized to bring about changes in an unsatisfactory situation. The crisis ended the coalition because that was the particular change which some of them were seeking.[119]

It began with an article in *Dagbladet* on 19 February which described the contents of a highly confidential report from Norway's ambassador in Brussels, Jan Halvorsen. In this the ambassador reported the EEC commissioner responsible for relations with the applicants as saying that he was pessimistic about a successful outcome of the negotiations if Norway maintained its demand for permanent special arrangements for the whole of Norwegian agriculture. The newspaper's original source was not established. What did eventually emerge however was that Per Borten had shown the Halvorsen report to Arne Haugestad of the People's Movement some days before the article appeared, allegedly in an unsuccessful attempt to convince him that there was no danger of Norway entering the EEC while he was prime minister. *Dagbladet* learned of Borten's indiscretion at a very early stage (on the day the article appeared, according to the journalist who wrote it), though the paper later corroborated Haugestad's denial that he, and thus by implication Borten, was its source. Borten however tried to conceal what he had done from his government colleagues, and managed to do so for a week after the article's publication — a week which he spent trying to persuade *Dagbladet* not to publish its damaging information about him, or if it did so then only accompanied by a denial that he, via Haugestad, was the source of its story. He failed, partly because both *Dagbladet* and Haugestad considered him unreliable on the EEC and wanted to see him and his government fall over this matter.[120] Meanwhile Borten's ministers, not knowing of their prime minister's indiscretion or secret negotiations with *Dagbladet* and Haugestad, had started inquiries into how the Halvorsen report could have reached the press. The government also discussed it without Borten giving any hint of his own part in the affair. When finally he did admit it, even then it was not to his government but in the form of a public statement put out hastily to anticipate the appearance of *Dagbladet's* revelation that he had shown the report to Haugestad. By insisting that Haugestad was not its source, the newspaper indirectly cleared Borten too. But by then the issue for his ministers was not so much Borten's original action in showing the report to the People's Movement, as the way in which he had deliberately misled his colleagues afterwards.

The Conservative, Christian and Liberal ministers accused him of disloyalty and demanded his resignation, despite the Centre party's threat to leave the coalition if he was forced to go. There were probably some politicians in these three parties who saw and took an opportunity to reshape the coalition, Borten himself having given them a strong argument with which to pressure the Centre party into abandoning him. But basically their reaction was a spontaneous one: they were not prepared to serve under a prime minister who treated his ministers in this fashion. It was immediate, unanimous and not related to their positions on the EEC. Some observers speculated that the pro-market ministers had seized this chance to get rid of Borten because of his unreliability on the EEC. Others went further and suggested that the Conservatives had deliberately brought about the coalition's fall because they saw in a Labour government the only hope of taking Norway into the EEC. The evidence did not support either view. The Conservatives certainly wanted to refashion the coalition under new leadership. But at this juncture they appeared to be reacting to events and, insofar as it was possible to chart a course through them, trying hard to hold together the coalition that was their only means of staying in office — which meant preventing the

Centre party from leaving it. The concessions the Conservatives made to the Centre party in the negotiations under Kjell Bondevik — they accepted a candiate for prime minister who was no more enthusiastic about EEC membership than Borten, they dropped their opposition to examining alternatives to membership, they agreed to the Centre party's demand that the government present a report to parliament on the Werner and Davignon reports — showed how far the Conservatives were ready to go to save the coalition. What they would not accept was the Centre party's demand that it be free to declare its opposition to membership immediately, even before the promised report was published. But nor would those Liberals and Christians, including Bondevik himself, who were later to campaign against membership. At the end of the crisis, as at the beginning, the position of the Conservatives, Christians and Liberals was determined primarily by considerations about the political condition and future of the coalition itself, not relations with the EEC. The question they faced at the beginning was whether they could continue under Borten, and they decided that they could not. The question at the end was whether there any longer existed a political basis for the coalition. And these three parties all more or less reluctantly came to the conclusion that there did not.

The reason that there did not was that the most determined anti-marketeers in the Centre party had recognised their moment for forcing the party out into open opposition — and had succeeded in doing so. Initially the Centre party's leaders had been unwilling to take such an extreme course; when it came to the point they hesitated, as in June 1970, to provoke the final break. Instead of carrying out their threat to leave with Borten, they won the party's approval, after a hard debate lasting several days, to enter the negotiations under Bondevik, their own choice as Borten's successor. It was at this point that hopes for the coalition's survival were highest — or from the point of view of those wanting to break out of it, the danger greatest. But the debate also produced an ambiguously worded declaration which made the party's continuation in government conditional on the coalition clarifying its policy towards the EEC and respecting the Centre party's position on it.[121] Interpretations of precisely what this meant in practice varied considerably, within the Centre party as well as in the other three. That section of the party disposed to join a Bondevik government seemed to understand it as endorsing a continuation of the previous policy of indirect opposition, at least until the promised report provided a formal pretext to call for a halt to the negotiations. This would give them time to see whether Britain's negotiations looked like succeeding; they also seemed to be hoping to win over most of the Christians and Liberals to their side during the preparation and consideration of the report.[122] This strategy, however, meant that at this stage they should merely require the other parties to acknowledge the Centre party's right to adopt a position in line with its programme during the forthcoming discussions on the report. To those Centrists who were pressing for open opposition this looked like a continuation of the slide into the EEC which they were determined to stop.[123] They insisted on the party declaring now, during the coalition negotiations, that it would oppose membership, and that whatever the contents of the forthcoming report, it would call for an end to the negotiations in Brussels. In the end it was their view that prevailed within the Centre party.[124]

The other three parties were willing to accept the first group's condition for continuing the coalition, but not that of the second. In other words, they were ready to go on with the uncomfortable compromises of the previous twelve months in the hope that the situation would eventually resolve itself satisfactorily. They were not prepared, however, to begin again under a new prime minister with this fundamental disagreement over the EEC publicly documented by one party having already announced an unalterable position prior to the formal government discussions on the subject. The coalition negotiations were therefore broken off.

If the coalition had survived this crisis, it could well have fallen at a later stage of the negotiations, as many afterwards maintained it would have done. But it might have managed to hold together and stay in office, in which case the outcome of the referendum might have been different — as some anti-marketeers had feared, and therefore worked so hard from their positions in the press, the Centre party, and the People's Movement to bring it down. As it was, the three middle-parties were freed from the constraints of government, and their leaders from the responsibility of carrying out a policy which they had recommended to parliament just eight months before. Freed from that responsibility it was easier for these leaders to abandon their previous policies — and also for their parties and voters to bring pressure on them to do so. The anti-marketeers' position had been improved in other ways as well during the fifteen months between the Hague summit and the change of government in Oslo. Labour's internal opposition was active and better organised. The People's Movement was already campaigning. The EEC's 'union plans' and fisheries policy had provided it with central themes for that campaign. Sweden's decision not to seek membership, announced officially in March 1971, had left the 'Nordic alternative' intact. Public opinion appeared to have stiffened against joining the EEC. And the EEC's offer of negotiations to those EFTA countries not applying for membership had begun to make a free trade agreement seem a credible alternative.

On the other hand, Norway now had a Labour government committed to completing the negotiations, if possible with an agreement it could recommend in a referendum. The anti-marketeers' hopes of stopping the negotiations looked less likely than ever to be fulfilled. On the contrary the new government could be expected to pursue them with vigour and determination to succeed. It was also likely to be forced away from its previously cautious line, however unwillingly, if only because it was now identified with the EEC negotiations and would have to win public and party support if it was to avoid a humiliating defeat in the referendum. Within its own party the government could call for loyalty and unity to support it in its precarious minority position. It was because they had foreseen all this that some anti-marketeers, especially in the Labour party itself, had always seen in a Labour government a much greater danger than the non-socialist coalition under Per Borten[125] — and that most pro-marketeers were still basically confident about the final outcome.

5. The negotiations concluded

The spirit in which the Labour government intended to conduct the negotiations was demonstrated very shortly after it took office, when the foreign minister, Andreas Cappelen, made his opening statement to the EEC council of ministers. He repeated his predecessor's request for permanent special arrangements for agriculture, and reminded them of their promise to take account of Norway's special interests in the fisheries sector. But his reference to these economic problems was subordinated to the broader political aspects of the enlargement negotiations. He spoke of the advantages for both Norway and Europe of the closer form of international co-operation being developed in the EEC. He also emphasised the importance his government attached to Norway participating in the unification of Europe. Norway belonged to Europe and had to look outwards, not only economically but politically, and join fully and actively in its affairs. The application for membership he described as a demonstration of this wish to participate in the EEC's future development.[1] Back home *Dagbladet* summed up the general impression made by this speech. There could no longer be any doubt, it said, that the Labour government's aim was to take Norway 'full speed ahead into the EEC'.[2]

In March 1971, though, the negotiations had scarcely begun. The EEC was still concentrating on Britain's problems. Norway, although it had described the EEC's fisheries policy as unacceptable and transitional arrangements for agriculture as inadequate, had not yet put forward any solutions. Work on them was well advanced but the political decisions were still outstanding. Here the new government faced a tactical problem. Its proposals had to be acceptable enough to the EEC to provide a basis for serious negotiations or membership would be impossible; but satisfying this criterion might well bring it into immediate conflict with the primary producers which it wanted to avoid at this stage. On the other hand, if it framed its proposals with too great a concern to pacify its critics at home, it ran two risks. It might alienate the EEC, thereby lessening the prospect of gaining good terms, perhaps even causing the negotiations to fail at an early stage. And it would raise expectations too high, handing the anti-marketeers an unrealistic standard against which to criticise the result if, as was probable, the Norwegians had to compromise on their original proposals during the negotiations. The government tried to steer a middle course between these extremes. As a result, however, it started off with proposals which seemed too far-reaching to the EEC (for terms contrary to EEC principles in one case, a complete revision of its policy in the other), yet which were still considered inadequate by many at home. The Six regarded them as Norway's maximum demand, its opening bid; the domestic audience as the very minimum to which Norway could agree. So essentially the negotiations became a matter of trying to find ways of bridging this gap which would be acceptable both in Brussels and at home.

For agriculture the government rejected the protection policy in favour of seeking a solution based on monetary compensation for the loss of income resulting from Norway's integration into the common agricultural market.[3] The coalition seems to have been working with this alternative too when it left office.[4] Nor would that necessarily have been incompatible with the continued national control of agricultural policy being demanded by the Centre party and producer organisations. For the principle of compensation could provide the basis for very different detailed proposals, some compatible with the common agricultural policy and EEC membership, others probably not. Here there were two key issues. Did the compensation have to take the form of price subsidies tied to particular products, which was the Norwegian system for its two main agricultural sectors, dairy products and grain, but was not permitted by the common agricultural policy? Or would the producer organisations accept a changeover to methods of financial support allowed under the EEC's rules? Secondly, where was the amount of compensation to be fixed, in Oslo or Brussels? These two questions, in turn, were only aspects of the basic question of whether the major decisions determining the level and source of agricultural incomes would continue under Norwegian control or be surrendered to the EEC's institutions. Like the formula 'permanent special arrangements' the compensation policy would support both pro- and anti-market positions. For the latter it meant arrangements necessarily in breach of EEC principles (or how could they be described as 'special'?), legally guaranteed as permanent, expressly under Norwegian control, and based principally on price subsidies as the best means of encouraging production and recruitment to the industry.

The government's version was presented to the EEC on 21 June,[5] by which time the main difficulties in Britain's negotiations had been resolved and the EEC was ready for serious discussions wth Norway. The government made it clear that it regarded these proposals as a minimum solution in domestic political terms. It said it had rejected the farmers' demand for a retention of import controls, and was seeking instead arrangements which, while solving Norway's particular problems, would be as much in conformity with EEC policy as possible. The proposals themselves were defined in general terms, which gave the government some room for manoeuvre in the forthcoming bargaining. Thus while the farmers' demand that price subsidies continue to be the main source of compensation was adopted, milk was the only product for which they were expressly requested. Even this would make a sizable inroad into EEC principles, as about half the compensation would be paid out in the milk sector; but at least it limited it to this one major exception. The government further asked to be allowed to continue the system of transport subsidies because of the long distances between producers and their markets in Norway. And while it agreed to the general principles of the special arrangements being settled in negotiations between the Norwegian government and EEC, it wanted the decisions about the concrete measures to implement them left to the government and producer organisations in Oslo. Reactions to these proposals were fairly predictable. Anti-marketeers immediately criticised the failure to specify whether Norway or the EEC would determine the total level of compensation.[6] The EEC's response was longer in coming, but it would obviously have difficulties in accepting them. Its rules, after all, excluded not only price subsidies, but also special arrangements for an indefinite period, let alone for a whole country.

The next three months were spent in discussions between the two sides. An important part of these consisted of visits to Norway, to see conditions at first hand, by EEC agricultural ministers and commission members responsible for preparing the recommendations for the council of ministers.[7] The EEC made it clear that it could not formally grant permanent exceptions from the common agricultural policy. Moreover the questions of price subsidies and which institutions, community or Norwegian, formally controlled agricultural policy in Norway, were as crucial from the EEC's point of view as they were for Norway's farmers and anti-marketeers.[8] The EEC was ready to go some way towards meeting the Norwegians' difficulties. But basically it was a question of finding formulas which would safeguard Norwegian interests without flouting EEC principles or undermining the common agricultural policy itself.

The first step towards doing this came on 19 October. In a formal statement the council of ministers recognised that Norway would have special problems as a result of membership, particularly its farmers' heavy income losses, and promised proposals to maintain the latters' living standards.[9] The proposals followed on 3 November.

Norway was to accept the common agricultural policy — which it had already said it would do. Some form of support system would be necessary because of the resulting drop in incomes, but the EEC would not agree to price subsidies linked to particular products, nor was the system to apply to the whole country: the type and level of support was to depend on the area and type of producer. However, the EEC promised unspecified 'suitable measures' to ensure regular milk supplies throughout the country. It also recognised the need for transport subsidies, for which it believed an appropriate solution could be found within the EEC's regulations. The existing support system would continue for a transitional period after membership while the details of the new one were worked out. Insofar as it became possible to solve Norway's problems within the framework of common policies, these were to replace the special arrangements. And the EEC's institutions would review their working.[10] Altogether the proposals represented a careful balance between giving the Norwegians terms which would probably diverge from the common agricultural policy on some points, and retaining the principle of EEC control and the common agricultural policy framework.

The final compromise was agreed in December 1971 and incorporated in a protocol which formed an integral part of the treaty of accession. The Norwegians gained some of their requests, explicitly or by implication. Thus the exceptions being granted to Norway were not described as permanent. But in the preamble the EEC acknowledged that it was permanent natural conditions and agriculture's importance for settlement which made transitional measures inadequate, and the government interpreted this as an implicit admission that the special arrangements would have to be permanent because the problem was of a permanent character. Similarly the protocol excluded the use of price subsidies in principle. In practice it opened the way for their retention in the important milk sector by stating that they could be among the measures used to maintain a level of milk supplies sufficient to meet the high Norwegian consumption level. The need for transport subsidies was again recognised. And existing support measures allowed under the common agricultural policy could be retained, while new ones based on it would be substituted for price subsidies in order to achieve what was described as the main objective, namely to prevent a fall in producers' living standards. The EEC, on its side, avoided an open breach of its principles by not describing the arrangements as permanent and by maintaining the provision that Norway's exceptions could be replaced by common policies at a later date if these proved capable of solving the problems documented in the preamble. Norway was to apply the common agricultural policy, apart from those exceptions specified in the protocol. The decisions regarding the new support system would be taken in Brussels, and its working subject to EEC examination. EEC competence and control, in other words, would be respected.[11]

In defending the agreement at home the government claimed that it would protect Norway's essential interests by maintaining the farmers' standard of living, the existing level and type of production, and the pattern of settlement based on it. The preamble, it said, guaranteed the EEC's permanent commitment to these objectives and so in effect the permanence of the special arrangements. Although formally the EEC's institutions would take the decisions about the new support system, in practice they would be worked out in close co-operation with the Norwegian authorities and agricultural organisations. The government explained that neither of these points could be explicitly stated because of the EEC's understandable concern to protect the principles on which it was based — principles which in Norway's case it had been willing to stretch a long way. Basically, though, the foreign minister argued, the protocol's acceptability depended on whether the Norwegians trusted the other members not to override their vital interests. It was this mutual trust and confidence which was the real foundation of the EEC, without which it could not function successfully. Recognising this the government for its part intended to act in a community spirit and recommend the agreement even though its guarantees were not as explicit as it would have liked.[12]

Confidence in the EEC, however, was what many Norwegians, not just confirmed anti-marketeers, did not have. The latter described the agreement as merely further proof of the government's determination to take Norway into the EEC whatever the cost. The farmers rejected it. The government, they said, had abandoned the principle of price subsidies as the main form of compensation — the only one that would attract people into the industry and prevent a fall in production. Only a system under which the bulk of a farmer's income came from the prices he received for his produce could achieve this. The proposed substitutes they described as little more than an EEC social security system which no self-respecting farmer would accept, and which failed to offer the attractive long-term economic prospects necessary to halt the decline in the agricultural labour force. Nor did they consider the protocol's commitment to maintain a vaguely defined 'standard of living' any substitute for the Norwegian parliament's commitment to establish parity between agricultural and industrial wages. As for the permanency of these arrangements, how could they be described as such if they were subject to EEC control and could therefore be revoked at any time? There would be little the Norwegians could do to prevent it once they had been integrated into the EEC's economic and monetary union. Nor could the arrangements be called 'special', for that logically meant a breach of the common agricultural policy and they were practically all in conformity with it. Even the price subsidies for milk — the major exception — were not guaranteed; anti-marketeers pointed out that the protocol only said they 'could' be used, not that they would be. And because the decisions were to be taken in Brussels, the Norwegians would be unable to ensure that they were. Indeed that was the most objectionable point. As soon as they joined the EEC, the control of policy would pass out of Norwegian hands. The new support system would not have been worked out by then. So they would be thrown onto the goodwill of the other members and EEC bureaucrats when it came to deciding the vital details of the system, only a vague outline of which was sketched in the protocol. Even after it had been set up the EEC could review it — and change it at will if it wished. Such a loss of control over their own affairs they described as totally unacceptable.[13]

No doubt any solution acceptable to the EEC would have been unacceptable to the anti-marketeers. But that they were able to raise such serious doubts in many other Norwegians' minds was due not least to the complicated, ambiguous formulas which had been required to reconcile Norwegian and EEC interests. That meant that much depended on the spirit in which the formulas were interpreted. Pro-marketeers regarded the guarantees as water-tight, politically if not legally. Anti-marketeers had no difficulty in pointing to loopholes through which they maintained the EEC could — and many implied would — evade fulfilling the guarantees which the government claimed to have obtained. And given the climate of public opinion by the end of 1971 it was very much easier to destroy confidence in the EEC than create it.

The same was true of the fisheries agreement concluded a month later after much more difficult negotiations.[14] As a result of the EEC's policy decisions in 1970 the obstacles in the way of a settlement had become much greater. The EEC was now defending an agreed common policy. No Norwegian government could recommend membership unless the principle of non-discriminatory access to members' fishing limits was either abandoned for the EEC as a whole or made inapplicable in Norway's case. The timing of the EEC's decision had made the issue even more sensitive than it would have been anyway. And the Labour party had important electoral interests among the coastal fishermen, whose livelihood was at stake, while its main political rivals for their votes were the two anti-market parties, the Centre party and Socialist People's party. The post of fisheries minister had been given to a director of the fishermen's powerful national sales organisation, Knut Hoem, an appointment obviously intended to reassure the fishermen that their interests would be heard within the government and fully protected in Brussels. But the appointment was a gamble. As long as Hoem vouched for the government's negotiating line by carrying it out, the fishermen would probably be reluctant to oppose it openly; and his recommendation of any final agreement would be invaluable, with the public at large as well as the fishing industry. But if Hoem felt unable to do either of these things, the government would have to choose between failing to obtain an agreement — and thus membership — or settling for one rejected by its own fisheries minister. A member of the Labour party, Hoem would be under heavy pressure to go along with a settlement regarded as satisfactory by his government colleagues. But in certain circumstances the outcome could well depend on which loyalty, political or professional, proved the stronger.

The fishermen wanted to keep their exclusive fishing limit and their producer organisations' considerable rights under Norwegian law, including compulsory membership, the handling of all sales of landed fish, and price and market regulating powers. The government's difficulty was to reconcile this with the EEC's 1970 fisheries policy and the weaker position of the Six's producer organisations, which had neither compulsory membership nor the Norwegians' price and market regulating competence. As in the agricultural sector, the government tried to draw up proposals which stood a chance of being accepted both in Brussels and at home. When presenting them to the EEC in May and June 1971 it again described them as an attempt to find community solutions to special Norwegian problems — this time however by changing EEC policy. To overcome the major problem of fishing limits it put forward two alternatives for a new EEC policy which would meet Norway's requirements. The first was based on the Treaty of Rome's provisions governing business establishment, and proposed to restrict fishing within a member state's limits to vessels registered and persons resident in it. If this was unacceptable to the EEC, however, it proposed that the EEC base its fisheries policy on exclusive national limits for all members. It rejected any solution based on a division of the coastline, with certain areas reserved for coastal fishermen and the remainder open to all EEC vessels.[15] An important point about both alternatives was that they left open the possibility of extending Norway's limit after joining the EEC, with the new areas also reserved for Norwegian or Norwegian-based fishermen. As for the producer organisations, the government wanted obligatory membership to continue in Norway and suggested that this 'closed shop' system be adopted throughout the EEC.

But it seemed to accept that the main price-setting powers would be transferred to the EEC's institutions.[16]

One obstacle to getting these proposals accepted was that the other three applicants did not support them. Their positions were rather different from Norway's. Britain and Denmark were predominantly middle and distant water fishing nations concerned to preserve or win fishing rights in waters off other countries' coasts. Norway also had important trawler fishing interests, its southwest fishermen being dependent on banks off the British and Irish coasts. But coastal fishing predominated and its interests were uppermost when it came to determining the country's position in international negotiations. Another difference was that Norway was the only major fishing nation in Western Europe which had not signed the London Convention of 1964. That had opened the way to twelve-mile fishing limits by permitting coastal states an exclusive inner six-mile belt but recognising other signatories' traditional rights in the outer six miles. Norway had not signed it because it would have entailed a derogation from the exclusive character of the twelve-mile limit it had already established in 1961. It was the London Convention which the Six had replaced among themselves by the principle of non-discriminatory access. But they and the other three applicants did at least have a common base in the convention, to which they were all still signatories, when they started negotiating — a base which Norway did not share.

Denmark accepted the 1970 fisheries policy, only requesting special terms for the Faeroe Islands and Greenland. Britain and Eire, with important coastal fishing interests, did not. Eire wanted to postpone discussion of the question until it was a member. Britain proposed a modified version of the London Convention, with access to the inner six miles restricted to fishermen established in Britain and the EEC's principle of non-discriminatory access applying in the outer six miles.[17] None of these positions were possible for the Norwegian government. It could not agree to the common fisheries policy as it stood. It could not postpone the matter because entering the EEC depended on finding a satisfactory solution beforehand. Nor was it prepared to accept the London Convention's 'six plus six' formula in the more liberal version which Britain was proposing because that would have opened the outer six miles of Norway's limits to EEC vessels. It was that formula however which finally provided the basis for an agreement between the Six and the other three applicants on 12 December 1971. The 1970 common fisheries policy was to remain in force, but during a ten-year transitional period all members would retain the six-mile exclusive limits allowed under the London Convention, while the applicants and France would also keep their exclusive outer six miles in certain specified areas where the coastal population was mainly dependent on fishing for its livelihood (though respecting other countries' traditional rights). Before the end of the ten-year period the commission was to present a report on the economic and social conditions in the areas in question, and on the basis of this the council of ministers would consider what arrangements might replace the transitional ones. There was thus no legal guarantee that they would continue: a new decision would be required to prevent the 1970 policy's principle of non-discrimination being applied in full.[18] But the agreement of 12 December was widely interpreted as marking the end of the 1970 policy and the beginning of a long renegotiation after enlargement.

Norway was not a party to this agreement. The Six had rejected its first alternative, the establishment principle, and it had then fallen back on the second, exclusive national fishing limits. The agreement between the other three and the Six was a significant step towards adopting this second alternative for the whole EEC; and in Norway's case a six-mile exclusive belt plus a further six miles reserved for its coastal fishermen would amount to an exclusive twelve miles in practice, because other nations' traditional rights within its fishing limit had been phased out over the previous decade. But the government held out for further negotiations after the others had settled, for two reasons. Though it had moved closer to accepting a division of the coastline, Norway and the EEC could not agree on where the dividing line should be. More seriously, they could not agree about the so-called revision clause, or what would happen after the ten-year transitional period. The Norwegians wanted a legal guarantee that this exception to the 1970 policy would continue after 1982 — in other words, that it would be permanent. As one minister explained to the press in Brussels: the government could not tell its fishermen that it had only got an arrangement for ten years, and that they would just have to wait and see and place their hopes on community goodwill for what happened after that. Only a treaty guarantee that the exclusive limit would continue after 1982 would be politically acceptable at home.[19]

In one respect, however, the government saw a definite advantage in the situation which had now arisen. The other three countries having concluded their negotiations, Norway could at last be treated as the special case which it claimed the EEC had already recognised it to be in the council of ministers' declaration of 22 September 1970. The Norwegians proposed a protocol, similar in some ways to that just concluded for agriculture. In this the Six were again to acknowledge the peculiar difficulties Norway faced because of geography and climate, which in the case of the fishing industry made the coastal population heavily dependent on this one occupation. They were also to recognise the 'vital' importance of this question to Norway, which should strengthen Norway's hand in future EEC negotiations and ensure that decisions on fisheries policy were subject to the unanimity rule. The transitional twelve-mile exclusive limit was to be understood as continuing after 1982 unless the council of ministers decided otherwise, instead of a new decision being required to prolong it; or at least there was to be a legal guarantee of it continuing in Norway's case as long as the conditions described in the protocol existed — that is, permanently. Finally the Norwegians wanted the exclusive twelve miles to apply to the whole coastline from the Russian border down to the most southerly point of Lindesnes.[20]

The EEC on its side was willing to sign a protocol which recognised Norway's special problems and interests in this sector. It was ready to give a political guarantee that the EEC's institutions would take particular account of them when the time came to revise the transitional arrangements. It was also prepared to include a prolongation of exclusive limits in certain areas as one of the measures which could be introduced after 1982. But it would not give Norway a legal guarantee that they would be prolonged, arguing that to bind a future council of ministers in this way would be contrary to the principles on which EEC decisions were taken. Nor would it give Norway the veto right implicit in describing its interests as vital. It also proposed a division of the coast considerably further north than the Norwegians wished.

The Labour government now faced the most difficult days of the whole negotiations. Its problem was essentially a domestic political one. It needed a guarantee for the period after 1982 which looked clear and convincing to ordinary fishermen and voters, not just to politicians and civil servants who understood how the EEC functioned and why it would go no further in its concessions to Norway. The revision clause also had to satisfy the fisheries minister, who would be the government's witness that it amounted to a permanent retention of the exclusive limit even it if did not expressly say so. Once again the difficulty was to find formulas to harmonise Norwegian and EEC interests and the EEC's unwillingness to spell out in readily understandable terms what it was in fact giving Norway. The importance the government attached to getting a satisfactory revision clause was demonstrated by the prime minister's visits to EEC capitals and Britain at the beginning of January 1972, when he tried to win understanding for his government's position. The Belgian prime minister tried to help with a letter assuring Mr. Bratteli that in Belgium's experience as a small member such political guarantees were always kept: the protocol's preamble, with its implicit recognition that Norway's problems could not be solved within the transitional period, was a 'real guarantee' that its fishing limit would not be opened up to EEC vessels after 1982.[21] But the EEC refused to spell this out in the protocol. A political guarantee couched in phrases easily open to anti-market attack had to suffice.

There was a brief break in the negotiations in the middle of January while the government consulted its party, parliament, the trade unions and fishing organisations. As the ceremony for signing the treaty of accession had already been fixed for 22 January 1972, a rejection of the EEC's final offer would mean acknowledging that Norway's negotiations had failed and it would not be joining along with the other applicants. In one sense the government's decision to accept it was a foregone conclusion, despite the tension of those days in political circles in Oslo. Both the government and the negotiating delegation were satisfied that a political guarantee would adequately safeguard Norway's interests, and that the EEC's fisheries agreements with the four applicants would be only the start of a fundamental reform of the 1970 policy.[22] That being so, they were most unlikely to allow the negotiations to break down over the revision clause. Fishing was certainly very important, but industry was more so, and both industry and shipping were arguing strongly for entry, as were most trade union leaders. The political and foreign policy arguments for membership were considered just as overwhelming. But still the decision was a difficult one. For while settling on the EEC's terms would allow the negotiations to be concluded, it could also so harm the government's chances of winning a referendum that the treaty would never be ratified.

On 15 January 1972 Norway and the EEC signed the fisheries protocol on the terms offered by the EEC. The revision clause stated merely that the EEC's institutions would be advised to take account of Norway's interests when considering what would happen after 1982, and that a retention of areas reserved for coastal fishermen could be among the measures adopted. A compromise divided the coast at Egersund, insignificantly further north in fishing terms than the government's original proposal.[23] The Norwegians delivered a formal declaration which served as their interpretation of the protocol. This said that the EEC had recognised Norway's special problems and had advised the commission and council of ministers to take their decisions in the light of them when revising the transitional arrangements. The EEC was based on the mutual confidence existing between its members, and that being so the government was certain that the other members would not adopt policies contrary to Norway's vital interests. The government regarded the solemn assurances in the protocol as a 'real guarantee' of the EEC's intention to take special account of the interests of Norway's coastal fishermen after 1982.[24] Formally this declaration was addressed to the Six. It was meant as much, though, for the audience at home, where in defending the protocol the government used the same arguments. The decision to accept a political guarantee, the foreign minister told parliament, was based on the government's confidence that the EEC did not act contrary to members' vital interests, and its recognition that the EEC could only succeed if its members' relations were founded on mutual trust.[25]

But confidence and trust no more characterised the reception of this agreement than they had the agricultural protocol. The fact that, formally, it sanctioned only a temporary exception to the 1970 policy was an invaluable argument for the anti-marketeers.[26] Again they described the terms brought home as a capitulation and as proof of the government's determination to join the EEC irrespective of the damage it would do to the primary sector. The so-called guarantee for the period after 1982 was no guarantee at all, because the EEC was not legally bound to honour it. Was the livelihood of Norway's fishermen to depend on foreign governments and civil servants in Brussels one day honouring political assurances given ten years before by their predecessors? And if a political guarantee amounted to the same thing as a legal one, why had the EEC been unwilling to describe Norway's interests in this sector as 'vital' and thus ensure it a veto over future policy decisions? It could only be because the Six wanted to leave themselves free to ignore those interests when the time came to fulfil the vague promises in the protocol. The latter only 'advised' the EEC's institutions to take account of Norway's interests — it did not instruct them to do so. And were those institutions not also bound to take account of other members' interests, which might well conflict with Norway's?[27] These negotiations, they said, had again demonstrated how limited Norway's influence would be inside the EEC, and how in the end it would always have to give way, even on such vital matters. After ten years of economic and monetary union its position would be even weaker.[28] Moreover, even this transitional exclusive limit had a serious disadvantage: their loss of the freedom to extend it during the next ten years. Probably, some argued, that was why the EEC had been willing to grant it at all. A general move to wider fishing limits seemed likely to come as a result of the forthcoming United Nations Conference on the Law of the Sea (UNCLOS). But Norway would be unable to take advantage of it because its limit would be fixed at twelve miles in an international treaty. Even if the EEC permitted it

125

to do so, the other members would certainly insist on access for their vessels to the area beyond twelve miles.[29]

An almost equally hostile reception greeted the agreement about the producer organisations. Here too the EEC had gone some way towards meeting the substance of the Norwegians' requests. In another tortuously phrased formula it had conceded that, because voluntary membership could lead to market instability in some countries, a member government would be free to name one organisation as the most representative and make its regulations and price levels compulsory even for fishermen who did not belong to it but landed their fish in the country in question.[30] That meant the Norwegian government could nominate the fishermen's national sales organisation (*råfiskelag*) and thereby achieve much the same effect as by insisting on compulsory membership. But the Six would not concede the principle of compulsory membership. For the fishermen and anti-marketeers nothing less would suffice. Only this, they argued, would ensure that all fish caught by Norwegian fishermen or, after membership, foreign firms established in Norway, was landed and processed in the country. Otherwise the latter, and even some Norwegian fishermen, might start landing it in the EEC countries to which much of it would be exported anyway. And that would threaten the raw material base of the small processing plants along the coast.[31]

In neither the agricultural nor the fishing sector had the government managed to obtain terms which satisfied or silenced its critics. It was equally unsuccessful in the other two sensitive areas, capital movements and business establishment. Here the Norwegians had two main fears, which were shared to some degree by pro-marketeers too. One was that the predominantly small Norwegian firms would be unable to compete with the larger foreign ones or would be taken over by them. The other was that a weakening of control over business establishment and capital movements would lead to a loss of control over the economy as a whole, and with it over the long-term development of Norwegian society. The Norwegian negotiators obtained transitional arrangements which allowed Norway to postpone implementing the EEC's liberalising directives: for two years in the case of foreign purchases of Norwegian shares and foreigns firms' long-term loans to Norwegian subsidiaries, for three years in the case of business establishment in Norway, and five years in the case of Norwegian purchases of foreign shares. The government argued that by using the time gained to strengthen state control and participation in the economy, particularly in the areas most threatened by foreign penetration, adequate control could be maintained over both foreign ownership and domestic monetary and credit policy.[32] The anti-marketeers disputed this. They predicted that Norwegian firms would pass into foreign hands. Norwegian capital would flow out to EEC countries with higher long-term interest rates, inevitably forcing up long-term Norwegian rates too, while control over the volume and direction of domestic investment would be lost. In short, the freeing of capital movements and removal of discriminatory regulations governing foreign investment and ownership would bring back the unbridled law of the market place to Norway's planned economy. The clinching blanket argument, with which all counter-arguments could be capped, was the EEC's proposed economic and monetary union. That would make the counter-measures promised by the government futile. For once the union had been implemented — once even the first three-year stage was completed — these last defences against foreign economic domination and international capitalism would be swept away.[33]

On 17 January 1972 the fishermen's national organisation unanimously rejected the protocol signed in Brussels two days before.[34] On the 19th came and even heavier blow for the government. After being subjected to intense pressure from both sides for several weeks, the fisheries minister, Knut Hoem, resigned. He said he would have been willing to accept the arrangements reached for the transitional period and for the producer organisations. But he described the revision clause as unsatisfactory on the crucial question of what would happen after 1982.[35] His resignation was a triumph for the opponents of membership. As *Dagbladet* wrote, 'Hoem was to have been the pro-marketeers best argument that the treaty was acceptable. Now he has become the anti-marketeers' witness that it is not.'[36]

On 22 January the prime minister attended the formal ceremony in Brussels to sign the treaty of accession along with the other applicants. In his speech Mr Bratteli said that his signature demonstrated that the government considered the terms satisfactory and would recommend them at home. But the final decision about membership would have to be taken by the Norwegian parliament and people.[37] In Oslo *Dagbladet* made the same point, only somewhat differently. 'Norway's engagement day' ran its headline on the 22nd: whether there would ever be a marriage would depend on the coming campaign and referendum. After Hoem's resignation it obviously felt more confident that there would not be.

6. Campaign and referendum

March 1971 - January 1972

Labour had taken office in March 1971 as a minority government relying on support from among the non-socialist parties to get its policies through parliament. Its strength was the lack of an alternative. Under the Norwegian system of fixed four yearly elections, the relative strengths of the various parties was unalterable until the next election in September 1973. Until the EEC issue had been settled the non-socialists would be unable to form a four-party majority government, and the middle-party alternative advocated by some anti-marketeers had fewer seats in parliament than Labour. In European policy the government's aim remained the same as it had been in opposition: to take Norway into the EEC with as little damage as possible to the party or to its chances of winning the 1973 election. Its strategy for achieving this was much the same. The doubters and uncommitted were to be held to the negotiating line by the injunction to 'wait and see'. The anti-marketeers were to be kept from leaving or splitting the party by a relatively conciliatory treatment. And the EEC was to be kept out of domestic politics. The polls showed that the party's official policy was unpopular, and bringing it to the fore would increase the risks of dividing Labour itself. It was the same combination of an unwavering course towards membership, but with tactics determined very much by party considerations.

This was seen at Labour's national conference in May 1971. The previous one in 1969 had voted overwhelmingly in favour of seeking membership negotiations with the aim of entering the EEC if Britain did so and the terms were satisfactory.[1] In May 1971 the leadership's aim was to hold the party to completing the negotiations in the face of the upsurge of opposition since the question was reopened as a result of the Hague summit conference. The anti-marketeers on their side had two objectives. One was to demonstrate their strength in order to encourage the wavering and deter the leadership from taking disciplinary action against them. The other was to have the 1969 resolution on European policy replaced by one rejecting membership, or one at least more favourable to open opposition activity within the party. The second objective was particularly important if they were to consolidate the position they had built up since the previous summer. The 1969 resolution, combined with the leaders' 'wait and see' line, could still prevent them welding together an internal opposition strong enough to withstand the full weight of the party organisation once the negotiations were completed. Ingrained discipline and loyalty were still major obstacles to those challenging the party's own government and programme.

The government won a majority for concluding the negotiations. It also succeeded in avoiding a head-on clash with the anti-marketeers, the tone of the conference debate remaining moderate. But it did this only by making concessions which weakened the position from which it would later take up the anti-marketeers' challenge. In contrast to the 1969 resolution on European policy which it replaced, the 1971 resolution was neutral as regards the party's ultimate objective. The point was specifically underlined by the minister who proposed the resolution, Per Kleppe, when he told delegates that they were not voting about the desirability or otherwise of membership, only about how best to handle the question: whether to break off negotiations as the anti-marketeers were proposing, or continue them in order to clarify the basis for the party's later decision on membership itself.[2] This neutrality was not simply a continuation of the 'wait and see' line. It was a retreat, even if regarded as a merely tactical one, because it weakened the pro-marketeers' base in the party programme and in effect sanctioned active opposition to membership within the party.[3] Moreover the premises on which the conference supported a continuation of the negotiations provided a more favourable position from which to argue against membership.[4] The resolution laid down that the final decision about joining the EEC was to be taken in the light of the party's principles and programme as a whole, not just the entry terms; that participation in European co-operation was not to prevent closer Nordic co-operation; and that it was not to be an obstacle to Labour achieving its long-term objectives at home, including the extension of democracy and equality and preservation of a pattern of settlement which the Norwegian people themselves wanted. It would be easy to argue that entering the EEC was incompatible with any or all of these objectives. There would also be ample opportunity to do so, because the resolution promised a democratic debate within the party before its position was finally settled.[5]

Labour's anti-marketeers were better armed for that debate after the May conference than they had been before it. Although the government's policy was unchanged — as its conduct of the negotiations in

Brussels showed — they had demonstrated their weight, one-quarter of the delegates having voted to break off the negotiations.[6] The programme was now neutral as regards membership. They clearly did not need to fear a tightening of party discipline, at least until the negotiations were finished. They could continue building up their position inside the party for the confrontation which would then come.

The government had however gained its immediate aim: it had party backing for the negotiations. In parliament there was a large majority for them too; if necessary the Labour and Conservative groups alone were large enough to block any move to halt them. Whether, however, there was still the three-quarters majority needed to ratify a treaty of accession was less certain. All the Centre party members would now vote against one, so would a few from Labour itself, and the leaders of the Christian and Liberal parties were under increasing pressure to do so too. So in parliament, as in its own party, the government's handling of the question revealed its concern to avoid activating potential opposition before the terms were known and before it was free to campaign openly for membership itself.

The major test of parliamentary opinion came a month after Labour's conference, when the government's report on relations with the EEC was debated in June.[7] The origin of this report was the Centre Party's successful insistence on one during the non-socialist parties' negotiations about continuing their coalition under Kjell Bondevik.[8] After Labour took office the Centre party pressed it to produce one instead, and it agreed.[9] But it avoided the sort of report which the Centrists wanted, namely one that concentrated on the EEC's plans for political co-operation and economic and monetary union and would have provided a field day for anti-marketeers in and outside parliament. Instead it embedded these sensitive questions in a positive review of the EEC's development and Norway's relations with it, devoting considerable space to rehearsing the arguments for seeking membership. On the subject of economic and monetary union the report simultaneously stressed the advantages of the EEC's plans and played down their importance. It described them as an attempt to restore stability to the international financial system, which Norway was particularly interested should be done because of its heavy dependence on trade and shipping. It was too early, though, to know what would follow the first three-year stage approved by the council of ministers on 9 February 1971, let alone whether the planned union would be established by 1980. The government promised however to reserve Norway's position regarding the most far-reaching interpretations of what such a union would involve, and it reminded parliament that once Norway was a member it would have a veto on the matter.[10] As for political co-operation, the report described the EEC's new system as going no further than the co-operation in which Norway already participated in other international organisations. It was a positive but modest step towards enabling Western Europe to assume a greater responsibility for east-west relations and international affairs in general, especially relations with the developing countries. But should it at any stage look like going beyond mere consultations, the government promised to lay the matter before parliament.[11]

During the negotiations in March the non-socialists had also agreed to examine the alternatives to membership. Tactically it was not in the pro-marketeers' interest to have an alternative worked out in detail, and the Conservatives had only reluctantly conceded the point in their effort to save the coalition. This particular legacy the Labour government did not follow up, although pressed to do so. It argued that until the non-applicant EFTA countries' negotiations with the EEC were further advanced, there would be no basis on which to judge what terms the EEC would offer Norway or what their effect would be. Again it adopted a conciliatory tone. It said it would follow the EEC-EFTA negotiations carefully and send a new report to parliament in the autumn session.[12] Labour's representatives in the foreign relations committee indicated that it would include a discussion of this question.[13]

The June report failed to satisfy the anti-marketeers. But it still partially fulfilled the purpose for which they had been calling for one since the previous autumn. Although it did not provide a pretext for stopping the negotiations, it enabled the Centre party formally to repudiate the line it had adopted a year before. Moreover the vote on the report provided the occasion for an anti-market demonstration of strength. The politically significant number was thirty-eight, the one-quarter which could block a treaty of accession. Seventeen had opposed negotiations in June 1970: seven Centrists, seven Labour party members, and three Christians. With all twenty Centre party members now against, the total was up to thirty. Unless there were large scale defections from Labour's parliamentary group, however, they would only reach thirty-eight if more Christians and Liberals joined them. Both parties had held national conferences during the period between the coalition's fall in March and the debate on European policy in June. These had revealed an increase both in general scepticism about membership and outright opposition to it. They had also shown that in both parties opposition came predominantly from new alliances between the radical and conservative wings: in the Christians' case between the youth section and west coast members,[14] in the Liberals' between the urban radicals and the rural section of the moderate wing of the party.[15] But at neither conference had there been a majority for breaking off negotiations. Both had supported their leaders' recommendation to continue negotiating as the only way to find out what terms Norway could get, but at the same time to look seriously at the alternatives to membership.[16]

The same pattern was repeated in parliament. The Centre party's representative in the foreign relations committee recommended changing the membership application into one for an industrial free trade agreement on the EFTA model. He maintained that the EEC's plans for an economic and monetary union pointed to a degree of integration that would probably be incompatible with the constitution, which only permitted parliament to transfer powers to an international organisation within 'a functionally limited field'. EEC membership would certainly be incompatible with the Centre party's objectives for Norway because control of its economy and resources would be lost to Brussels. He wanted the negotiations broken off immediately because continuing them would bind the Norwegians 'bit by bit' until finally they had no real choice in the matter.[17] The Christian and Liberal representatives on the committee did not support him. They joined Labour and the Conservatives in recommending a continuation of the negotiations. But whereas the former wanted a parallel investigation of the alternatives, the two large pro-market parties rejected this.[18]

For the government the Conservatives' support was at once an advantage — for with twenty-nine members they were the largest group after Labour — and a source of some embarrassment. The Conservatives on their side were well aware of the difficulties this *de facto* alliance was causing the government within its own party and its propaganda value for the anti-marketeers. That was probably one reason why they did not try to establish a more open and formal co-operation for the referendum campaign, judging that keeping their distance was the best way of helping the government to hold its party and voters to its policy. It perhaps explained too why the Conservatives, in parliament at least, were so restrained about challenging the Labour leaders' defence of membership as a means of strengthening socialism in Western Europe and building a socialist EEC. But such self-restraint could not disguise the fact that on the major issue of the day the leaders of the two parties stood side by side. It was there for all to see in the voting figures and the similarity of so many of their arguments.

The Centre party's proposal to end the negotiations was defeated, and so was the joint Christian and Liberal one to examine alternatives to membership. But the first won thirty-seven votes, just one short of the required one-quarter, while fifty-five members supported the second. Of the thirty-seven who wanted negotiations restricted to a free trade agreement, twenty were from the Centre party and eight from Labour, while four Christians and five Liberals went against their parties' official policies. The Liberals included the party's two vice-chairmen and the chairman of the party committee studying Norway's relations with the EEC. As in 1970 the debate also showed others who clearly did not like the idea of entering the EEC but were unwilling to break with their parties' policies of waiting to see what terms the negotiations produced before approving or rejecting membership.[19] The anti-marketeers themselves put their real support in parliament at between forty and forty-five.[20] Moreover the June 1971 vote came after the main obstacles to British entry had been cleared out of the way. That it had made no difference was a commentary on Britain's diminished influence in Oslo. It was also a blow to the pro-marketeers, who had been counting on it to win over some of the waverers and now realised that the British argument for Norwegian entry was not going to help them as they had expected it to do.

One consequence of the pro-marketeers' weaker position in parliament was to make the referendum even more important. Winning it might now be the only way to get a treaty of accession ratified. The expectations of just a year before had been reversed. Then parliament had looked largely united, even if the Centre party was again having serious internal difficulties over the question, and the task had been to win over the voters. Now it seemed that the voters would have to be brought in to subdue the growing opposition in parliament. But that meant the referendum result would have to be regarded as binding and conclusive. As most pro-marketeers still thought they would win it, despite the public opinion polls, they had little difficulty in accepting this. It was not so simple however for the anti-marketeers, many of whom still feared they would lose the referendum if the government managed to complete the negotiations with terms it could recommend. The June 1971 vote started off a revision of their calculations too. Before it, most anti-marketeers had treated the referendum as binding, because they saw winning it as their only hope of staying outside the EEC, but now a binding referendum if lost, would nullify the gains they had made in parliament.

So a debate began about how binding the consultative referendum should be, a debate which continued right up until the referendum itself. The pro-marketeers insisted that parliament must respect the outcome however small the majority one way or the other. They promised to do so themselves — to do otherwise, they said, would make a mockery of consulting the people; and they pressed the anti-marketeers to declare in advance that they would do so too.[21] Some anti-marketeers did.[22] Others refused to commit themselves, arguing that parliament must retain its constitutional responsibility for the final decision.[23] Others said they would respect a 'clear' majority for membership, leaving unclear how large that would have to be.[24] On this point some argued that a three-quarters majority for membership should be required in the referendum as in parliament. Others spoke of 60 to 70 per cent of the 80 per cent who would probably vote,[25] while one Labour member said he would only respect a majority among the 'Norwegian workers of town and country'.[26] It was obvious that some anti-marketeers were rehearsing the arguments with which they could ignore a majority for membership, or at least cast doubt on its democratic validity. The voters were being frightened by scare arguments about unemployment, some said; they were being inadequately and misleadingly informed, said others; and they all maintained that Labour party voters were being forced to vote against their real convictions by misplaced loyalty to the prime minister, Trygve Bratteli. Despite this, however, it remained unclear until the end just what the anti-marketeers in parliament would do in the face of a 'yes' majority. Most of them probably did not know themselves and would only make up their minds when the result had been declared.

According to the polls, public opinion had been stable since the sudden drop in support for membership at the beginning of 1971. Some 12 per cent wanted to join the EEC, nearly 50 per cent had no opinion, and the rest opposed it. Even among Conservative voters only 44 per cent supported membership in September 1971, while the percentage was much lower among Liberal, Labour and Christian voters (14 per cent, 12 per cent, and 6 per cent respectively).[27] The local elections of that month also brought encouragement to the anti-marketeers. This was the election Labour had been hoping would pave the way for victory in 1973, and which with over 50 per cent in the March 1971 poll it had seemed to have a good chance of winning. Both sides in the party had tried to keep the EEC out of the campaign, and so had the equally divided Christian and Liberal parties. The Centrists had used it, but it was the Socialist People's party which had campaigned hardest on it.[28] The result fulfilled its hopes after several months of rising support in the polls. Although the result could not be explained solely in terms of the EEC issue, the pattern of shifts between parties was clear enough to point to it having been important, especially for the pro-marketeers' losses. The SPP and Centre party gained compared with the 1969 election. Labour and the Conservatives lost ground. So did the Liberals, though that appeared to be part of a secular decline. The Christians, whose public

pronouncements on the EEC were so cautious, remained stable. Labour, which had won 46 per cent in 1969, fell to 41.7 per cent, losing
heavily in the fishing constituencies where the Centre party made its
most marked gains. On the right Labour lost to the Centre and
Christians, on the left to the SPP, which now re-emerged as a dangerous attraction for left wing anti-marketeers.[29] This election, moreover, had seen the phenomenon of joint lists of SPP and communist candidates united in fighting EEC membership. If transferred to
the national level, the threat to Labour's left flank could become even
more serious.[30]

The following winter months were dominated by the final stages of
the negotiations in Brussels, which brought more aid to the anti-marketeers' campaign. While the government gave up first its request for
general price subsidies for agriculture, then its opposition to dividing
the coast, and finally its attempt to get a legal guarantee for exclusive
limits after 1982, the anti-market press headlined capitulations and
retreats and the abandonment of vital national interests.[31] Public disputes about the precise meaning of key clauses in the protocols for
agriculture and fisheries were carried on between the two sides'
French language experts, the anti-marketeers accusing the government of trying to disguise its surrenders by misleading translations.[32]
The reliability of the civil servants responsible for the negotiations
was called in question, and like the government they were portrayed
as so anxious to enter the EEC as to have become blind to what was
happening or, even worse, negligent of Norwegian interests. By the
time the negotiations were finished in January enough confusion
had been created about the real meaning of the protocols to serve
the anti-marketeers' main purpose of raising a barrier of public
suspicion against government arguments on the subject, while the
pro-marketeers were hardly helped by the unfamiliar EEC terminology
in which the agreements were couched.

In October the British house of commons voted in favour of membership by a majority of 112. But that made little impression in
Norway now, and the anti-marketeers pointed to the fact that Britain's
Labour party had opposed it.[33] More important were other events at
home. The Liberal party's committee on European policy published
its report, and half the members came down against membership.[34]
In November 1971 came the conclusions of a committee set up by
the government itself, under the chairmanship of the deputy governor
of the Bank of Norway, Hermod Skånland, to examine the probable
consequences of the EEC's plans for economic and monetary union.
As far as the public debate was concerned, the Skånland committee's
most damaging conclusion for the pro-marketeers was that it thought
it realistic to assume that the EEC would establish such a union, even

if it took longer than the ten years foreseen.[35] This gave official support to the anti-marketeers' main campaign theme and the premise on which many of their objections to membership were now based, namely that within a short time the EEC which Norwegians were being asked to join would be transformed into a supra-national union with their country reduced to the status of a peripheral and powerless region. In January came the fishing organisations' rejection of the terms brought home for their industry. Then came the resignation of the fisheries minister: conclusive proof not only for anti-marketeers but many ordinary voters that the terms were not good enough whatever the government claimed to the contrary.

Throughout these difficult months the government held firm to the strategy laid down in March. In Brussels it negotiated hard for the essentials of what it needed in order to sign a treaty. At home it maintained its 'wait and see' line and gave its internal opposition a relatively loose rein, while itself remaining immovable about the course on which it was set. Even after the September elections, with party morale deteriorating and some backbenchers talking of returning to opposition so as to end Labour's identification with the EEC negotiations, the government gave no hint of being willing to compromise.[36] 'He [Bratteli] regards this as just a little passing difficulty which we have to get over, like in 1949 [over NATO]', was the impression one Labour anti-marketeer had in December 1971.[37] The party leadership appeared confident that once the negotiations were over and it gave the signal to start campaigning, the polls would move in its favour and most party members fall in behind the official policy. Just before Bratteli left for Brussels to sign the treaty of accession came the blow of Hoem's resignation. But Labour's national executive had approved the terms thirty-two to three and the parliamentary group with only nine of its seventy-four members voting against.[38]

Nevertheless on balance the pro-marketeers' starting point for the last stage of the campaign had been weakened during the previous ten months. In the Labour party the opposition had continued to consolidate its position, and after enjoying comparative freedom for so long would be difficult to call to order even if the leadership was ready to risk the conflict that doing so would probably provoke. Labour's anti-marketeers were now too numerous to discipline without serious consequences for the party — especially with the SPP revival on the left. Nor did the relevant conference resolution provide much support: that contained only a commitment to negotiate and then conduct a democratic debate about membership in the light of the party's programme as a whole. In parliament too the anti-marketeers' position was stronger, with the Christian and Liberal parties looking even less likely to support membership than they had done in March. The agricultural organisations would almost certainly reject the terms, just as the fishermen had done. And the People's Movement had now occupied the field practically unchallenged since August 1970.

On the other hand, the negotiations had been concluded and the treaty of accession signed. Powerful economic organisations wanted to see it ratified, including the national trade union organisation, industry, shipping and the employers' federation. Above all, the government was now committed to working for ratification. That meant the Labour party organisation, so far deliberately held in check, would at last be actively campaigning all out for membership. Few on either side doubted what the effect would be once it was set in motion. That explained the continuing confidence of the pro-marketeers in the face of the public opinion polls and the fundamentally defensive attitude of the anti-marketeers. The latters' campaign since 1970 had been very much a pre-emptive strike aimed at capturing some strongholds from which they could fight a defensive holding action once Labour's organisation moved against them. In the coming months until the referendum their essential task would be to hold onto what they had gained: to withstand majority decisions in favour of membership in the Labour party, to get the already widespread opposition in the Christian and Liberal parties formalised into official policy, and to hold onto as much of their large lead in the public opinion polls as possible. As for their chances of ultimate success, one of Norway's leading modern historians, Jens Arup Seip, summed up the general view when he wrote at the beginning of 1972: '. . . if Bratteli wants us to be members, we will be. He can do just as he likes because he controls the [Labour] party and, through the party, the voters who support it.'[39]

The arguments[40]

What were the arguments of each side by this stage in the long debate about membership? After nearly two years of the third round there was little new to be said by either side. All that was left was elaboration, simplification and repetition. The prominence given to various arguments changed over the course of the campaign, sometimes in response to external events, sometimes as a consequence of changing campaign tactics. Thus Sweden's negotiations for a free trade agreement attracted considerable comment in the later phase of the campaign, and while Labour began by emphasising specifically socialist reasons for joining the EEC rather than foreign and security policy ones, by the end the emphasis had been reversed. But essentially it was the same main arguments which ran through the debate from beginning to end.

How they were formulated depended of course on the level at which the debate was being conducted. At one level — in parliament for example — it remained throughout a relatively intelligent if repetitious debate, with room for nuances and qualifications. At the popular level — outstandingly represented by the literature of the People's Movement and the many pamphlets produced by *ad hoc* groups around the country — the arguments were at best oversimplified, at worst and all too often a travesty of the facts designed to exploit people's fears and arouse national feelings. The character of the campaign at this level — increasingly emotional, extreme and intolerant — probably owed something to it taking place to some extent outside the framework of the major political parties, especially on the anti-market side. The arguments were the more complex ones of responsible politicians and experts degraded to slogans for mass consumption. And as the campaign reached its climax the slogans increasingly took over — on both sides.

Each side had its chief slogan, the one which summed up and encompassed all its particular arguments. 'We cannot stay outside', was the pro-marketeers'. 'Sovereignty' was the anti-marketeers', as it was in the other applicant countries.

As one supporter of membership conceded, 'We cannot stay outside' was hardly an heroic or positive platform on which to go to the country. But in his view it was the only argument which had ever succeeded in overcoming the Norwegians' deep-seated reluctance to participate in new forms of international co-operation; and many other pro-marketeers seemed to agree with him.[41] Essentially, 'We cannot stay outside' meant that Norway was too small, too exposed strategically, too dependent economically on the outside world, to be able to isolate itself and be self-sufficient. They might not like such close involvement with other countries, but the disadvantages of not joining the many organisations of international co-operation, especially Western co-operation, were so great that they would just have to overcome their instinctive preferences and do so. Most pro-marketeers probably manted to join the EEC for other and more positive reasons as well. In particular, many saw a challenge, a wider European stage for action, and felt themselves sufficiently part of Western Europe to want their country to stay in the mainstream of its development. They used such positive arguments as well, Labour's early emphasis on building a socialist Europe being only one example of many. But their overriding theme was a negative one: the many reasons why Norway would suffer if it stayed outside an enlarged

EEC which included Britain and Denmark; why there was no acceptable alternative.

One serious weakness of this approach was that in the circumstances of 1972 it was not difficult for their opponents to persuade many people that, on the contrary, Norway could manage very well outside the EEC. The real disadvantages of staying outside were not easily expressed in simple, effective slogans, and when the attempt was made the result was all too often an easy target for the anti-marketeers. At a time when the average Norwegian voter was more affluent than ever before and oil was being discovered in the North Sea, warnings about unemployment and lower growth rates made less impression than they would have done ten years earlier, especially as there were reputable economists ready to say that the economic arguments were inconclusive. At a time when detente was the main theme of east-west relations and Norway's NATO membership in no obvious danger, it was not immediately evident why Norway's long-term security should be undermined if it refused to join a group of mainly continental countries with neither a defence policy nor the means of effectively defending Norway's vulnerable northern region. The pro-marketeers were not the only ones to base their campaign on raising fears about what would happen if the voters rejected their advice. So did the anti-marketeers. The only difference was that the pro-marketeers' warnings proved less effective than their opponents'. Another weakness of the 'We cannot stay outside' argument was that it made little appeal to the younger, self-confident Norwegians of the early 1970s, who were by then a significant section of the electorate and an even more important active factor in politics. Having only known prosperity and peace, most of them were unimpressed by arguments which concentrated on how to maintain them. They were not frightened by warnings about a slightly lower growth rate or weakening Norway's political ties with Western Europe. On the contrary, that was what many of them said they wanted.

Having settled on an approach which sought to persuade Norwegians that it would hurt them more to stay outside the EEC than join it, the pro-marketeers might have been more successful if they had pursued it consistently. But for various reasons they did not. In particular they were cautious about pursuing the security argument for membership during most of the campaign. The Conservatives were less reticent in this respect, pointing to the long-term implications of the EEC's foreign policy co-operation for the work of the Atlantic alliance, and the danger that Norway might find itself excluded from European defence co-operation at a time when American forces in Europe looked like being reduced. But even they were careful about pressing such arguments, for there were a number of risks attached to doing so. One was that the EEC's unpopularity would affect public attitudes towards NATO if they became too closely identified in people's minds; and Norway's NATO membership was far too important to be put at risk. Indeed for those who regarded EEC membership partly or even primarily as a means of consolidating Norway's place in the Atlantic alliance, it would be self-defeating if support for NATO was weakened as a result of the referendum campaign. Linking the two together might of course have the opposite effect: NATO's popularity might help the EEC. But there was the real danger that it would merely hand an effective argument against NATO membership to those who wanted to end it. Starting a debate about the connection between Norwegian security and EEC membership might also make people more aware of just how little able to defend Norway the Western Europeans actually were. That in turn could lead them to question whether such close political ties with the EEC were necessary. Why not just trade with Western Europe and rely on the United States for security? For Labour there was the additional risk of sharpening existing party differences over security policy. The youth organisation, for example, which was playing so prominent a part in organising opposition to joining the EEC, was also against Norway's NATO membership. The main obstacle for Labour's leaders initially, however, was probably the general tone of the party's pronouncements on foreign affairs since the late 1960s. Having concentrated on stressing the desirability of detente and, since 1969, the progress being made towards achieving it, a reversal to pointing out the dangers of Norway's position and the continuing threat from the east was not easily or suddenly undertaken.

During much of the campaign therefore the pro-marketeers played down the one argument — that joining the EEC was necessary for the Norwegians' security and place in the Western world — which might possibly have split the anti-marketeers, or at least seriously embarrassed them. Drawing attention to the Soviet Union's growing naval strength in the north might even have made an impression on the fishermen and voters up in that stronghold of opposition to EEC membership. The neutralist anti-marketeers recognised this potential weakness in their coalition with NATO supporters like the Centrists and Christians. That was presumably one reason why they made so little reference in the public campaign to what was one of their main motives for working against EEC membership, namely the hope that preventing it would be the first step to taking Norway out of NATO too. With most pro-marketeers and the neutralist anti-marketeers holding back on security matters lest their arguments prove counter-productive, the field was largely left to those who were as strongly for NATO as they were against the EEC. With their reliability on NATO beyond doubt they were well placed to reassure the voters that a 'no' to the EEC would not alter Norway's Western orientation. Indeed, according to them NATO gave the Norwegians the security to vote 'no'. Nor, they said, would it be a change of course in Norway's post-war foreign policy as the pro-marketeers were claiming. This had been an Atlantic policy, not one orientated towards continental Europe. It had been based moreover on co-operating with other Western countries, not participating in supra-national union-making. Some of these pro-NATO anti-marketeers even turned their opponents' argument on its head, maintaining that the EEC could endanger NATO and Norway's security. Would the Americans still be so ready to defend Western Europe if that European defence co-operation about which some pro-marketeers talked produced a defence community, perhaps armed with Anglo-French nuclear weapons? Whether described as merely unnecessary to Norway's security or a positive threat to it, however, the conclusion was the same: entering the EEC would not make the Norwegians any safer.

Only relatively late in the campaign, when the pro-marketeers' other arguments seemed to be making little impact on the public opinion polls, did they at last bring the security arguments right to the fore. They insisted that Norway's allies would indeed regard a 'no' to the EEC as a break with the country's foreign policy. That in turn would raise doubts about the continuity of its security policy, a risk which the Norwegians could not afford to take in their exposed strategic position. Security, they pointed out, was not merely a matter of formal military agreements, as the anti-marketeers seemed to think. Rather it presupposed a feeling of solidarity between countries, a solidarity which engendered loyalty and a willingness to come to the others' defence. Was it not obvious that EEC members would feel more solidarity with each other than with outsiders? The EEC's political co-operation would also lead to it playing a more important role as a community inside the Atlantic alliance. That in turn would lead to decisions being increasingly prepared or even taken in bilateral discussions between the EEC and the United States, with other alliance members left on the sidelines, unable effectively to make their views heard. And far from European defence co-operation weakening NATO, as long as it remained within the Atlantic framework (and were the British or Germans likely to go outside it?) such co-operation would strengthen NATO by enabling the Europeans to carry a greater share of the common defence effort. In short, joining the EEC would anchor Norway more securely to the West, while adopting a neutral position towards the EEC could very well result in Norway drifting away into a neutral position towards

NATO as well. Many pro-marketeers really took this view of what was at stake in their relations with the EEC. But by the time they said so it was too late to make the impression it might have done had they argued their case consistently ever since 1970. By 1972 the counter-arguments were well prepared and well known. And the fact that they were using the security argument so prominently only when they were in obvious difficulties made it easier for their opponents to label it a mere scare tactic.

They applied the same description to the pro-marketeers' economic arguments. On the whole these were the same ones which had been used throughout the 1960s to explain why Norway could not stay outside an enlarged EEC without meeting serious disadvantages. The country's prosperity depended on industry and shipping, which in turn depended on export markets and the maintenance of liberal international shipping policies. The enlarged EEC would be taking 60 per cent of Norway's industrial exports, and a much larger percentage in some key sectors. If Norwegian industry was to achieve a greater degree of specialisation and technological sophistication, it had to have guaranteed access on competitive terms to a large and expanding market. It also needed the stimulus of an advanced industrial milieu such as the EEC's. As a member Norway would participate in drawing up common policies in sectors of vital importance for it such as industry and energy. And it would be able to join in solving those problems of modern industrial society, such as pollution, which individual countries could not master alone. For Norwegian shipping exclusion from the EEC could have serious consequences. An EEC which included Britain would be employing some 60 per cent of Norway's shipping services, yet would have sufficient tonnage to meet its own carrying requirements if it wished. That could be a temptation to protectionism, and it was therefore important for Norway to be in a position to defend liberal policies from inside the EEC's institutions, where the crucial decisions would be made. The prospect of being a modest producer of high cost oil was not regarded as having altered the primary importance of industry and shipping. Indeed it provided an additional argument for joining the EEC, namely that only guaranteed access to a large market could justify the heavy investment required to build up a petrochemical industry. As for agriculture and fisheries, the entry negotiations had taken care of their interests, and the fishing industry would benefit from duty-free access to a market of 250 million people. Nor should it ever be forgotten that it was the prosperity of Norway's industry and shipping which financed the expensive support measures that alone kept much of the primary sector profitable.

As the EEC's negotiations with those EFTA states not applying for membership got underway in 1971, the pro-marketeers devoted considerable effort to exposing the disadvantages of a free trade agreement. Here the Swedish model was the one generally used by both sides. Its immediate disadvantage for industry would be the longer transitional periods for major exports like metals and paper. Pro-marketeers also warned that in any free trade negotiations following a rejection of membership, the Norwegians must expect that those economic interests in the Six which had prevented Norway receiving the standard tariff reductions in the Kennedy Round negotiations of the 1960s would make their influence felt again. The result would be a cut in profits, and behind the protective barriers put up against Norwegian goods the EEC would build up its own competitive industries like France's aluminium industry. Moreover, a free trade agreement would not give the market security of membership because of the 'protection clause' which the EEC would insist on including. This, a feature of the other agreements, permitted it to introduce protective measures against EFTA exports if these caused disturbances in EEC markets. The uncertainty thereby created would make long-term planning difficult and discourage investment. Even more serious would be Norway's exclusion from the industrial and technological co-operation which the EEC was expected to develop, and participation in which some pro-marketeers claimed would be one of the major economic benefits of membership. Shipping would be in a weaker position to defend its interests. The fishing industry would forfeit access to a large free market and the opportunity of exporting more of its catch in the more profitable processed form because of the EEC's high tariffs on processed fish. That in turn would mean less jobs in processing plants on land than there would be if Norway was in the EEC. As for agriculture, which was so intent on staying outside in order to keep its protection against imports, Sweden's negotiations had demonstrated that the EEC would probably demand concessions here too in return for the market opportunities it would be offering to Norwegian industry.

At the popular level these arguments were often simplified to the claim that only membership could protect Norwegian jobs and living standards. A 'yes' vote would save them from unemployment and economic stagnation. A 'no' vote would open up a future of economic uncertainty, with export industries and shipping threatened, firms establishing inside the EEC in order to avoid tariff barriers, and imports of foreign capital drying up. But just as in the debate about the consequences of a 'no' for Norway's security policy — where the pro-market argument was finally reduced to the slogan 'a 'no' vote will set Norway adrift from the West'[42] — there were plenty of politicians and experts on the other side to argue the contrary.

They pointed out, for example, that it had not been conclusively proved that EEC membership would stimulate economic growth in Norway or staying outside necessarily be an obstacle to it. Growth was anyway an economic objective which had to be balanced against others, like resource conservation. They also had to consider what type of economic system would be producing the growth. Would it help or hinder the achievement of important non-economic objectives like greater equality, more participation, a harmonious social development, and a balanced distribution of population? Norway's postwar economic performance gave no grounds for the pessimism displayed by pro-marketeers about a future outside the EEC. When other Western European countries had experienced economic difficulties in 1971, Norway had maintained its stable growth rate and low unemployment. Some economists had attributed this to the adaptability of a small economy like Norway's and to the range of control mechanisms which Norwegians had developed in response to their country's particular problems and objectives. Were these advantages to be abandoned? The pro-marketeers, they said, seemed to be implying that staying outside the EEC would cut Norway off from international economic co-operation, which was nonsense. As for shipping, its interests could be adequately protected within existing international organisations like the OECD. In short Norway did not need to join the EEC for economic reasons. A free trade agreement would protect its trading interests, and the longer transitional periods for some industries would be a merely temporary disadvantage, more than offset by the permanent advantage of retaining a greater degree of control over their own economy than they would have inside the EEC.

It was precisely this last claim which the pro-marketeers argued against most strongly. On the contrary, they said, they would have less genuine control over their own affairs outside than inside the EEC. Indeed that was one of the main reasons they wanted Norway to go in. For a small country heavily dependent on trade for its prosperity and on allies for its security, the choice was not between dependence and independence, but between dependence with or without an opportunity to influence those decisions of other countries which were going to affect it whatever it did. EEC membership would mean surrendering some formal national decision-making powers. But in return they would gain a voice in the joint decisions of other states. The most serious disadvantage of a free trade agreement was that their economy would be integrated into the EEC market without them having a say in the decisions and regulations governing that market. It would be integration without influence, and all the more dangerous because the appearance of independence would be maintained. It would be the equivalent in the economic sphere to the probable consequences of a free trade agreement for Norway's position in the Atlantic alliance (as long that is, as Norway had not drifted away from it). The outer forms would remain the same: national economic control in one case, formal alliance procedures in the other. But the reality would be different. Norway's businessmen and civil servants would find themselves having to follow EEC regulations and adjust to policies drawn up in Brussels. Its diplomats would find that the real decisions had already been taken elsewhere: in the EEC's foreign policy consultations or in prior negotiations between the EEC and the United States. The sovereignty of a Norway outside the EEC would be an illusion.

The anti-marketeers did not deny that Norway's dependence on EEC markets would lessen its freedom of action. Of course Norwegians would have to adjust to decisions taken inside the EEC. Of course they would be influenced by them. But this would be nothing new. When had they not been affected by the policies of their neighbours? It was because Norway's trading interests in EEC markets were so important that they were advocating a free trade agreement. They did not want to cut Norway off from the EEC. On the contrary, they wanted to co-operate in any areas where it was in their mutual interest to do so. If Norway became isolated because it had chosen to stay outside the EEC, it would be because the EEC had isolated Norway. But they saw no reason why it should want to do so.

They denied that they were rejecting membership out of a spirit of isolationism and nationalism. The reason they did not want to join the EEC was that doing so would reduce their chances of retaining or creating the type of society that they wanted in Norway itself: a society suited to the Norwegian people's traditions and history, their geographical position and their country's economic structure. They admitted to disagreeing among themselves about many aspects of what that society should look like. But they claimed to be united in wanting Norwegians to be free to form it in accordance with their own values. To do this, however, they had to retain control over the key decisions in the economy. They had to control credit and taxation policy, capital movements, income transfers, regional policy, interest rates, the distribution of resources, and the rate at which they were exploited: in other words all those decisions which determined where industries were located, the viability of small communities and small producers, the economic relations between social groups, and the ownership and use of natural resources. In the EEC this would be impossible, because these were precisely the powers which were to be transferred to Brussels under the plans for economic and monetary union. In Norway, moreover, the government enjoyed considerable powers to regulate the economy and thereby the country's social development. The very nature of the country had required it if Norway was to be developed into a balanced economy, and most Norwegians had accepted it in order to achieve their economic and social objectives. Only to a limited degree therefore was there scope for the free play of market forces. The EEC's objective, on the other hand, was to liberate these forces: to free the movement of labour and capital and remove restrictions to free competition. These were very different economic principles and priorities and expressed social values and produced societies which differed in some important ways from Norway's. Yet in the EEC it was these principles which guided the formulation of common policies. Quite apart from having to apply alien principles to their economy, how much influence could the Norwegians expect to have on the EEC's policies? Even at the present level of integration it was the large states which dominated the EEC, and exceptions to EEC policies were not permitted, as the entry negotiations had just demonstrated. With the establishment of the economic and monetary union there would be supranational decision-making and the veto would go. Pro-marketeers who claimed that Norwegians would still be able to control their own economy and society inside the EEC had overlooked or chosen to ignore the logic of the organisation's development.

EEC membership, according to the anti-marketeers, would steadily and profoundly alter the conditions under which people lived and worked in Norway. The EEC's free-market principles would mean centralisation, greater labour mobility and rationalisation. People would be forced to move to jobs where capital chose to invest, concentrated in large urban areas as on the continent and having to compete with foreign workers forcing down wage levels. The settlement pattern would be drastically altered as coastal fishermen were driven out by foreign trawler fleets, small farms abandoned, and fishermen and farmers forced to seek work in industries far away. Large areas of the country would be depopulated and lie unexploited. Food prices would rise steeply as consumer subsidies were removed and Norway had to import food at prices higher than those in world markets. House prices and rents would rise as long-term interest rates were driven up to EEC levels. So the ordinary Norwegian would be worse off even if the country achieved a marginally higher growth rate as a result of joining the EEC.

Their culture and language would suffer too. Foreign books and papers would swamp the Norwegian market. *Riksmål* — Oslo Norwegian — would finally win out against *landsmål* as the rural population was driven into the towns and the country way of life disappeared. Even this standardised Norwegian would be reduced to a minority tongue spoken by a mere four million of the EEC's 250 million inhabitants. When Norwegians went to Brussels they would have to speak English or French or German because hardly any foreigners would be able to understand Norwegian, let alone speak it. Yet it was in Brussels that all the important decisions affecting their lives would be taken — taken by foreign bureaucrats and politicians who would probably have never even visited Norway and could not speak with its inhabitants in their own tongue. What chance would the ordinary Norwegian have of making his views heard then?

These were the anti-marketeers' negative arguments for voting 'no', their equivalent to the pro-marketeers' warnings about the consequences of not voting 'yes'. But the anti-marketeers' ultimate success was due not only to the undoubted impact of these dire predictions. Important too was their ability to unite on a positive platform, however vague and generally formulated. They claimed to be fighting EEC membership not merely to avert dangers but in order to achieve certain specific social and political objectives. At home they wanted more democracy and equality, a better use of resources and an avoidance of the problems of urban and industrial concentration. EEC membership, according to them, would be an obstacle to this because the EEC exemplified all the worst features of modern industrial society: concentration, bureaucratisation, and the individual's loss of influence within his community and workplace. Abroad the anti-marketeers declared they would work for an international economic system which helped the developing countries instead of exploiting them and for forms of economic co-operation which brought the Nordic countries together instead of splitting them. Again they described the EEC as a serious hindrance to achieving these aims, because it was an economic and political power bloc which appropriated an unfair share of the world's resoures and deepened the conflict between rich and poor nations.[43]

This platform gave their campaign the appearance of a broad national front. Within it sectional interests acquired national significance and small extreme left-wing parties like the SPP and communists could be active without alienating non-socialist voters. It based the anti-market campaign on values and objectives which their opponents could not attack directly because they enjoyed a place in all the parties' programmes. All the pro-marketeers could do was dispute that membership would be an obstacle to achieving them. But that shifted the public debate onto issues chosen by the anti-marketeers instead of those on which the pro-marketeers wanted to focus attention. The Labour party's socialist arguments for membership had been in part an attempt to anticipate this challenge by basing the party's support for entering the EEC on fundamental social and political principles, not just economic and foreign policy considerations. But being aimed specifically at the Labour party, it could not provide the basis for a national platform on which all pro-marketeers could unite, such as the anti-marketeers had created for themselves. On the contrary it split the pro-marketeers' efforts, while not even achieving its aim in the Labour party itself.

The anti-marketeers' positive reasons for voting 'no' may not have made much impact on the average voter. Those voters already inclined to oppose membership were probably more impressed by arguments showing that staying outside the EEC would not harm them economically or reduce their security, while it would harm the interests of the fishermen and farmers if they went in. But the general aims set out by the anti-market side were doubtless an important factor in mobilising the many people, especially young people, who did the active campaigning. For the issues on which they concentrated — regional policy, local democracy, decentralisation, environmental and resource questions, helping the developing countries — had already been taken up by the more radical sections of Norway's political parties and academic community before the EEC debate began, the campaign itself merely giving the discussion about them a much greater impetus. The campaign may have been heavily financed by the agricultural organisations, and without the primary sector's self-interest in preventing membership the outcome could well have been the same as in Denmark. But many of those who campaigned to keep Norway out of the EEC believed they were fighting for something, not just against something. It was that which created the sense of idealism and purpose which infused much of their activity and was such an important factor in their victory.

January-September 1972

As this last phase of the campaign opened, however, most Norwegians, wherever they stood on the question, still expected it to end with a majority for membership: in the end Labour's organisation and the loyalty of its members and voters would surely reverse the consistent message of the polls and give a victory for the government.[44] But, even assuming that a majority could have been found for membership (and the post-referendum polls produced one for several months),[45] both the Labour party and the pro-marketeers generally had started their campaign much too late to win an easy victory in the time left. After eighteen months their opponents' position was too well entrenched for that. They might have succeeded had they used all the remaining time to campaign for public opinion and had they agreed among themselves on tactics and priorities. But instead

148

much of the time was used in bringing their own organisations to the point where they were ready to go out and win over the voters. Moreover Labour's leadership, divided at this crucial stage, failed to pursue a clear and consistent policy, either towards its internal opposition or in its handling of the national campaign. Veering between concilation and firmness, between giving priority to EEC membership and party unity, it largely neutralised its own efforts and never succeeded in regaining the initiative from its opponents.

The government enjoyed the tactical advantage of being able to determine the timing of the referendum and therefore the length of the campaign. The anti-marketeers wanted it held as soon as possible in order to give the pro-marketeers less time to catch up. That meant in May or June before the long summer holidays.[46] But the government argued that this left insufficient time for the party and parliamentary preparations prior to the campaign, and set an autumn date, 24 and 25 September.[47] Given the habitually systematic approach of the prime minister, Trygve Bratteli, this time probably was required to go through all the various formalities which had to precede the referendum: the Labour party's special local party conferences had to be held, then the national one, legislation had to be passed in order to hold the referendum at all, the government had to prepare and present its report on the negotiations to parliament, parliament had to debate it, and then in late June the towns would start emptying for two months as the Norwegians left for their holidays. But it gave the impression of a government trying to gain time. The later date also had another, more serious, consequence, which probably outweighed the advantage of a few extra months campaigning. Once a time of the year had been chosen for the referendum which almost exactly coincided with that at which the fixed four-yearly national and local elections were held, the Labour party's campaign timetable became that followed in such normal elections: first the various party conferences to agree on policy in the spring, followed by a low level of activity in the summer, and then a short intense campaign of four to five weeks in late August and September.[48] It was a well-established procedure which had served the party well for years. Whether it was suited to such a very different political situation as a referendum in which the party had a lot of ground to catch up before polling day was at least open to question — but does not appear to have been questioned. Instead the wheels were set in motion in February and from then on the organisation ran along its accustomed course. So for much of the nine months the party was not seriously campaigning, which was probably an important factor enabling the anti-marketeers to maintain their position as well as they did.

Nor did the government gain another advantage it had hoped for from the later date. During 1971 it had been expected that the Danish referendum would be held in June 1972. As Danish public opinion was more favourable to EEC membership than was Norwegian, Norway's pro-marketeers had been hoping that a Danish majority for entry would influence the Norwegian electorate when it came to vote afterwards. Early in 1972 however the social democratic government in Copenhagen decided to postpone its referendum until after the Norwegian one, apparently as a concession to its own anti-marketeers who were calculating on a Norwegian 'no' perhaps tipping the scales in their favour in Denmark.[49] The Labour government in Oslo therefore lost the help it had anticipated from Denmark. Norway's anti-marketeers were also provided with a new variation on the Nordic alternative theme for use in the last stage of the campaign. The Norwegians, they said, would be deciding the future of the Nordic area because a 'no' majority would improve the chances of a similar result in Denmark, and thereby open the way for a revival of Nordek: '25 September — a chance for the Nordic countries'.[50]

By the time Labour's special national conference on the EEC was held in April, the pro-marketeers had suffered several more setbacks. The first followed immediately on the ending of the negotiations, when at the end of January Labour's anti-marketeers established their own organisation for the coming campain, the 'Labour Movement's Information Committee against Norwegian Membership of the EEC'. Its founders' intention was to avoid the charge of extra-party activity and provide a platform for those party members who felt uncomfortable about working outside the party in an organisation like the People's Movement, including those who disliked the People's Movement and some of the political forces in it. The Labour Information Committee's objective was to persuade Labour voters that they could vote 'no' without being disloyal to the party's basic aims and ideals, and that neither their jobs nor the country's security would be endangered if they did so.[51] Its establishment, an open breach of party regulations, demonstrated the self-confidence of the internal opposition by early 1972 as well as their determination to ignore the majority conference decisions which no one doubted the government would win for its policy in the coming months. The Labour Information Committee was a Labour party organisation aiming to defeat party policy and persuade Labour supporters to vote contrary to the advice of the party's leaders. Yet the latter were unable to enforce normal party discipline, because they were unwilling to risk the probable consequences for party unity. The Labour Information Committee demonstrated the limits of the leadership's control over the party by 1972, and that those non-socialist pro-marketeers who were relying on Labour to take Norway into the EEC were placing their hopes on an organisation which was no longer functioning with its renowned solidarity and effectiveness.

Then in March the Liberal party's national conference rejected membership, followed by the Christian People's party in April. Both parties were still divided. A majority of the Liberal members of parliament (eight to five) favoured joining the EEC, including the chairman, Helge Seip, but opponents predominated in the national executive and at the national conference (128 to 95); the polls showed Liberal voters almost evenly split.[52] The Christians' parliamentary group and national executive were evenly divided, but both the past and present chairmen, Kjell Bondevik and Lars Korvald, now came out against entry, followed by a clear majority at the conference (93 to 64), while Christian voters also continued to reject entry by a substantial margin.[53] Both parties now stood officially on the anti-market side. In both this position was based on general social and political arguments: the EEC's economic system and objectives would mean a sharpening of the forces of competition and faster pace of change, an increase in the pressure on resources, even more concentration of people in larger communities, and a weakening of the economic basis for a pattern of settlement which permitted local democracy and cultural diversity to flourish. However, while the Liberal anti-market arguments were stamped by an anti-capitalist, populist outlook, the Christians on the whole revealed an essentially conservative desire to preserve the existing society and way of life. Both parties left their members free to campaign as individuals on either side, and the national organisations were to be kept out of the campaign. In this way they hoped to bring their parties unscathed through the coming climax of the campaign.[54]

For Labour's leadership these decisions made the situation much more difficult. With all the middle-parties now opposed to membership, Labour's alliance with the Conservatives was even more lonely and politically awkward than ever. Both the Liberal and Christian People's parties were magnets for anti-market Labour voters who stood in the middle or on the right of the party. Moreover their decision to treat the conference policy resolutions on the EEC as only a recommendation to members and voters, not as binding on them, was an example to which Labour's own anti-marketeers could now point when claiming the same freedom. So was the decision not to mobilise the party organisations exclusively on one side when the parties were divided over the issue.

With the Christian and Liberal conferences over, the anti-market coalition was complete. Its main pillars were the primary producers, the left socialists, the radical populists of the Liberal and Centre parties, and the conservative economic, social and cultural forces in all three middle-parties. The urge towards national independence, the economic self-interest of the farmers and fishermen, anti-capitalism, lay protestant fundamentalism, the new economic and social movements which had been winning ground since the late 1960s: all now stood united in opposing Norwegian membership of the EEC. A large part of the country's politically active and better educated youth and of the academic community were on their side. In the People's Movement they had a national mass organisation which had been campaigning for eighteen months, and in the Labour Information Committee an organisation established inside the Labour party itself. In parliament their number had risen to about forty-four by the time the government's report on the EEC negotiations was debated in June 1972[55] — from seventeen in June 1970, to thirty-seven a year later, and now six more than the blocking quarter they needed. To a large extent all these different groups had overcome their disagreements on other issues and were working together inside parliament and outside it. They were still a minority of the Oslo political elite, perhaps even of the broader national social and cultural one. But they were nonetheless a formidable and well-organised minority, able to draw on reserves of talent, enthusiasm and conviction which more than made up for what they lacked in numbers.

Against them the pro-marketeers had no national cross-party organisation until the spring of 1972, while Labour and the Conservative party continued their separate campaigns. The two parties' representatives in the foreign relations committee joined together to produce a common recommendation on the government's report in May,[56] but otherwise Labour was as concerned to maintain its distance as it had been since 1970 and the Conservatives to cause as little embarrassment for the Labour pro-marketeers as possible. As their alliance was plain for all to see however (providing a prominent theme of anti-market cartoons, for example), this probably no longer helped Labour much with its own members and voters, if it ever had done, while it was a serious obstacle to establishing an effective national pro-market platform to counter that of the anti-marketeers. That the basis for such a platform existed was demonstrated by their joint position in the foreign relations committee: by 1972 the arguments they were using in favour of membership were so similar as to be expressed in a single recommendation. Yet party considerations — Labour's overriding concern to minimise its internal conflicts and the seemingly unbreachable psychological barrier created by decades of politial confrontation — prevented its translation into an open alliance for their common objective such as their opponents had established. This was no doubt partly because their confidence in ultimate victory created the illusion that it was unnecessary, whereas it was precisely the anti-marketeers' consciousness of their weak starting position which had been so potent a force in making them put aside their equally deep differences.

One result was that when at last a national organisation to campaign for membership was established in the spring, it contained no prominent public figures from either party in its leadership. 'Yes to the EEC' was supported by some Labour and Conservative politicians, but only in their individual capacity.[57] Its leaders were not well-known figures and scarcely had time to become so. The organisation had to be built up, members recruited, literature prepared: all the preparations made which the People's Movement had completed in the winter of 1970-71. Not until the early summer was 'Yes to the EEC' ready to campaign, but even then its leaders postponed any serious activity until after the summer holidays.[58] Again it was probably over-confidence which was partly responsible for this 'too little, too late' approach: they were so sure that at some point the public opinion polls must swing in their favour under the combined impact of the government's authority, Labour party loyalty, the Labour and trade union EEC conferences, and the campaigns of these two powerful organisations. Even the pro-marketeers' national organisation, in other words, seemed to be relying on Labour to carry Norway into the EEC.

But by the late spring Labour's organisation had scarcely progressed beyond the first stage of its strategy for winning the referendum, namely the promised broad democratic party debate which was to culminate in a majority for the government's policy at the special conference in late April. Moreover, differences had appeared within the leadership over how to handle the question. No one doubted that the preliminary local party conferences would produce majorities for the government's recommendation and send delegates to the national conference who were mostly committed to supporting it, although the anti-marketeers did succeed in mustering substantial minorities even at the local level.[59] The real issue in April was not whether EEC membership would become official party policy, but how much pressure the leadership would then put on its members and voters to support that policy. Would the conference decision be made binding on members? Would the government turn the referendum into a question of confidence?

Re-imposing party discipline by drastic methods like expulsion had obviously been ruled out because of the size of the opposition and the serious split this could lead to. Even the establishment of the Labour Information Committee had not met with disciplinary action. The question was whether it would even be possible without serious repercussions for the leadership to require that the opposition follow standard party practice and respect a majority conference decision once its position had been defeated. Labour anti-marketeers insisted that the EEC issue was so unique and of such importance to them that the party rules would have to be waived. They could point to the example of the Christian and Liberal parties which had seemed to acknowledge this, and the risk the question posed to their parties, by leaving members free to campaign and vote according to personal conviction. The second question, whether the government should link its fate to the outcome of the referendum, had arisen as a result of press speculation and remarks made by individual ministers and party leaders.[60] The anti-marketeers argued strongly against it, their natural fear being that loyalty to Bratteli and the Labour government would prove stronger for many ordinary members and faithful Labour voters than their wish to stay outside the EEC. They argued that the referendum was solely a test of voters' views on the EEC, and this should not be confused by bringing in other, quite extraneous, issues. Turning it into a question of confidence would impose intolerable conflicts and unfair pressures on Labour supporters. If members of parliament were to respect the voters' advice as the pro-marketeers were insisting they should, then the government ought to do the same, and if the vote was 'no' continue in office to negotiate the free trade agreement which a majority of voters had shown they preferred. In Denmark, the anti-marketeers pointed out, the social democratic government had expressly said it would not resign if its recommendation to vote for joining the EEC was defeated.[61]

The leadership seemed to be divided on both questions. The party's general secretary, for example, had said that conference decisions on the EEC should be binding like all other decisions, and that the government should declare its intention of resigning if defeated in the referendum.[62] Bratteli's predecessor as chairman and prime minister, Einar Gerhardsen (himself a supporter of membership, but with a son who, as chairman of Labour's youth organisation, was actively campaigning against it) argued that on this particular issue the normal rules should be waived and no pressure brought to bear on Labour supporters in the form of a question of confidence.[63] Among those who took the harder line were perhaps some who did so because they were beginning to feel less confident about the outcome. But other motives were probably just as important: some ministers closely identified with the negotiations felt they could not continue in office if membership was rejected,[64] and some party officials no doubt simply disliked the flagrant breaches of party rules and indiscipline.[65]

154

On the other side, among those taking a softer line, motives were probably similarly mixed. Some were still so confident about the outcome that they considered it unnecessary to use methods which would afterwards make it much harder to reunite the party. Others simply regarded party unity as the highest priority, and if Norway could only be taken into the EEC by methods which seriously threatened it, then they preferred to stay outside. Bratteli did not even indicate, let alone impose, a clear line amid all the statements and speculation. So when the national conference met the result was a compromise resolution which covered over the unresolved disagreements with formulas capable of meaning one thing to pro-marketeers and another to anti-marketeers.

The majority in favour of membership was 227 to 73.[66] On the question whether members now had to support what had become official policy, the resolution said that 'in the months to the referendum the task must be to persuade the voters to support the party's policy'. On the face of it this seemed to maintain the standard party practice and could be used to require the minority at least to stop actively working against conference decisions. But the general view was that a compromise had been reached under which, while Labour's national organisation would campaign for membership (in contrast to those of the Christian and Liberal parties), individual party members would be free to engage on either side. By that stage the most the leaders seemed to be hoping for was that once they had won the referendum (as most still expected to do) the minority would accept defeat and stay within the party. As for the issue of making the referendum a question of confidence, here the anti-marketeers obtained a passage in the conference resolution, to which they attached importance, which said that whatever the result of the referendum the party would not cease its struggle to control the country's democratically elected institutions. Their interpretation of this was that the government would continue in office even if defeated.[67] That Bratteli himself did not necessarily accept this interpretation, however, was made clear in his subsequent statement that the government would take its decision on the matter only after the referendum and in the light of its outcome. So the question remained open — and with it the implied threat that voting 'no' could be helping to put a non-socialist government back into office.

Labour's anti-marketeers however now had an argument to use against such a step, and one moreover which they could base on the conference resolution itself. But it was another event at the special conference which gave their campaign for Labour opinion an immeasurable boost. For they won not merely official toleration of their opposition to party policy, but the stamp of approval for it from none other than the former chairman, Einar Gerhardsen, himself. Taking as his starting point the simple facts that many Labour voters were against joining the EEC, yet the party could not afford to lose their support if it wished to retain power, he told the conference that,

'. . . if the party had not had any well-known members and officials who were opposed to membership we would have had to get some, in order to make it clear to all that one can belong to Labour and vote for Labour even if one votes 'no' in the referendum.'[68]

With that the party's most respected 'elder statesman' gave the green light to opposition; indeed his words seemed positively to encourage it. This passage became the Labour anti-marketeers' answer to the party's campaign slogan 'Labour voters are 'yes' voters'. Not so, was their reply, Einar Gerhardsen himself has said that loyal party supporters can vote 'no' with a good conscience. Gerhardsen may have contributed in the long term to achieving what was presumably his main objective, namely preventing the EEC issue tearing the party apart and permanently losing it many of its voters. But as far as his successor's immediate aim of taking Norway into the EEC was concerned, he had dealt it one of the most serious blows it suffered during this last phase of the campaign.

By early summer the anti-marketeers could also take encouragement from the public opinion polls. In the first two months after the ending of negotiations there was a slight shift towards the pro-marketeers. Then between March and April the decisive, long-awaited swing in Labour opinion towards the government seemed to have begun: among Labour voters in April a clear majority of those who had made up their minds said they would vote 'yes', while support was even higher among party members. In the population as a whole the anti-marketeers still had a majority: 55 per cent to 45 per cent.[69] But they were losing ground with five months still to go, and the general expectation was that the trend would accelerate after the Labour and trade union conferences had come out in favour of membership. Instead the balance of opinion remained stable. The anticipated further swing to the pro-marketeers failed to materialise in May. In June the polls were still recording the April balance between the two sides. Then came the summer holidays with campaigning at a low level and nothing likely to happen which could be expected to make an impact on public opinion.

But still the Labour leadership kept to its timetable, according to which the second stage of its campaign, that aimed at the electorate as a whole, would not really get underway until late August. Pro-marketeers outside the party who were relying on Labour to bring

156

some movement into the polls again, began to show signs of impatience and nervousness. Were the party's leaders over-confident, or were they too bound by their organisational procedures and fixed plans to change them in the face of this seemingly unshakeable anti-market lead? Was the party to continue receiving such priority that even at this stage anything likely to exacerbate its internal conflicts would be avoided? And if that was the case, could the government win?

When campaigning resumed in August, however, the tone sharpened and each side's efforts reached an unprecedented level of intensity. This was partly due to their closeness in the polls. The pro-marketeers still had a chance of catching up, but would have to fight hard now to do so. The anti-marketeers, perhaps for the first time, scented victory but knew they could still lose it on the very last lap. Spurred on by this neck-and-neck race to the finish each side redoubled its efforts, flooding the country with pamphlets and broadsheets distributed by many thousands of voluntary campaign workers. With the arguments known and nothing new to say about the EEC or Norway's relations with it, all that was left was to sharpen and drive them home, or to find new supporting evidence for well-known points. The anti-marketeers, for example, made much of Iceland's extension of its fishing limit to fifty miles on 1 September: Norwegians, bound by their treaty with the EEC, could neither follow Iceland's example nor even support the Icelanders, despite the fact that they were fighting the same battle as Norway's own coastal fishermen. French atomic tests in the Pacific highlighted the EEC's potential as a nuclear power: did the Norwegians really want to be submerged into a European superpower with nuclear weapons? A speech in London by the EEC commission's energy director, Ferdinand Spaak, setting out the commission's ideas for a common energy policy — off-shore oil to be a community resource, freedom of establishment, non-discrimination as between members' oil companies, EEC control of exploitation — provided a last minute sensation under the headline 'The EEC wants control of Norway's oil'.[70]

The simplifications and tougher campaign methods were most noticeable however on the pro-market side because of its previous comparative restraint in this respect. The security arguments were brought strongly to the fore, encouraged by the prime minister himself in a speech on the theme of war and peace in Europe at Televåg, a village which had been razed to the ground and its population deported during the war. Although Bratteli undoubtedly had the theme of reconciliation between the former wartime enemies of Western Europe very much in mind (himself having nearly died in a concentration camp during the war), equal prominence was given to the theme of Norway's place in the West and the security this provided against a repetition of the country's wartime experience.[71] One thousand war veterans signed a declaration of support for EEC membership (a controversial step which brought protests from other veterans). The foreign minister had already claimed that membership would increase Norway's security.[72] Now 'Yes to the EEC' asked menacingly in a newspaper advertisement: 'Which countries will be our allies in the long-term if Norway stays outside the EEC?' A 'no' would be a gamble with Norway's future, the advertisement went on. How would Norway replace the export markets from which a 'no' would exclude it? How would they secure the jobs put at risk? How could shipping interests be safeguarded if Norway lost its influence on international shipping policy by voting 'no'? And — it asked — what government would Norway have after 25 September if it voted 'no'?[73]

Uncertainty about this was the other reason for the harsher climate of the last few weeks. For as the final phase opened Bratteli had turned the referendum into a vote of confidence after all by announcing on 22 August that the government would resign if its recommendation was rejected, and that the Labour party would not assume responsibility for negotiating a free trade agreement.[74] The Conservatives had already indicated that they would not do so either: that would be a task for the parties which had opposed membership. But as the three middle-parties could at most muster only forty-seven of parliament's 150 seats, the position now being taken up by the Conservative and Labour parties meant that a 'no' would plunge the country into a political crisis with no majority government in sight. It seemed to many anti-marketeers that their opponents were trying to conjure up the picture of a 'no' being followed by something close to political chaos at home in addition to no agreement with the EEC.

Whether Bratteli's decision was merely the formalisation of a situation which others had created and he felt he had no choice in the end but to follow; whether it was a last attempt to secure a majority for membership as many anti-marketeers claimed; or whether, as he said on 22 August, he had simply come to the conclusion that if the voters rejected such a central part of the government's policy, the political basis for its continuation would have been removed; whatever the explanation, the effect was to increase the bitterness with which the last weeks of the campaign were fought. This was especially so within the Labour party, where the anti-marketeers maintained that Bratteli had acted contrary to the conference resolution of April and put them and many ordinary Labour voters in an

158

intolerable situation.[75] They regarded this as one last desperate effort to force voters to vote contrary to their convictions: Labour voters out of loyalty, the electorate generally out of a fear of the political consequences of voting 'no'. For Labour anti-marketeers and voters Bratteli's announcement made a vote against the EEC equivalent to a vote to topple their own government, and many deeply resented being subjected, after such a light rein during the previous two years, to this sudden conflict between party loyalty and personal conviction.

But this was its only consequence for the referendum, to add to the bitterness and divisions created within the Labour party during the last weeks of the campaign and to lend those weeks a greater intensity because of the uncertainty which faced the country should the anti-marketeers win. The announcement's impact on voting behaviour in the referendum itself was largely neutralised by the way in which months of speculation had pre-empted it, so that when it finally came it was, however much resented, scarcely unexpected. The arguments against making the referendum a question of confidence — unfair pressure, respect for the people's decision, the Danish example — were well known, while Labour's voters knew that Einar Gerhardsen had advised against it. Some also argued that as Labour was a minority government, its life expectancy was short anyway.[76] For most anti-marketeers and many ordinary voters the question of whether or not to join the EEC was quite simply more important than keeping a Labour government in office or avoiding a post-referendum political crisis. When the result was known on the night of 25 September it had had scarcely any effect on the stable figures recorded by the public opinion polls since the spring. The 'no's' had won by 53.5 per cent to 46.5 per cent.

The result

The most striking feature of the result, when combined with other polls and surveys of voters' intentions, was the clear division between the rural and urban areas.[77] Whichever test was applied — regional voting figures, degree of urbanisation, size and type of community, occupation, cultural characteristics — the general pattern held good. Support for membership increased with urbanisation and decreased the smaller the community and the more heavily it was dependent on the primary sector. Only one region produced a majority for membership (of 59.9 per cent), and that was the capital and area around the Oslo fjord; in the north 71.1 per cent voted against it. Sparsely inhabited communities were overwhelmingly against, more densely populated ones less so, while urban areas were generally in favour. Fishing and agricultural communities returned big 'no' votes;

people employed in typical city occupations like the professions and civil service produced 'yes' majorities. Voters speaking *landsmål*, supporting teetotalism, or belonging to the fundamentalist Protestant movement — all groups whose strength lay in the rural areas — were more inclined to vote 'no', whereas people in the large towns who spoke *riksmål* and took a liberal position on moral and religious issues were more frequently found supporting EEC membership than opposed to it. Economic interests, cultural outlook, and geographical location had reinforced each other to produce this result. It gave only an incomplete picture of the forces on each side, of course; people in the cities, especially radicals and young people, had also opposed membership. But although incomplete it undoubtedly reflected a fundamental line of conflict over the EEC.

The left-right axis in Norwegian politics was also reflected in the result, although not as strikingly. Surveys indicated that voters taking a left-wing position on questions like greater state control and public ownership were less favourable to EEC membership than those opposed to them. But the differences at voter level were not as marked as among politicians and those actively engaged in the referendum campaign. Moreover a substantial majority of the Labour supporters who voted in the referendum had cast their vote for membership, and whatever the pressures of personal and party loyalty that had contributed to this result, it undoubtedly blurred the picture. Where left-wing sentiment had been most important was in the campaign itself, where by splitting the Labour party and undermining the authority of the leadership it had probably prevented the majority among Labour supporters from being even higher.

After the intensity of the campaign, the turnout was low by Norwegian standards, falling from nearly 84 per cent in the 1969 election to just over 79 per cent. This was frequently interpreted as demonstrating the difficulty many voters had experienced in reconciling the frequently conflicting pulls of traditional party loyalty, local community, economic interest and views of family and acquaintances, especially supporters of the deeply split Labour, Liberal and Christian parties. However, such conflicts had not prevented a high turn-out in the northern fishing communities, whose inhabitants often voted for the pro-market Labour party. Indeed the numbers voting in the strongly 'no' peripheral areas of the north were even slightly higher than normal, by contrast with the sharp drop in areas of the country where opinion was more divided. This seemed to point to the degree of consensus in the voter's own community as having been an important factor in determining whether he voted and how he voted. Where the consensus was high and the community small, as in the fishing communities, the individual's hesitations and

160

conflicts of loyalty were more easily overcome, partly perhaps because the pressures on him to do so were correspondingly stronger. It was probably harder for the uncertain voter to make up his mind when his local environment was more evenly split.

Indeed many voters appear to have rather resented being forced to make up their minds on such a complex and important issue. Or at least they thought that the elected politicians should have assumed the responsibility for the decision. Polls showed that 43 per cent of the electorate thought the question of EEC membership should not have been made the subject of a referendum at all, while among members of political parties the percentage was even higher, 51 per cent.[78] Far from demanding a greater say in decisions affecting their lives, many 'men-in-the-street' seem, on this occasion at least, to have only wished that the politicians would give the country a clear lead and take the decisions entrusted to them by the constitution.

The politicians, however, had put the question to the people, and the people had voted 'no'. What had produced this result?

History and geography had combined to make 'no' a natural reaction for many Norwegians. Centuries of foreign domination had given the anti-marketeers' slogan of *selvråderett* (sovereignty) a profound emotional appeal. Their recent independence, intense patriotism, small numbers, and peripheral location had also injected a proud, touchy defensiveness into many Norwegians' reactions to anything, be it neighbouring states or foreign economic interests, which might possibly infringe this independence. This was not true of all Norwegians, of course. Those living in the larger southern coastal communities engaged in shipping and trade, and those with international experience and connections, tended to be more open, self-confident and relaxed in their dealings with the outside world. But the nationalistic, defensive attitudes of so many of their countrymen were a real and important factor which those responsible for conducting Norway's relations with the rest of the world had to take account of, and which created a permanent tension in the foreign policy of a country whose economy was so internationally orientated.

Insofar as Norwegians did look out beyond their own coastline, it had not traditionally been southwards towards continental Western Europe, despite the latter's commercial importance for them. It had been either towards the other Nordic countries, towards Britain, or overseas, and especially over the Atlantic towards America. The last was particularly important. Many Norwegians had close personal links with America, and since the second world war its Atlantic orientation had been the outstanding feature of Norway's foreign policy — one moreover which received genuine and widespread popular support.

Whatever the advocates of EEC membership argued to the contrary, it was not staying outside the EEC which struck many Norwegians as a break with their country's traditional foreign policy, but rather the prospect of becoming closely tied to continental Europe.

The country's economic and social development had produced deeply conservative groups who saw a threat to their cultural and moral values and traditional way of life in too close a contact with the urban, secular societies of industrial Western Europe. These were the fundamentalists, the *landsmål* speakers and the supporters of temperance, who were already having an uphill struggle at home as Norway was industrialised and modernised. The feeling that Western European society was in many ways alien from their own was however a much more widespread one. It was a diffuse, often unarticulated sense of possessing a different style of life and different values which could be lost unless they consciously tried to preserve them. When the anti-marketeers warned them about foreigners buying up their mountain huts and lakes and crowding out their empty countryside and national language, they touched on a sensitive nerve. They aroused defensive reactions in Norwegians living far away from the southwest bastions of cultural conservatism.

Then there was the dislike of remote government in a country of great distances, where almost a thousand miles of difficult terrain separated Norwegians in the north from the centre of government and political life in the south. This had long been a source of tension between capital and provinces. The provinces had put up a long struggle for more decentralisation of power and a greater share of the country's resources of capital and skilled manpower. For them EEC membership meant the prospect of even remoter government, even less influence over government policy, of losing even the gains they had made in recent years. It was understandable that they resisted it.

Foremost in doing so were the farmers and fishemen. Both saw, correctly, that their power to influence the conditions under which they worked would be curtailed when the key decisions were being taken in Brussels in inter-governmental package deals based on commission proposals. Both were convinced that the EEC's common policies would damage their interests as they conceived them and that the special arrangements negotiated were inadequate. Neither was ready to surrender what they had won at home in return for the less than precise assurances of foreign governments to safeguard their living standards. Their opposition to membership and the determination with which they pressed it were together one of the most important reasons why the referendum ended as it did — some would say the most important. Their powerful organisations formed the core of resistance around which other groups coalesced. Their opposition split the non-socialist coalition, and, in the case of the fishermen, the Labour party. Theirs was the hard core of economic self-interest behind the anti-market campaign. And their organisations' success in persuading their members, and many others, that membership would spell disaster for the primary sector was an important factor in producing the high turn-outs and high 'no' votes in the many small fishing villages and rural communities.

But the farmers and fishermen made up only a small percentage of the population. It seems unlikely that alone they could have prevented Norway joining the EEC. In some districts they were helped by the self-interest of other groups dependent on the primary sector. They were also helped by the solidarity (some would say the greater pressures to conform) of the small communities characteristic of much of Norway outside the few larger towns. They had allies in the conservative cultural groups of the southwest and the small extreme left-wing parties. But even this alliance of essentially rural economic and social forces, left-socialists and communists would have been hard pressed to win a referendum alone.

That was why the social and intellectual climate in which the third round of the EEC debate took place was so important for the outcome. When the campaign opened these groups were not alone. They had many and influential allies, in the heart of the 'centre' as well as elsewhere. It is a myth that the Norwegian establishment was overwhelmed by the 'periphery' in September 1972, if the establishment is understood as extending beyond the narrow bounds of parliament and the central administration. The referendum was won by an alliance of the economic and cultural 'periphery' — the primary sector and the rural conservatives — and important sections of the country's intellectual and political elite. During the period between the second French veto and the Hague summit conference a radicalisation of social and economic views had been taking place which particularly affected younger people, academics, and the Liberal, Labour and Centre parties. Before the EEC debate began, there was another debate underway about what kind of society the Norwegians had, and what kind they wanted, stimulated partly by similar developments elsewhere, partly by specific Norwegian problems like those of the north. This debate was accelerated and intensified by the question of whether or not to join the EEC because, believing as many did that membership would have profound consequences for their economy and society, it seemed to face them with a clear choice of social priorities. Thus the future of their farmers and fishermen came to be regarded very much as a test case of social values. That, in turn, profoundly influenced the EEC debate. The EEC came to symbolise all that many of those engaged in this debate rejected for Norway at home and abroad. Prominent academics provided the books and articles which argued their views. Young people took up the ideas with enthusiasm, and journalists popularised and spread them. All pressed them — and opposed EEC membership on the basis of them — with the fervour of social reformers, their combination of professional standing, zeal, determination and ability providing an essential ingredient in the anti-marketeers' ultimate success.

Other features of the context in which the campaign took place were important too. By 1970 British influence had declined both in political circles and in that wider network of organisations involved in Norwegian policy-making; among the young, British policy was largely irrelevant. Norwegians were prosperous in a booming world economy whose demand for their exports and shipping services seemed insatiable. Security hardly seemed a serious problem either in a Europe absorbed in discussions and negotiations about detente. So the decisive factor in pushing Norway towards Europe a decade earlier, Britain's decision to join, was no longer so potent, while the economic and political climate was hardly helpful to those trying to persuade Norwegians that the economic and political dangers of voting 'no' were so great as to overshadow all other considerations. Especially as one of these was the apparent prospect of a powerful, supra-national EEC within a relatively short time. The years of the referendum debate in Norway coincided with the years when the EEC was going through its most ambitious, dynamic phase since the late 1950s — a phase which culminated in the Paris summit conference in October 1972 and then ground to a halt eighteen months later in the face of political realities, British renegotiations, and international economic recession. Enlargement was to be accompanied by a 'deepening' of the EEC, and this produced the plans for economic and monetary union and political co-operation which figured so prominently in the referendum campaign. This was the background against which the Norwegians debated their relations with the EEC, and it probably had a considerable, if incalculable, impact on its outcome. Had the campaign taken place in 1967 or 1977 the result might have been the same. But the EEC they were talking about would have looked a rather different one.

There were thus a number of long and short term factors working for a 'no' to membership when the EEC opened up the way to it in December 1969: history, geography, primary sector interests, the international and economic situation, the prevailing social and intellectual climate. But that did not mean the referendum result was a foregone conclusion. The high percentage of 'don't know's' recorded in the polls pointed to many people, even if predisposed to vote 'no', being at least open to influence. It pointed to the campaign being a major factor in the result.

After September 1972 pro-marketeers tended to talk of the campaign having been 'dominated by huge *ad hoc* organisations of supporters and opponents'.[79] This is incorrect as a description of the pro-market side. The leaders of the Labour and Conservative parties did not lose control of their parties' campaigns in the way that the anti-market politicians lost control of the campaign on their side, where the People's Movement was led by men of sufficient political skill to become a major independent force. The pro-market equivalent, 'Yes to the EEC', organised too late and had people of insufficient political stature at its head to acquire such a position during the months it was active. The view that the established pro-market politicians lost their grip on developments had a certain truth in it, however, in that they appeared to be increasingly out of their depth in so abnormal a political situation. In the Labour and Liberal parties they lost control of important sections of their own members, with serious consequences for the outcome.

Over-confidence and a division of effort and objectives characterised and weakened the pro-market campaign from the beginning. It is understandable how this happened. Many of them did not recognise until late in the campaign how deeply split the Norwegian establishment was. Nor did they appreciate how well-organised, determined and skilled their opponents were. The idea that Labour's leaders and organisation would meet large scale organised resistance within their own party or be defeated by an *ad hoc* organisation run largely by amateurs was probably inconceivable to many, themselves included. Their arguments for membership seemed so irrefutable to themselves that they obviously found it difficult to imagine a majority of their countrymen refusing to heed them, especially the economic ones. Unlike their opponents, the men directing the pro-market campaign were mostly professional politicians. So they had party as well as national interests to take care of. Labour's leaders, in particular, had a party and electorate in which deep divisions had appeared over this question. They were naturally concerned to prevent this leading to organisational splits and lost votes. As professional politicians they also seemed to be inhibited from acting outside the usual norms of Norwegian politics, unlike many of their opponents. And most of them were politicians whose outlook had been formed two or three decades earlier. Probably many of them found it difficult to take seriously and therefore recognise the political force of the newer themes their opponents were campaigning on.

It was in the Labour party that the consequences of this combination of over-confidence and party interests were most serious because of the sheer size of the party's support in the country. In order to avoid a serious confrontation, the opposition was allowed a latitude which it proved almost impossible to restrict in the final stage of the campaign. The relative priority of EEC membership and party unity, and disagreements about how to handle the opposition, split the leadership and produced an impression of indecision and weakness. The prime minister's sudden display of firmness at the very end merely aroused the anti-marketeers to furious and self-righteous indignation. Party considerations largely determined the arguments used. For the first year or so the security aspects were played down in favour of social arguments which divided the pro-market side yet left Labour voters and anti-marketeers unconvinced. Party interests prevented formal co-operation with other pro-market groups, espesially the Conservatives, other than on an individual basis in 'Yes to the EEC' and, at the very end, the parliament's foreign relations committee. Confidence in the final result made tactical retreats seem relatively unimportant, and a late start to their campaign equally so. They seemed sure that once they did begin campaigning public opinion would swing their way and enable them to overtake their opponents in the eight months between signing the treaty of accession and referendum day. But it turned out that they had left it too late.

The anti-marketeers did not win merely as a result of their opponents' errors of judgement, divisions, and tactical mistakes, although these were a considerable help. They won also because of their better campaign strategy, their unity, and their success in attracting and mobilising people. They started campaigning early, much earlier than their opponents. They concentrated on the one issue which united them, ignoring or suppressing the many others which divided them or which the pro-marketeers could use to split them. They were much more successful in establishing a common organisation. Only Labour's anti-marketeers displayed the usual Labour reluctance to work outside their own party organisation, though even the Labour Information Committee collaborated with the People's Movement. The anti-marketeers succeeded in creating the impression that they were fighting for a positive, coherent set of social values. They managed to portray their campaign against the EEC as part of a longer-term one for a better Norway. They were able to put at rest many people's anxieties about the economic and political consequences of voting 'no'. Knowing their countrymen as they did, they put at the heart of their campaign the simple elemental appeal to national feeling and national independence. They campaigned vigorously and cleverly, exploiting all the means at their disposal to by-pass and neutralise the largely pro-market controlled media and reach the voters. They were not diverted from their objective by other considerations or conflicting objectives, especially the party objectives so important on the pro-market side. Some displayed a total lack of scruple about the methods or arguments they employed. Above all they had the active, enthusiastic support of many Norwegians who normally played little or no part in politics but threw themselves into the campaign against EEC membership. Some did so quietly but to considerable effect by influencing their own circles of acquaintances, colleagues and friends. Others staffed the campaign organisations, worked at the 'grass-roots' level on which the campaign leaders laid such stress, or provided the expertise, professional competence, and well-known names needed to counter the official arguments of government and administration.

Apart from their own campaign, the anti-marketeers were helped by a number of events at home and abroad. The EEC's decision on fisheries policy in June 1970 was one. Another was its choice of the word 'union' to describe the closer co-operation it was seeking to establish, a word conveying very different things to a Norwegian and, for example, a Frenchman. Sweden's decision not to seek EEC membership was hardly unexpected, but it added to the anti-marketeers' arguments against Norway doing so either, left closer Nordic co-operation as an alternative to a Western European orientation, and provided in Sweden's free trade agreement a model for a Norwegian alternative to membership. The Danish government's decision to hold its referendum after Norway deprived the pro-marketeers of what might have been decisive help, if the Danes had voted before Norway's polling day in the same way as they did after it. Commission statements on the sensitive subject of oil policy just a few days before 25 September provided additional aid and succour to the EEC's opponents. At home Knut Hoem's resignation was a major gain for the anti-marketeers. Some of them also believed that the fall of the coalition government had helped them, because it freed the middle-parties for opposition and created clear fronts on the EEC. If that was so, then Per Borten's indiscretion in February 1971 was one more of those fortuitous events which they skilfully turned to their advantage. As for the entry terms, they helped the anti-marketeers in two ways. The first was the EEC's refusal to give the government the revision clause in the fisheries agreement which it asked for. The other was the complicated, imprecise expressions used to clothe the delicate balance of compromises and concessions in the agricultural and fisheries sectors. The special protocols may indeed have given the Norwegians what the government claimed they did. But it was not immediately obvious to ordinary Norwegians from a simple reading of the texts.

However, having enumerated the reasons which probably contributed to the pro-marketeers' defeat in September 1972, it should be remembered how narrow that defeat was. In the period between the conclusion of the negotiations and polling day they caught up from 12 per cent in the polls to 46.6 per cent of those who voted. It is also worth recalling that membership was rejected by a minority of the electorate, only 79.2 per cent of those entitled to vote having done so. With hindsight some pro-marketeers say today that their basic mistake was not over-confidence or indecisive tacking between national and party interests, but the fact that they tried to take Norway into the EEC at all. From the narrow party point of view of the Labour and Liberal parties that might be so, as both emerged badly split, the latter irrevocably. But if by that they mean that the result was pre-determined in December 1969, then it is a very doubtful proposition indeed. Those trying to take Norway into the EEC certainly started with certain heavy disadvantages, and they added to them by their own mistakes and divisions. But what might the outcome have been if the Danes had voted first? Or if the coalition had carried on and remained responsible for the negotiations? Or if Hoem had not resigned ? Or if Einar Gerhardsen had given his successor as party chairman and prime minister the loyalty and support he himself had always required from his party? That a majority for membership was not an impossibility was demonstrated by the fact that the polls recorded one for several months after the referendum. So it is not inconceivable that if one or more of these events had gone the pro-marketeers' way instead of their opponents', they would have won on 25 September. Then, of course, hindsight would have looked differently on their campaign. 'Wait and see' would have appeared to have been the right strategy after all and their late campaign start not a display of complacency but of steady political nerves and professional timing. There are many 'if's' which it will never be possible to answer. But when the story of the events leading up to the referendum is put together one thing at least is clear. The result was too close to have anything inevitable about it. History, geography, the prevailing economic and political climate set the context in which the decision was reached. But the decision itself was very much the outcome of a long, hard political struggle which the supporters of membership only just lost.

PART TWO

7. The free trade agreement

The Korvald government

With the referendum over the Norwegians had to negotiate a free
trade agreement to replace the treaty of accession which had been
rejected. It was the situation about which so many conflicting predictions had been made during the campaign. Supporters of membership
had described such an agreement as likely to be disadvantageous
economically and an insidious threat to that control over their own
affairs which the anti-marketeers had emphasised so strongly during
the campaign. The opponents of membership had held it out as an alternative which would safeguard both their trading interests and their
national sovereignty. Now it was to be seen who would be proved
right by events.

Uncertainty was the main feature of the weeks immediately following the referendum. The Norwegians could not be certain what
the EEC's attitude would be to re-opening negotiations, even if
private contacts and statements by EEC representatives were encouraging.[1] The political situation was even more uncertain. The prime
minister, Trygve Bratteli, maintained his threat to resign if the government's European policy was rejected, and it was unclear which party
or parties would or could form a new government. On the economic
front the Norwegian kroner weakened temporarily[2] and there were
rumours of firms planning to leave the country and establish themselves inside the EEC.[3] The electorate too seemed uncertain about the
wisdom of its choice on 25 September. Very soon afterwards public
opinion polls started recording a slight majority in favour of membership, influenced perhaps by the Danish vote for membership one
week after Norway's 'no'.[4] This left Norway the only Western European member of the Atlantic alliance, apart from Iceland and Portugal, outside the EEC.

Norway was also the only EFTA country without a treaty regulating
its trade with the EEC after 1 January 1973. The others had all

negotiated free trade agreements which would come into force on that date.[5] These provided for a first round of tariff reductions on 1 April 1973. Also in April, new uniform rules of origin would come into effect in EFTA countries' trade with the EEC and with each other.[6] So unless Norway had an agreement by then it risked complications in the Swedish market, as well as losing its duty-free access to the British and Danish markets and endangering its competitive position in those of the original Six. Obtaining a free trade agreement had become an urgent matter.

But it was a task which none of the parties that had supported membership would undertake. They argued that as their opponents had worked for this situation they must now deal with the problems created by it. This did not go unopposed inside the Labour party, where the anti-marketeers urged that the party should stay in office, identify itself with the negotiations for Norway's new relationship with the EEC, and thereby take an important step towards healing the party's divisions and winning back its lost voters.[7] However Bratteli and the other leaders stood firm. They would not be responsible for negotiating the type of agreement they had campaigned against, and they would remain in office only as long as it took to find a new government. The Conservatives also refused to join the government which was to negotiate a trade agreement. So did the Liberal party's chairman, Helge Seip.

Of the parties which had opposed membership, the Centre party was unwilling to govern alone but ready to join a coalition.[8] The position of the Christian People's party was complicated by its divisions during the campaign, in which a minority of its leading politicians had continued to work for membership even after the national congress had rejected it in the spring. Once the referendum was over the Christian pro-marketeers agreed to join the others in forming a government to obtain a trade agreement. But their position would be difficult unless it also included other politicians who had supported membership: that is, the pro-market majority in the Liberals' parliamentary group. Initially therefore the CPP made its participation in a middle-party coalition conditional on it including all thirteen Liberal members, not just the five anti-marketeers.

The Liberals were split over whether to enter the coalition. Helge Seip rejected the idea and was supported by the other seven who had campaigned for membership. The anti-market minority in the group argued that, as the party's national congress had voted against membership before the referendum, the pro-marketeers should now be ready to join the other two middle-parties which had also opposed it. The Liberals' national executive backed the minority and gave it a mandate to enter into coalition negotiations with the Christians and the Centre party. After that the divisions opened up by the referendum were unbridgeable. Two months later the pro-market members broke away and formed a new party, eventually called the New People's party.[9]

Faced by this split in the Liberal party, the Christians dropped their condition of pro-market Liberal participation and joined the anti-market Liberals and Centre party in forming a government which took office on 12 October. Apart from the Christians' chairman, Lars Korvald, who became prime minister, it consisted of six ministers from the Centre party, four Liberal ministers and three Christians. In parliament it had only thirty-eight of the 150 members (twenty Centrists, fourteen Christians and four Liberals), a base so narrow as to rule out such a middle-party government in normal political circumstances. But the Korvald government resembled its Labour predecessor in being invulnerable until it had completed the main task for which it was in office. In the latter's case it had been to carry out parliament's mandate to negotiate EEC membership. The Korvald government's task was to negotiate a free trade agreement, the mandate for which came from outside parliament, from the referendum majority of 25 September. That extra-parliamentary mandate was its strength. All the pro-marketeers had promised to respect the referendum result and support the trade negotiations even though they themselves would not undertake them. On this question the Korvald government knew it could rely on the votes of all the parties represented in parliament. Its other source of strength was the lack of an alternative. The opposition parties could not offer one as long as the treaty was being negotiated because none of them were willing to take office until it was signed and ratified. Only after that would the government be in danger. It was generally thought likely to fall if at any time during the five or six months between ratification and the election in September 1973 a majority in the opposition parties decided it was in their interest to bring it down. In the event, despite a major crisis in the spring, they decided it was not, and the Korvald government stayed in office until the election.

Another guarantee of the government's position as long as the negotiations continued was the change in Labour's policy towards Europe once the referendum was lost. Labour's leaders now gave top priority to restoring the party's unity and strength in the country, which their attempt to take Norway into the EEC had so badly shaken. To this end they not only accepted the referendum result, as they had promised to do. They abandoned the aim of EEC membership for the foreseeable future. They declared the question settled and removed from the realm of practical politics. Norway's relations with the EEC had now to be based on the free trade agreement, and Labour promised to support the government in its efforts to obtain as good a treaty as possible.[10]

Party interest was not the only reason for this change of policy. Many prominent Labour pro-marketeers still believed membership would have been the best course for Norway and made no attempt to conceal it.[11] But nearly all had been deeply shaken by the bitterness and deep divisions of the campaign and saw the overriding national priority as being to re-unite the country. That this priority coincided with Labour's own party interest was considered entirely natural because of the way in which Labour contained within itself many of those economic, social and regional divisions which had come into conflict over the EEC.[12] The new policy did not stop the party's leaders from pointing out the disadvantages of a free trade agreement.[13] Indeed they were almost bound to do so in order to justify their previous opposition to one. But they knew that such criticism could boomerang and be more damaging to themselves than the government if it further alienated those Labour anti-marketeers who were still sceptical about the party's commitment to living with a trade agreement. Thus the leadership was intent on defusing the EEC issue and removing it from the forefront of domestic politics, rather than keeping the subject alive by a stream of criticism. What criticism the Korvald government had to face from Labour was moderate, both in tone and substance. As the government was well aware, Labour had more to gain from demonstrating its commitment to the free trade alternative to its own supporters, than it had from scoring party points in parliament by attacking the terms brought back from Brussels.

The negotiations

The government's aim was to have a free trade agreement ratified in time to join the other EFTA countries in the first tariff cuts on 1 April 1973.[14] Its application for negotiations was sent to the EEC immediately on taking office. The EEC on its side agreed to negotiations in principle at the Hague summit conference on 20 October, and then formally when the council of ministers met on 7 November. Preparatory discussions began soon afterwards, and by early February the council of ministers was able to approve the commission's mandate for the negotiations, which began on 16 February and continued until the agreement was initialled on 16 April.[15] Although the original target date was missed, interim agreements with Britain and Denmark ensured the continuation of Norway's free trade with them until a treaty came into force. In March the EEC also decided to give

Norwegian industrial products 'area status' under the new rules of origin when they came into force after 1 April.[16] The agreement, approved unanimously by parliament on 24 May 1973, came into effect on 1 July, and on the same date the first tariff cuts took place between Norway and the original EEC members. Apart from the three months delay in making the cuts — an insignificant factor in the boom conditions for Norwegian exports in 1973 — the period between the referendum and the entry into force of Norway's free trade agreement had thus been managed without any of the disadvantages, except perhaps uncertainty, predicted by some pro-marketeers.

The basic framework and terms of the treaty were already fixed before negotiations began by the EEC's agreements with the other EFTA countries.[17] These provided for free trade in industrial products and certain processed agricultural ones after a transitional period, which was four and a half years in most cases and eleven or seven years for those categorised as 'sensitive'. The latter were imports against which the EEC wished to give its own producers a longer period of protection, and included such important Norwegian exports as paper products (eleven years), primary aluminium, ferro-alloys and zinc (seven years). The sensitive products were subject moreover to a system of so-called indicative ceilings: import quotas above which, during their transitional periods, they could be subjected to the full instead of reduced tariffs. In the British and Danish markets, however, only paper would meet a re-introduction of duty on imports below the ceilings; and even in this case Britain and Denmark were allowed to make available to Norway duty-free quotas which at their maximum were expected to cover most imports. The free industrial trade provided for by these treaties was conditional on applying the EEC's rules of competition as well as its rules of origin. Separate treaties with the European Coal and Steel Community (ECSC) provided for free trade in these products too after the normal four and a half years. The parties could re-introduce protective measures in certain defined circumstances, such as balance of payments difficulties or a breach of the rules of competition; if necessary this could be done unilaterally.

In principle agricultural products, including fish, were excluded from the free trade introduced by these treaties. However, the EEC had required certain unilateral concessions from Sweden, Switzerland and Austria for its agricultural exports, while (of particular interest to Norway) Iceland's agreement included fish because of this commodity's predominance in its exports to the EEC. The Icelandic agreement gave its processed fish duty-free access to the original Six and provided for tariff reductions for its fresh fish. In Norway it was noted, however, that the EEC had made the implementation of these concessions conditional on a satisfactory resolution of Iceland's dispute with some EEC members following the unilateral extension of its fishing limit to fifty miles in September 1972.

The only institutional link which these treaties established between the EEC and each EFTA state was a so-called joint committee. The function of this committee was limited however to observing the treaties' implementation, and its importance as a forum for more general contacts was illustrated by the fact that it was not required to meet more than once a year. Potentially more significant were the evolution clauses included in all but the treaty with Finland. In these the parties declared their willingness to examine ways of extending their co-ooperation to fields not covered by the trade agreement, if both sides considered it in their interest to do so. The Swiss, Austrian and Icelandic evolution clauses specifically restricted such a possible extension to economic matters. Sweden's by contrast left the range of possibilities open, only setting as a condition that each side's freedom to determine its policy in the areas concerned was not undermined.

Although the agreements were basically similar, each had been tailored in some respects to the special economic and trade structure of the EFTA country in question. Iceland's agreement on fish was one example, Sweden's evolution clause another, while Switzerland had not adopted the ECSC's pricing system for steel. The Korvald government's aim in the negotiations was therefore to secure similar adaptations in areas of special importance to Norway. The EFTA free trade agreement model as such it accepted from the outset.[18]

Politically the government's objective had to be to secure terms which vindicated the anti-marketeers' claim that a free trade agreement would protect Norwegian economic interests as effectively as membership. Those who were still advocating membership would ensure that this particular claim was not forgotten when the agreement was brought home.[19] If possible the terms also had to be as good as those Sweden had obtained, because it was the Swedish agreement which had served as the anti-marketeers' model during the campaign. Fish had to be included too. These, after all, were the political parties which had laid such emphasis on providing a secure future for the fishing industry. And they had to vindicate their campaign claim that Iceland's agreement showed how the EEC would in practice be willing to negotiate substantial reductions for Norway in this sector.

Yet at the same time the negotiations presented the coalition with the delicate task of balancing the sometimes conflicting interests of industry, fisheries and agriculture. The major economic interests at stake in these negotiations were those of the traditional exporting industries against whose products the EEC was requiring extra protection. Yet Norway would also be seeking concessions for its fish, and this, by adding to its list of requests, might make the EEC less willing to accommodate it in the industrial sector. EEC concessions on fish were also likely to be conditional on Norway making unilateral concessions on agricultural imports, as other EFTA countries had done. This could bring the interests of the two primary industries which had fought side by side against membership into direct conflict in the subsequent trade negotiations. The negotiations seemed fraught with potential embarrassments for political parties which had presented themselves as the special protectors of agriculture and fisheries, and now found themselves responsible for defending and balancing all the country's different economic interests.

In the event the problem proved less difficult for the government than it might have feared. The EEC modified the original list of concessions it wanted for its agricultural exports to Norway.[20] The Norwegian agricultural organisations, while doing their best to limit the concessions, knew that they had fended off the much greater evil of the common agricultural policy and could rely on the Centre party to bring back the best terms that could possibly be got. Industry recognised from the outset that the fishermen's interests would have to be a high political priority for parties which had fought so strongly for the primary sector during the referendum. The government was also helped by being largely spared the attacks which might otherwise have come from the Labour party. What helped it most, however, was that all involved — industry, agriculture, fisheries, the opposition parties and its own — knew that the negotiations had to succeed. Norway would have to pay the EEC's price for a treaty which it needed far more than the EEC did. This time the Norwegians would be in no position to reject the EEC's final offer.

They all recognised the weakness of their country's bargaining position. Norway was the *demandeur,* needing a treaty as soon as possible in order to maintain its competitive position in its major export market. For the EEC the Norwegian market of four million was of only small importance. The scope for EEC concessions was anyway strictly limited by its agreements with the other EFTA countries. The Nine appear to have displayed no noticeable ill-will towards a country which had just chosen not to join it after a campaign in which its institutions, treaties, objectives and practical working had been repeatedly criticised. Germany was well disposed at the highest level, and the new Nordic member, Denmark, was active on Norway's behalf.[21] But as these were not membership negotiations, individual members could more easily take a hard line in defending their particular interests, as did France over aluminium for example. They were under no pressure to make special exceptions or stretch EEC principles in order to accommodate the vital interests of a prospective member.

During the referendum campaign oil had been mentioned by some anti-marketeers as a trump card which could overcome this weak negotiating position.[22] But the politicians responsible for the negotiations ruled out seeking trade concessions by means of bargains that might weaken national control over this new resource. Indeed any other line would scarcely have been compatible with their campaign theme of national sovereignty.[23] Norwegian oil policy was still under review and any deals now would foreclose parliament's options when it came to decisions about such basic questions as where to land the oil and whom to sell it to. On the EEC's side, some at least had the impression that the Norwegians were still unaware of the bargaining potential of their oil.[24] Whether oil played any part in the EEC's own attitude towards these commercial negotiations a year before the Arab oil embargo and oil price rise in the winter of 1973-74 is uncertain. If it did, then the effect in terms of trade concessions seems to have been minimal.

There was one means of strengthening its hand which the Korvald government did attempt to use. In secret bilateral contacts with the French during March 1973 it reminded them in general terms of the link which it regarded as existing between France's position in these trade negotiations, particularly on aluminium, and the quite separate negotiations then taking place about a possible Norwegian purchase of the French rocket system Crotale.[25] The *demarche* may perhaps have contributed to the slight softening in the EEC's position on primary aluminium early in April, when an extra duty-free 're-export quota' was linked to the annual quantity of EEC aluminium imports from Norway which was guaranteed access at reduced duty.[26] But even if there was such a link, the benefit in terms of concessions was small. The main effect of bringing Crotale into the negotiations was seen at home. It was the government's handling of this question which proved to be the trigger for the political crisis anticipated for the spring when the free trade agreement negotiations were out of the way.

The negotiations themselves largely revolved around the three areas in which the Norwegians set out to obtain modifications to the standard EEC agreement with the other EFTA states: the terms for sensitive products, fish exports, and shipping. As a matter of principle the Norwegians opposed the system of sensitive products.[27] This was hardly surprising as it would hit them harder than either their EFTA competitiors or the EEC if the Norwegians were to apply it

176

to their imports from the EEC. But the precedent set in the other treaties ruled out the Nine giving Norway duty-free access for all its exports after the normal four and a half years. So the Norwegians concentrated on reducing the length of the transitional periods and obtaining the highest possible indicative ceilings. What they wanted was better terms than those given to the other EFTA states. Their main argument to support this claim was that because products like paper, aluminium and ferro-alloys made up such a large share of Norwegian exports to the EEC — 34 per cent as compared, for example, with 24 per cent in Sweden's case — the same terms would in practice place Norway at a competitive disadvantage. They also argued that duty-free Norwegian exports would present little threat to EEC producers because of steadily rising EEC demand for these products, approaching limits on hydro-electricity development in Norway, and Norway's inadequate raw material base for paper production. For their fish exports the Norwegians requested the same treatment as Iceland, arguing that fishing was just as important for settlement and employment in large areas of Norway as it was in Iceland. They also argued that fish occupied a large enough place in Norwegian-EEC trade to justify its inclusion in the treaty: 41 per cent of Norway's exports of fish and fish products would be going to the Nine, representing some 10 per cent of Norway's total exports to the enlarged EEC. The same applied to shipping. Over half Norway's tonnage was usually occupied within the enlarged EEC area at any one time, and some 40 per cent of Norway's income from the Nine came in the form of shipping earnings. So although these were strictly commercial negotiations, the Norwegians argued that the EEC's importance for their economy in the shipping sector justified its inclusion in some form or other. The form they proposed was the establishment of a formal consultation procedure for shipping questions, either within the framework of the treaty itself or by an exchange of notes. The main point was that Norway wanted a guarantee that the EEC would consult it on questions concerning international and EEC shipping policy.

Shipping was only one of the subjects which were not included in the EEC-EFTA trade agreements, but on which the Korvald government said Norway would be interested in establishing formal co-operation with the EEC. Others were international financial questions, environmental matters, research, technology and industrial policy; Norway would take these up later on the basis of the evolution clause in its agreement, which the government wanted modelled on Sweden's. On the need for such an open-ended clause the government agreed with the opposition Labour, Conservative and New People's parties, arguing that the greater economic integration and dependence which would follow the freeing of industrial trade made close co-operation in other related areas necessary too.[28] It was an argument which contrasted oddly with some of the anti-market statements made during the campaign. There were other anti-marketeers — Per Borten, for example, and the left socialists — who parted company with the government on this point. They did not want an evolution clause at all. In terms reminiscent of the campaign which had just ended, they warned that it could be a means of 'tricking' Norway into the EEC 'through the back door'.[29]

With the referendum won, however, most of those who had opposed membership showed no reluctance about co-operating with the EEC along traditional lines in any areas where it seemed in Norway's interest to do so. Indeed both in Brussels and at home they stressed how such co-operation had been and remained a 'cornerstone' of Norwegian foreign policy, and one which the referendum result had in no sense weakened.[30] Some former pro-marketeers claimed to see in such declarations a 'normalisation' of their opponents' attitude to the EEC: the responsibilities of office, they suggested, had made them wiser.[31] In fact there was no contradiction between what most responsible middle-party politicians had said during the campaign and what they were saying now. They had never said they wanted to isolate Norway from the EEC. What they had insisted upon, was that any co-operation be confined to specific, limited areas without the commitments of membership. And it was only limited functional co-operation for which they were asking now.

The final terms of Norway's trade agreement[32] represented less than the government had asked for. Some 34 per cent of Norway's exports to the Nine were given sensitive status. Indeed, far from treating the Norwegians more favourably, the EEC had added to the list some major exports enjoying normal transitional periods in the other EFTA agreements, notably wrought aluminium, magnesium and silisium carbide. Its primary aluminium exports were given a low ceiling of 190 000 tons for 1973 compared with the 372 000 tons exported to the nine countries of the EEC in 1972. The EEC justified this by reference to the Norwegian aluminium industry's low energy costs and close links with powerful North American multinational concerns. On the other hand, as the government pointed out when defending the agreement at home, the ceilings would not come into force automatically and would normally rise by 5 per cent a year. By the middle of 1977 only 15 to 20 per cent of Norway's exports to the Nine would in fact be subject to duty because of Britain's and Denmark's optional duty-free quota system for paper products, and because beneath the ceilings Norwegian sensitive products would still enter these two former EFTA markets duty-free. The inclusion of petrochemicals with a normal transitional period seemed to disprove pro-market-eers' warnings that Norway would eventually find this major poten-tial market prohibitively protected. To demonstrate that not only Norwegian exports would suffer from longer transitional periods, the government had drawn up a similar list of sensitive products from the EEC which subjected some 12 per cent of the original Six's exports to Norway to the same disadvantage. The Norwegians had succeeded in getting fish products included in the tariff reductions, even if their opening request for terms comparable with Iceland's had had to be modified by the exclusion of fresh fish and some important fish products. When the negotiators came home it was with an agree-ment which gave very low tariffs to some 80 per cent of Norwegian exports of fish products to the EEC and enabled the government to claim that, as in the case of petrochemicals, the pro-marketeers' gloomy predictions had been proved wrong.

As those who had campaigned for membership pointed out, how-ever, Norway had to pay a price for these concessions.[33] The tariff cuts for fish were conditional on there being no major changes in the general terms of competition prevailing at the time the treaty was entered into. By this the EEC meant the maintenance of Norway's twelve-mile fishing limit, for whose extension pressures were building up following Iceland's unilateral extension to fifty miles and with the United Nations Conference on the Law of the Sea due to hold its first negotiating session in 1974. In the agricultural sector Norway had to give tariff reductions and extensions of its unrestricted import periods to a range of EEC market garden products. It also had to give a general commitment to facilitate the import of EEC wines and spirits. Even if the last concession was considerably less onerous than the doubling of Norwegian wine imports originally demanded by the EEC, it was still an embarrassment for a government with a CPP prime minister.

Shipping was the one sector in which the Norwegian negotiators had made no headway at all, and where the government's critics claimed to see their predictions beginning to be fulfilled.[34] Much time and effort had been expended without success in Brussels and the other EEC capitals in trying to get the Nine to agree to a formal consultation procedure for shipping questions. The EEC rejected the idea from the start, giving two reasons for doing so. As yet it had no common shipping policy. Even if it had one it could not assume obligations towards a non-member state which would have the ef-fect of curtailing its freedom when drawing up EEC policies. Countries outside the EEC could not be guaranteed the right to be consulted before decisions were taken. In the end the Norwegians had to be content with making a formal unilateral declaration re-iterating their desire to strengthen co-operation on shipping matters.[35] The Nine's position was a disappointment to those who were hoping that the evolution clause could be used to open up areas not covered by this trade agreement. It indicated the limits of what might be achieved by means of that clause. It also checked any unrealistic expectations of the joint committee developing into an important forum for questions outside the commercial sphere.

Despite this, Norway's need to extend its relations with the EEC beyond mere trade matters was a prominent theme in the parliamentary debate about the agreement after the conclusion of the negotiations. Not only those who had campaigned for membership emphasised this point. Coalition spokesmen too now described it as one of the main ways of overcoming what — with the referendum won — they were ready to concede was the main disadvantage of the free trade alternative. This was Norway's lack of representation in the EEC's institutions at a time when free trade would be increasing its dependence on the EEC and the Nine were expected to be developing common policies for ever more areas of their economic, social and political affairs.[36] The old referendum arguments still had some life in them however, and resurfaced on both sides. Thus while acknowledging this disadvantage, coalition spokesmen claimed that it would be outweighed by the advantage of retaining national control over areas where membership would have meant surrendering it: over agriculture and fisheries, social, regional and energy policies, trade relations with third countries, even foreign policy in view of the EEC's plans to coordinate that too.[37] The opposition parties replied by pointing to Norway's adoption of EEC rules of competition and the constraint on extending its fishing limit, describing them as only two outstanding examples of how in reality national control would become an illusion as the necessity of adapting to EEC policies increased in pace with economic dependence.[38]

Yet despite this rehearsal of well-known arguments there had been a noticeable narrowing of the distance between many on each side during the six or seven months since the referendum. All except the left socialists were now more or less agreed about the basic problem facing a small country whose relations with the Nine were based on a free trade agreement. This large majority was also able to agree on at least the general lines of how to meet the problem. Expanding Norway's co-operation with the Nine in sectors beyond the ones regulated by the present agreement was one. Extending their channels of communication and information in Brussels and the other EEC capitals was another. Both were part of that 'active' European policy which all agreed Norway would now have to pursue towards the Nine.[39] 'Active' however only described the manner in which they intended to defend Norway's interests. It left vague the content of the policies they would so actively pursue. That would depend on developments in the EEC and in Norway itself.

There were still deep disagreements over policy towards the EEC, but their lines had shifted since September 1972. The differences which had always existed within the anti-market coalition had become visible, with the non-socialist parties on the whole ready to go further and faster in developing Norway's relations with the Nine than were their neutralist, socialist allies. More important was the split which had opened up on the pro-market side. Here the ten-year-old alliance between Labour and the Conservatives on Europe had ended immediately after the referendum. On the key issue of whether membership was still a realistic option which pro-marketeers could continue to work for, Labour now stood with the coalition parties against the Conservatives and the New People's party. Labour's new position had brought about a fundamental change in the political landscape by depriving the supporters of membership of the majority they had commanded at the political level since 1962.

Labour's post-referendum line, that the issue was decided and debate should cease, had been hardened by subsequent events. The leadership was still having difficulties with the party's anti-marketeers. To the left of Labour, a Socialist Electoral Alliance had been formed between the Socialist People's party, the Communist party, and a group of anti-marketeers who had broken away from the Labour party.[40] The general election was only a few months away, so Labour's criticism of the trade agreement was confined to practical problems it could create for Norway. Its spokesmen avoided comparisons with membership, arguing that such comparisons were irrelevant because membership was no longer a realistic alternative.[41] As soon as the trade agreement was ratified, Labour committed itself not to re-open the question of membership during the next four-year legislative period, and with that the party had officially buried the issue until 1978 at the earliest.[42]

The Conservatives and New People's party kept their campaign promise to respect the referendum result and voted for the trade agreement as both a logical consequence of that promise and an economic necessity. But in their programmes for the 1973-77 parliament they said that they would continue to work for EEC membership and would call for a new referendum if there was clear evidence of a change in public opinion on the subject.[43] They too promised to cooperate in solving the problems raised by a trade agreement. But unlike Labour they said they would not stop publicly arguing that the best long-term solution to these problems would be to replace it by membership.[44] The explanation for the difference between their positions and Labour's at this time was not to be found in the genuine-ness or otherwise of their previous support for membership. Rather it lay in domestic politics. In 1973 neither the Conservatives nor the New People's party judged that maintaining their support for EEC membership would threaten vital party interests. Labour did. When quite soon afterwards the Conservatives came to see their commit-ment to membership as a serious liability, they modified their posi-tion accordingly.[45]

Although Labour and the coalition parties were now describing comparisons with membership as irrelevant, that was the standard which spokesmen for industry, business and shipping used when judging the free trade agreement. Inevitably their arguments were still heavily influenced by their positions in the recent referendum campaign. They pointed to all the disadvantages and costs of the trade agreement which could have been avoided by entering the EEC. There was the additional tariff burden for the traditional export industries, which they put at some one billion kroner for aluminium and paper products alone. There was the uncertainty built into the agreement in the protection clause, the indicative ceilings which the EEC might or might nor enforce, the EEC's right to interpret the rules of competition, and the way the EEC had reserved the right to change the terms for petrochemical imports when a common energy policy was drawn up. Uncertainty about future markets, they war-ned, could hold up investment decisions and necessary rationalisa-tion measures in Norwegian industry. Most serious of all however was Norway's exclusion from the multitude of decisions which the EEC would be taking about economic questions in the years to come, decisions which would have a steadily greater impact on economic activity in Norway itself. As the sphere of EEC common policies widened, industry and business in Norway would be forced to adapt to these policies in order to avoid being placed at a competitive disadvantage in EEC markets. Yet they would have no voice in their shaping. They would be excluded too from the network of EEC-based contacts between private economic organisations. Increasing-ly isolated, subject to a permanent process of adjustment, they would find control over their own affairs slipping out of their hands. Shipping was described as only the most outstanding example of how limited would be the Norwegians' possibilities to protect their interests when the EEC came to draw up common policies in areas of importance for the country.[46]

In May 1973 it seemed that the comparisons and arguments could continue for years to come, but the opposite happened. Within a year the debate had almost ceased, in public at least. By the time most industrial trade had been freed in July 1977 the debate belonged

182

to history for most people. The reason for this was partly political. By 1974 not even the Conservatives wanted to keep the question of membership alive. It was also economic however. Economic events had forced even those former pro-marketeers who still regretted the referendum's outcome on political grounds to acknowledge that, in the short term at least, its economic consequences had not confirmed their campaign predictions.

Living with the free trade agreement

In the three or four years after the referendum a combination of skilful management, oil, luck and external events beyond their control produced an economic performance which seemed to prove that the anti-marketeers had been right when they argued that Norway could manage perfectly well with a free trade agreement. Even the problems which became increasingly worrying after 1976 — a worsening balance of payments deficit and low international demand for Norway's traditional exports — were recognised to be a consequence of the general international economic situation, not Norway's position outside the EEC.[47]

From an economic point of view the Norwegians could not have chosen a better time to reject EEC membership. After the short international recession of 1971 the Western industrial economies were all simultaneously enjoying the boom which was to peak in 1973 and then be brought to an end in 1974 by domestic anti-inflation measures and the consequences of the oil price rise. With demand strong in their European markets, Norwegian exports had grown faster than the OECD average in 1972 and they continued to expand in 1973. Not tariffs but insufficient capacity to meet demand became the problem facing many export industries in the year after the referendum.[48] The sensitive products about which so many fears had been expressed did well too, their exports growing rapidly well into 1974.[49] So during the eighteen months or more after the referendum Norway's economy and electorate benefited from the stimulus and optimism generated by an unprecedented level of international activity. Growth and success provided an ideal atmosphere for healing the country's divisions. They proved as effective in silencing the complaints of industry and business as party interest had become in silencing the politicians.

But the international recession which followed was perhaps even more important for confirming the 'no' of 1972. For while in the EEC growth levels dropped and unemployment rose, Norwegians continued for two or three years to enjoy steady growth, low unemployment and rising real living standards. Even in the trough of the international recession in 1975, with their export industries and shipping hard hit, gross national product rose by some 3 per cent and private consumption by 4 per cent.[50] The comparisons strengthened the optimism and self-confidence fed by the preceding boom and were widely regarded as providing yet additional vindication of the anti-marketeers' arguments. The EEC's poor performance lessened its attraction even for former pro-marketeers. It was during 1974 that many began saying that perhaps, after all, it was 'for the best that it all turned out the way it did' ('. . . best at det gikk som det gikk').[51]

Their growing disenchantment with the EEC was reinforced by the different economic priorities revealed by the recession. While the EEC countries put cutting inflation and balance of payments deficits before full employment, in Norway full employment and steady growth remained the first priorities. While governments in the EEC were resorting to deflationary policies, Norway's Labour government was introducing measures to maintain a high level of domestic demand and imports, subsidising production for stocks by the export industries, and financing the resulting balance of payments deficit by borrowing abroad itself and assisting the private sector to do likewise. As in the 1971 recession, large reserves were one factor enabling it to do so.[52] A more important one though in this much deeper and longer recession were the off-shore oil reserves, which now became for the first time a major factor in the country's general economic performance.

Both the proven size and the value of these reserves had increased considerably in the two years since the referendum. Early in 1974 the Norwegian North Sea sector's estimated reserves were one to two billion tons, with an annual production rate of fifty million tons of oil and forty million tons of oil-equivalent of gas possible by 1981-82.[53] As domestic oil consumption was only nine million tons, most of Norwegian production would be available for export in some form or other. After the giant Statfjord field had been declared commercial in August 1974, the estimates of reserves nearly doubled.[54] At the same time the quadrupling of oil prices by OPEC increased their value to Western Europe as a close and secure non-OPEC source. Actual production from the Norwegian sector in 1973 was only one and a half million tons[55] and three years later it was still no more than thirteen and a half million,[56] but the indirect economic and political impact of the reserves was already out of all proportion to these production figures.

They were the security which made it easy for the government to raise medium-term international loans on advantageous terms at a time when nearly half the country's tanker fleet was laid up and its traditional export industries' products piled up waiting for an improvement in their international markets.[57] Oil kept foreign capital flowing in and investment levels above international standards.[58] Actual off-shore activity and the psychological boost from oil, combined with the expectation of an imminent up-turn in the international economy, helped to keep general business confidence relatively buoyant until well into 1976, long after it had sunk to depression levels in other countries.

The radical change which oil produced in the Norwegians' view of their country's future was just as significant for their attitude to the EEC as were the unfavourable comparisons with their own success. The oil embargo and price rise at last focused public and political attention on the implications of their new resource, and this awareness was further heightened by the Statfjord announcement and oil policy debates in 1974.[59]   Oil moved into the centre of the stage, firing imaginations, capturing the headlines, and opening up prospects whose dimensions could hardly have been foreseen in 1972. For years the Norwegians had argued among themselves about whether their small country on the north-west periphery of Europe could afford to stay outside the EEC. Now they found that they would soon be enjoying the highest per capita income in Europe, and that the revenues from oil would be so large that their main problem would not be whether they were inside or outside the EEC but how to manage this new resource in a way that would avoid drastically altering their economic and social structure. Compared with such a perspective and such a problem the tariff levels and transitional periods for their traditional export industries paled into insignificance.

Oil also diminished the importance which these industries would have for Norway's economy in the future. They would remain major items in foreign trade for years to come, and would be important for regional settlement and employment, but by the mid-1980s oil and gas were expected to be providing a quarter of total export earnings.[60] Other factors would be limiting the role of the traditional export industries by then as well, like environmental limitations on hydro-electricity development and steeply rising production costs as the abundant supplies of cheap energy dwindled. Spreading protectionism in international shipping was also putting the future of this revenue earner in doubt, even before the crisis brought on by the depression and international over-capacity hit it. So in the long run these two sectors, whose interests had played such a prominent role in the free trade agreement negotiations, would be less important to Norway, whatever their importance in the medium term. This may have been another reason why in general so little public or political attention was paid to the way the trade agreement was working.

The main economic reason though — as distinct from the political one of ending the debate about Norway's relations with the EEC — was that on the whole the agreement had been put into effect so smoothly. With only a few exceptions, the anxieties expressed about its economic consequences had proved exaggerated. Much of the negotiations in 1973 had centred on the ceilings for sensitive products: the quantities of Norwegian exports for which the EEC guaranteed entry at the reduced duty and above which it could introduce the full external tariff if it wished. In practice the commission made no use of this possibility for discriminating against imports from Norway during either 1973 or 1974; with demand so strong the EEC's own producers were hardly threatened by foreign competition. Even during the subsequent depression the commission had, by the end of 1976, imposed the ceiling on only one occasion. This was in 1975 when under heavy pressure from the EEC's paper producers, it decided to introduce them on a range of paper imports if these exceeded the ceilings fixed for that year. At the time this was worrying for the Norwegians, not only because three Norwegian products were affected by it, but as a possible precedent for other protective measures. However the commission's harder line was in fact directed mainly against Sweden, which had imposed import restrictions on shoes, and in practice it had little effect on Norwegian exports. More anxiety was caused by Norway's failure to obtain the maximum duty-free quota for its paper exports to the important British market, the British government also having come under pressure for protection from its producers as the depression deepened. Once again, however, the real effect of this on Norwegian exports proved to be slight.[61] The aluminium industry's fears also proved to have been exaggerated. The EEC did not impose the ceiling. And the primary aluminium producers were able to utilise the additional duty-free 're-export quota' by establishing a processing plant inside the EEC which, under this scheme, was able to import its raw material from Norway duty-free.[62]

The exception to this predominantly problem-free picture was one of the fish products, hardened fats used for margarine production, which the EEC had refused to include among those benefiting from tariff reductions. Its exclusion meant the re-introduction of duty in the British and Danish markets. Here the Norwegian exporters found themselves gradually forced out as the tariff was progressively raised to the EEC's level of 17 per cent. The Norwegians kept up the argument about hardened fats in the joint committee until 1975. Then they gave it up, perhaps judging that the commission's liberal position on more important exports should not be put at risk.[63]

Calculations about the extra tariff burden involved in the free trade alternative had been much used by pro-marketeers and industry during the referendum campaign and when criticising the trade agreement afterwards. In the event neither the effect of the longer transitional periods nor that of the tariff reductions after 1973 were easy to identify, and were probably of comparatively little importance at a time when factors of much greater significance for the terms of trade were changing so drastically. The violent swings in demand for Norway's exports and shipping services were incomparably more important for the general level of export performance. Similarly, currency instability and the kroner's appreciation against the dollar and pound probably had more impact on exports than tariff level changes. When, for example, the Norwegian authorities decided not to devalue along with the dollar and Swedish kroner in February 1973, industry's own estimates were that the resulting competitive disadvantage would cost it some 700 million kroner.[64] Shipping, with its earnings in dollars, was hit by dollar devaluations. Again, Norwegian production costs rose faster than those in most other OECD countries after 1973, and this offset to some extent the advantages gained from freer industrial trade.[65]

Such factors as the level of international activity, currency movements and higher production costs were also a much more serious source of uncertainty for Norwegian industry and business than was the trade agreement. Trading from outside the EEC instead of inside it led to planning difficulties for some firms, because marketing conditions could be changed by EEC decisions, with the preparation of which it was not always possible to keep up to date. However in 1973 Norway's federation of industries opened an office in Brussels, one of whose main functions was to keep firms at home informed about commission proposals which might affect them. Individual industries set up similar offices. Associate membership of the EEC's industrial and employers' organisation also helped to keep firms in Norway abreast with developments in the Nine. This tended to become more difficult in proportion to the extension of EEC harmonisation to new areas. But by and large firms managed to adjust easily enough to such things as new production standards and labelling regulations.[66] As a consolation for what difficulties they experienced, they knew that the uncertainties and adjustments would have been all the greater had the Nine succeeded in harmonising their economies as rapidly and comprehensively as was planned in 1972.

Their failure to do so was the main reason why, during the six years following the referendum, Norway's lack of influence on EEC policies proved much less of a disadvantage than had been feared. Another was that Norwegian interests were indirectly defended inside the EEC's institutions when they happened to coincide with those of some member states, as in shipping matters for example. Moreover partly because of the EEC's lack of common policies in some important sectors such as shipping and energy, the most important international negotiations continued to take place in organisations where Norway was represented. After 1974, for example, the OECD's International Energy Agency became the central forum for Western energy policy negotiations, and while Norway had an association agreement with the IEA, one of the leading EEC countries, France, remained outside it. France's refusal to join the IEA along with the rest of the Nine was an example of how on some questions they went their separate ways, co-operating with countries outside the EEC instead of each other. Another important instance was exchange rate policy. While Britain, France and Italy mainly operated independently of the EEC's fixed parity system (the 'snake'), Norway had been linked to it in one form or another since May 1972. For Norway the 'snake' provided an important measure of exchange rate stability with some of its main trading partners after the collapse of the Bretton Woods system and limited the difficulties it might have experienced operating alone.

Currency questions were one of those on which the Norwegians had said they wanted to extend their co-operation with the EEC beyond the free trade agreement. In this case they were able to do so. But that was due to the peculiar circumstances prevailing in the international monetary system at the time, not to any general willingness on the part of the EEC to establish formal co-operation with Norway on a whole range of non-commercial subjects. On other questions they were less sucessful. Within the framework of the joint committee meetings the Norwegians regularly proposed taking up issues such as the environment and shipping, but on the whole to little avail. This was partly because of the EEC's own difficulties in arriving at common policies for these questions, but even if its progress had been greater, the response would probably have been just as unforthcoming. The fundamental obstacle on the EEC's side remained what it had been during the trade agreement negotiations: the EEC's objection in principle to giving non-member states a right to be consulted about its decisions in advance. In 1977, in the depths of the crisis in European shipping and with protectionism spreading, the EEC at last agreed to hold regular talks with Norway about shipping, but such talks, although useful, were still far from the formal consultation arrangements the Norwegians had proposed in 1972-73.[67]

However, if the EEC was not prepared to go much beyond the trade agreement, its members were more than ready to do so on an individual basis — and increasingly so as the potential of Norway's continental shelf became clearer. The oil and gas reserves changed not only the Norwegians' view of themselves, but also the Nine's view of Norway. Norway became a potentially significant supplier of energy, a valuable market for off-shore equipment, and an area for profitable off-shore exploration and production. The French were the first to initiate economic discussions, at senior civil servant level, in 1974. The other countries soon followed, the most important from Norway's point of view being the West Germans, with whom by 1976 they were involved in formal and detailed negotiations about long-term energy and industrial co-operation.[68]

Oil thus developed into the bargaining counter which the Norwegians had not been ready or able to use during the trade agreement negotiations. In the years which followed they became more than willing to use it in order to obtain concessions in other areas. At the same time, however, oil was one of the forces which was steadily integrating the country ever more tightly into the EEC's economic sphere of influence. For the EEC would be the largest market for Norway's oil and gas exports, while the industrial co-operation the government was seeking in return for the promise of future energy supplies would only intensify at the production level a process which free trade was already speeding up at the commercial level.

So in reality the problem of economic integration without the rights and influence of membership was being intensified in the years following the referendum, as those pro-marketeers for whom this had been a strong argument for joining the EEC had predicted. The anti-marketeers had been proved right about the short-term economic consequences of staying outside the EEC, but the long-term integration which it had been their main concern to prevent was nonetheless taking place, if more slowly, more patchily, and with much less public awareness and political comment than if Norway had joined the EEC on 1 January 1973. The dilemma had not become acute or attracted much attention for several reasons. The EEC's progress after enlargement had been much slower and fraught with problems than anticipated. Those who had supported membership in 1972 found it politically inconvenient to draw attention to the way events were proving them right. And the confidence bred by oil and their comparative economic success during much of the post-referendum period enabled most Norwegians to avoid taking the question seriously.

This, in turn, enabled the political parties and political system gradually to cover over the fissures opened up by the question of the country's relations with the EEC. As long as the EEC remained at its existing level of economic integration; as long as the process of Norway's integration into the EEC's economic system was slow and silent, and did not formally or blatantly infringe the Norwegians' control over their own affairs or threaten the interests of those who had fought against membership; as long as these conditions held, the problem would probably remain beneath the surface of political life. But they could change, and perhaps quite suddenly. In 1968 few had anticipated the radical change in French policy which within a year had opened up the way to negotiations about British entry and raised in acute form the question of Norwegian membership. It was not to be ruled out that the EEC's development would again alter course, and in a way that would starkly expose the dilemma of a non-member's integration without representation; the revival of plans for closer monetary co-operation in 1978, for example, opened up just such a possibility. Whether, if that happened, Norwegian politicians would be able to deal with the situation in any other way than by continuing to pretend that the dilemma did not exist — as with but a few exceptions they had come to do — was one of the main questions raised by the successful 'return to normal' after the political upheavals of the referendum.

8. Politics and the EEC

By the time of the 1977 election Norwegian politics seemed to have returned to the broad pattern of the 1960s, before they were thrown into disarray by the question of EEC membership. There had been some changes. But the politicians who had made a return to pre-referendum normality their main priority after September 1972 had been more successful than many at first thought possible. There were several reasons for this. They included most of the establishment politicians and large parties. They, not the populists and left socialists, proved to be the ones with the main forces in the political system on their side: when the EEC question had been resolved, the lines of conflict created by it turned out to have been confined to this one issue, and the former pattern gradually reasserted itself. The two parties which had supported membership, Labour and the Conservatives, were ready to abandon this objective as the price of regaining the positions they had occupied before the referendum campaign. Even more than is normally the case in foreign policy, it was largely domestic priorities and party interests which set the framework and limits for Norwegian policy towards the EEC after September 1972.

1972-75

During the two years after the referendum the prospect of a return to the stable system of the 1950s and 1960s hardly seemed promising. Injecting the EEC issue into Norwegian politics seemed to have led to party fragmentation, a volatile electorate, political instability, and a new pattern of political forces. There were radical changes in the centre and on the far left and right. There was a general election which was widely interpreted as marking the beginning of a new political era. The fundamental question was whether the referendum had brought about a permanent change in the political system or only caused a temporary upset. Had it served to speed up and clarify longer term trends which had already been undermining the stability of the post-war period? Or would the instability, the new tensions and the altered balance of forces turn out to be relatively short-term phenomena which it would be possible to contain within the old system, given time, skilful political management, and the removal of their cause, the question of Norway's relations with the EEC?

Left socialists and 'green' populists of the Centre and Liberal parties put forward the first interpretation of the referendum result. According to them the Oslo political establishment had been defeated over the EEC because the anti-market coalition expressed the dominant future trends in Norwegian society.[1] Labour, the Conservatives and the Christians, on the other hand, claimed that what they were witnessing was only a temporary disturbance in the political system, and, although they obviously feared that it might not be, set about doing their best to make sure it was. Those in the Centre party who had supported the four-party non-socialist co-operation of the 1960s and seen it collapse in 1971 with reluctance, hovered uneasily in between, eager to exploit their party's referendum victory but averse to letting the party's more radical wing dictate its policy and alliances afterwards. These various interpretations of what had happened on 25 September 1972 were of course seldom the product of objective analysis. Rather they were themselves political platforms for the coming struggle to shape and control the post-referendum political system.

Whether the effects of the referendum proved to be temporary or permanent, however, there was no doubt about the force of its immediate impact. The Liberal party's split in November 1972 was the first major event directly following in its wake and attributable to it. Defeated in their attempt to prevent the party entering the Korvald government and then in their effort to have the national executive's decision retrospectively condemned, a majority of the Liberal members of parliament, including the chairman Helge Seip, broke away and formed the New People's party.[2] The split more or less followed the lines from the referendum, and therefore also in part the older division between the party's radical and moderate wings, whose disagreements over a wide range of domestic and foreign policy questions had crystallized around that of EEC membership. In this respect the EEC issue had merely brought to the surface and intensified tensions long existing within the party. Similarly the personal rivalries which seem to have played a part in the final struggle for control of the party's organisation[3] had been a long-standing feature which the referendum merely heightened to breaking point. In both cases differences over European policy had been as much catalyst as cause in the final break. Whether the party would have split without that catalyst cannot be known — probably not — and certainly not at that time or in that way.

The same could be said about the action of a group of Labour anti-marketeers who left the party in the spring of 1973 and then joined the Socialist People's party and the Communist party in an alliance for the forthcoming election.[4] Most of Labour's anti-marketeers stayed with the party, their fundamental loyalty never in serious doubt whatever their differences with the leadership, intent on changing their party's policies not leaving it. Had it not been for the referendum those who did leave might never have made the break either, despite their dissatisfaction with much in the party's domestic and especially foreign policy. It was the referendum which brought their grievances to a head, embittered personal relations and finally alienated them from the party.[5] Without it, as with the Liberals, the tensions might have continued to be contained successfully within the old party framework.

On the right too it was the referendum and its aftermath which triggered into organisational form frustrations which were of longer standing. Discontent with the high levels of taxation had been a growing force in Norwegian politics since the 1960s, as it had been in the other Scandinavian countries, and as in Denmark the tax burden had not fallen during periods of non-socialist government. In Denmark Mogens Glistrup's anti-tax party came to prominence in 1973. In Norway the post-referendum atmosphere of political febrility and abnormality, in which the established parties were being successfully challenged and new parties and political alliances formed, provided the setting in which support could be found for a party based on a single issue, lower taxes, and a colourful personality, Anders Lange. Without the upheavals of the previous two or three years it seems most unlikely that Anders Lange, an old national conservative politician who had agitated on the fringes of political life since the 1930s, would have enjoyed the success he achieved.

Of perhaps as much importance as the after-effects of the referendum which took an organisational form were those which left the party structure intact, but affected the ideological debate and the balance of forces inside the major parties. In the Labour party, defeat was followed by a period of debilitating quarrels and mutual recriminations. The nomination process for the 1973 election kept open all the campaign wounds, with the anti-marketeers claiming a larger number of safe list seats in recognition of their victory.[6] The ideological issues raised by the EEC debate continued to be thrashed out, while the Socialist Electoral Alliance intensified the pressure on Labour to move leftwards in competition for the left wing vote. Inside the party and by the public at large the debate became personalised around the two most likely successors to Trygve Bratteli when he retired as chairman and prime minister: Odvar Nordli, leader of the parliamentary group and generally regarded as representing the party's moderate, establishment wing, and Reiulf Steen, party vice-chairman, the youth organisation's candidate, and the non-socialists' radical bogyman. With Bratteli expected to retire early in the 1973-77 legislative period, his authority, already undermined by the referendum defeat, was further weakened. The result of all this was that for the eighteen months or so after the referendum the party was dogged by an intensifying ideological debate linked to a sharpening campaign for the leadership.

The Centre party had emerged victorious from the referendum and regained office as a result. But it had also come out of it more divided than before and with the balance between its various groups altered. Both the conservative agricultural lobby and the radical populist wing, which was strongly represented among the younger party members, had been strengthened, partly at least because of the way the party had deliberately emphasised populist and agrarian themes as part of its campaign against EEC membership. With the referendum over, the differences between these two groups and the party's more pragmatic wing came to the surface. They did not cause any serious difficulties in the period immediately following the referendum. Nor did they prevent the party electing a representative of the last group, Dagfinn Vårvik, as chairman at the party's national congress in Bodø in April 1973. At Bodø the party was also able to unite in rejecting co-operation with the Conservatives.[7] Two years later, however, the tensions were to erupt into a serious dispute over this very question of relations with the Conservative party, because of the way it was closely linked with the Centrists' own continuing debate about the party's ideological identity and place in the political system. It was then that the altered balance of forces within the party really made itself felt. It was this effect of the referendum which was ultimately to prove the biggest obstacle to establishing a credible non-socialist alternative to Labour.

The election in September 1973 turned out to be as much of an 'EEC election' as some had feared and others hoped.[8] The EEC had only been made an issue by those anti-marketeers who saw an advantage in keeping the question alive, notably the Socialist Electoral Alliance. On the pro-market side the Conservatives were already anxious to suppress it in order to open the way for co-operation with the other non-socialist parties if they won an overall majority. More important were the indirect effects of the referendum. Many voters had lost confidence in the parties they normally supported. Old loyalties had broken down and political identities become blurred. The behaviour of the electorate had become less predictable and stable. The outstanding feature of the election result was the large number

194

of anti-marketeers who switched their vote away from pro-market parties, mainly at Labour's expense but also at the Conservatives'. Pro-market voters were less inclined to change party, but even they had been affected by the general mood and become more volatile. In both cases it was reactions to the EEC issue which seemed to have been the decisive factor initiating a switch of vote. Which party the shifting voter then chose to support was a complex interaction between the party's position on the EEC and its position on the two main domestic issues of the 1973 election, abortion law reform and taxation.

The election's outstanding losers were Labour, the rump Liberal party, and the New People's party. Labour lost a quarter of a million votes, falling from 46 per cent of the poll in 1969 to 35 per cent, and winning only sixty-two of the 155 seats in parliament compared to seventy-four of the previous parliament's 150 seats. Not since 1930 had Labour sunk to so low a share of the vote. Whereas the old united Liberal party had won thirteen seats in 1969, the anti-market Liberals won only two and the New People's party one. Both were removed as significant forces in the centre of Norwegian politics. The Conservatives held on better and kept the same number of seats, but even they lost 2 per cent of their 1969 vote. All the anti-market parties except the Liberals improved their positions. The Centre party gained one seat, the Christians six, and the Socialist Electoral Alliance entered parliament with sixteen, making the last two parties the election's clear winners. So too was Anders Lange's party, which entered parliament with four seats and 5 per cent of the votes, isolated and ignored there by the other parties, but a warning to them that something had gone wrong with the political system and a pressure on them to relieve the grievances which had put Anders Lange there.

Analysis of the election result showed that Labour had lost to left and right. On the left former Labour voters supplied nearly half the Socialist Electoral Alliance's 11 per cent of the vote. On the right, although Labour picked up some votes from the New People's party, it lost anti-marketeers to the Christians and Centrists and pro-marketeers to the Conservatives and Anders Lange's party. The losses to Anders Lange were particularly worrying, and strengthened the impression that Labour's broad coalition was disintegrating at either end: 32 per cent of Anders Lange's votes had come from Labour, compared with 22 per cent from the Conservatives.[9] The regional distribution of Labour's losses were hardly surprising after the referendum. They were heaviest in the solidly 'no' north and in the traditionally more radical industrial region of Telemark. Fishermen and small farmers had deserted the party. Support among manual and white collar workers had fallen, while most first-time voters had gone either right or left, only just over a quarter voting for Labour compared to half of them in 1969. Whether this signalled a permanent weakening of the party's position, or was an exceptional and therefore reversible defeat explicable mainly in terms of the referendum would depend on how many of these sources of loss were consistent with long-term voting trends.[10] In the primary sector Labour had been losing to the middle-parties and sometimes to the Socialist People's party for some years. The referendum campaign had only accelerated this trend. Losses among the much more numerous white collar and manual workers had previously been slight, however, and the sharp drop in support among young people was also new. The question facing the party was whether the 1973 losses in these last two groups signified a trend independent of the exceptional circumstances created by the referendum — a consequence of workers becoming more affluent and youth more highly educated. Nobody could be sure in 1973. Nor could anybody know what the Socialist Electoral Alliance's future would be. Its constituent parties and groups were planning to merge themselves into a single party. However improbable it seemed that the Communist party would dissolve itself, the threat to Labour was obvious and taken seriously by its leaders.

The way in which the upheavals of the referendum had sent Labour 'no' voters over to anti-market parties and 'yes' voters to the Conservatives or Anders Lange was repeated in the pattern of losses and gains for the other parties. Conservative anti-marketeers transferred to the Centre and Christian parties. New People's party voters, if they switched, voted for the parties which had campaigned for membership. The Christians' sizable gains were partly due to the way in which it had succeeded in retaining its own pro-market voters (a tribute to both the strength of its ideological foundations and its way of handling the EEC issue) while at the same time gaining anti-marketeers from other parties; the abortion issue and its chairman's increased standing after a year as prime minister also helped. On the left the switches between parties were almost wholly attributable to the referendum.

After the election it was the Socialist Electoral Alliance's sixteen seats which gave it and the Labour party together a majority of one over the six non-socialist parties (seventy-eight to seventy-seven). The middle-party coalition which had been in office since the referendum had forty-three seats. A revival of the co-operation between them and the Conservatives was still politically impossible. Even together however the four parties would have commanded only seventy-three seats. Labour, although the election's loser, was still the largest single party with sixty-two seats. A coalition between Labour and some other party, whether the Socialist Electoral Alliance or one of the middle-parties, was ruled out by them as well as Labour, which still held to its tradition of only governing alone. A minority Labour government was therefore the only possibility. Labour announced that it would seek support from the other parties from issue to issue. They, in turn, declared that they would give or withold it on the same terms. On that basis Trygve Bratteli formed his second government, which took office on 16 October 1973.

Labour's weakness in parliament was that if the three largest opposition parties - Conservatives, Centrists and CPP - and the Socialist Electoral Alliance voted together against the government, they could muster a majority of eighty-six to Labour's sixty-two. Its strength was that this majority could not be translated into an alternative government. It would be a negative majority because the Socialist Electoral Alliance and the other three parties would never coalesce, and the non-socialist parties alone were in a minority. The Socialist Electoral Alliance would also find it difficult to justify putting and keeping in office a non-socialist minority government. On the non-socialist side, the Centre party's opposition to co-operating with the Conservatives seemed as strong as ever. Combined with disagreements over a series of major domestic issues in 1974, this not only seemed to rule out the establishment of a credible non-socialist alternative for the 1977 election, but was an important factor enabling Labour to govern in the 1973-77 period by means of shifting majorities for the various parts of its programme.

In this situation the Labour government had to perform a difficult balancing act between left and right, both in parliament and in its own party.[11] If it leant too far in one direction in order to gain support there, it risked losing it on the other side. Policies which would staunch the losses to the Socialist Electoral Alliance contained the danger of uniting the non-socialists, which would limit Labour's ability to divide and rule in this parliament and risk conjuring up a united non-socialist challenge in 1977. Policies aimed at attracting middle-of-the-road voters and non-socialist support in parliament could frustrate Labour's efforts to recover its losses to the Socialist Electoral Alliance, and even drive more Labour voters in a more radical direction. These, then, were the two dangers for Labour. On the right the revival of an alliance which included the Conservatives. On the left the creation of a strong, united left socialist party. If either materialised it would be a serious embarrassment. If both materialised, Labour would be squeezed to a medium-sized, **left-of-centre social democratic party** excluded from government except in coalition with the blocs to its left and right.

In its strategy to avert this threat Labour assigned to the Conservatives a key role. Their *de facto* alliance on the EEC was regarded as having been an electoral disaster. So now the Conservatives were re-installed as Labour's principal ideological opponent.[12] This was intended to clarify the left-right conflict as the dominant one in politics, refurbish Labour's socialist identity, and stimulate the left to unity by emphasising issues which divided socialists from non-socialists. Stressing the Conservatives' liberal free enterprise character was also intended to isolate them further from the middle-parties. Labour tried (not always successfully, as the bitter struggle over abortion in 1973-74 showed) to avoid conflicts with the middle-parties in order to keep them closer to Labour than to the Conservatives, and because moral and cultural issues such as this had been shown to divide Labour's own voters. The government made no attempt, at least publicly, to reach a formal agreement on parliamentary co-operation with any of the middle-parties. Bratteli himself, with an eye to the party's position after 1977, tried to encourage a party debate on the subject, but met with little response.[13]

Binding co-operation with the Socialist Electoral Alliance was ruled out, even if its votes were needed on questions like abortion and bank socialisation.[14] A consistent Labour theme during 1974 and 1975 was the need to re-unite the working-class movement, but by that Labour's leaders did not mean establishing an organisational or political link with the Socialist Electoral Alliance. Such a re-unification could only come about as far as they were concerned by democratic socialists returning to the Labour party, where they rightly belonged.[15] If the party's leaders were uncompromising on this point, however, in other respects they showed considerable flexibility in their efforts to win back the left-wing vote. Their defeat over the EEC had left them cautious and willing to compromise. Dissenting voices were listened to more readily, even anticipated, and the necessary real or apparent adjustments in party policy made in order to quiet them and avoid damaging conflicts. Particular attention was paid to the views of groups alienated from the party or its leaders by the referendum, like the fishermen, young people, and those members who stood to the left of the leadership on many questions of domestic and foreign policy.[16] The issues of particular concern to these groups — primary sector interests, decentralisation, 'quality of life' questions, national control of natural resources, the Third World — figured prominently in party speeches and gained more influence on party policy.

This did not seem to be helping Labour much in the eighteen months after the election. In early 1974 the public opinion polls showed that it was supported by only one-third of the voters, and it remained at this level for the remainder of the year.[17] Equally serious was that the Socialist Electoral Alliance seemed to have stabilised at around 11 to 12 per cent. A major and perhaps permanent shift in the balance of power seemed to have taken place on the left of Norwegian politics. The only bright spot for Labour was that while almost half the electorate supported the non-socialist parties, their disagreements over policy and the distrust and personal acrimony created by the events of 1970-73 were a formidable obstacle to them offering anything more than a small middle-party alternative. Many began to think that the referendum had indeed profoundly altered the political system. Insecure minority governments or fragile coalitions appeared to have replaced the long post-war run of stable and, with the exception of 1961-65, majority governments, based on a powerful Labour party on the left and four medium-sized parties on the right. Worried parallels were drawn with the similar situation in Denmark.

1975-77

Yet two years later, as the campaign for the 1977 election began, the picture looked rather different. The contours of the older pattern had re-emerged. The polls showed Labour approaching its 1969 level. The Socialist Electoral Alliance had split and its support fallen to that of the Socialist People's party in the 1960s. On the non-socialist side, the Conservatives, Christians and Centrists were negotiating about co-operation in the event of them winning a parliamentary majority. In other words, it was beginning to look as though the party system might have only been severely strained by the referendum not radically altered, and that it was now righting itself as silence gathered about the question of relations with the EEC.

The lowest point for Labour had been 1974 and the spring of 1975. The policy debates and mutual recriminations had continued unabated. On top of them had come the long-drawn-out process of choosing a successor to Trygve Bratteli, who in June 1974 announced his intention of resigning at the national congress in April 1975.[18] Bratteli had combined the offices of party chairman and prime minister, as his predecessor, Einar Gerhardsen had also done. This time it proved impossible to unite the party behind one candidate. In a compromise the chairmanship went to Reiulf Steen, while the position of prime minister was to pass to Odvar Nordli when Bratteli eventually resigned that too.[19] The struggle for the leadership harmed the party with the voters by strengthening the impression that it was deeply divided over ideology and personalities. Despite their popular identification with rival wings of the party, however, both Steen and Nordli stood well within the middle ground of social democracy. Both had supported EEC membership. Both, in their own ways, had taken care to keep open their channels of communication with the party's anti-marketeers. The differences between them were more those of personality and political style and of having come to the top by different routes. Nordli had risen through local government, parliament and ministerial office. Steen had come up mainly through the youth organisation and party headquarters. The younger, more radical and usually anti-market party members generally supported Steen. But that was more a reflection of these factors of style and personality, and his ability to get on with them, rather than of differences between himself and Nordli over important questions of domestic and foreign policy.

Steen became chairman just a month after what could have been regarded as another blow for the party. In March 1975, the Socialist Electoral Alliance, meeting at Trondheim, transformed itself into a political party.[20] In fact the disagreements displayed at Trondheim raised Labour's hopes that this threat would never materialise, or at least not in a serious form. Soon after the 1973 election the communists had agreed to change the alliance into a party during 1975, and to dissolve their own organisation by the end of 1976.[21] They had done this under heavy pressure from the Socialist People's party and former Labour party members, but the preparations for the new party highlighted the basic differences between the socialists and communists over ideology and organisation. At Trondheim these were only covered over by unsatisfactory verbal compromises and postponing decisions. The communists themselves were divided about whether or not to dissolve their party. There were indications that the Soviet Union did not approve of such a step,[22] and there were Norwegian communists who did not like the idea either. The communists who supported a united left party argued that by joining the Socialist Electoral Alliance in 1973 they had at last managed to escape from their post-1949 political ghetto and exert a real influence on national politics. They wanted to consolidate this progress. To demonstrate the new weight the alliance had given the communists, they pointed to the way in which, within it, they had nearly toppled the government just a few months before, when they joined forces with the non-socialists to oppose the terms on which Labour was proposing to buy back part of the shares owned by Alcan, the Canadian company, in Norway's largest aluminium works.[23]

They were right in arguing that participation in the alliance had enabled the communists to play a more active role in Norwegian politics than they had done since the 1940s. But from Labour's point of view one of the main lessons of the Alcan crisis of December 1974 was the way it exposed the divisions between its left wing opponents. Four months before the Trondheim conference openly documented the disagreements between socialists and communists, the chairman of the Socialist People's party broke with the rest of the alliance's parliamentary group in the crucial vote on re-purchasing Alcan's shares, and supported the government. The hopes raised in the Labour party by this were confirmed in March 1975, with further confirmation following during the rest of the year. While Labour's own internal difficulties subsided after the resolution of the succession issue, the Socialist Left's quarrels became increasingly public and acrimonious. In the middle of 1975 the contrasting images being presented to the public began to be reflected in the monthly party polls. Labour began a slow but steady climb up from its lowest point of 32 per cent in May 1975. The Socialist Left started an equally slow but relentless descent from the seemingly stable level of support it had maintained since October 1973.

The Alcan crisis had also exposed the divisions to the right of Labour. It was the last-minute reversal of position by a section of the Centre party's parliamentary group that had been mainly responsible for saving the government. The failure of the non-socialist parties to stand together in this crisis had underlined their inability to offer an alternative to Labour more than a year after the election. The Conservatives had marked their interest in putting together such an alternative even before the elction.[24] So had the Christians who, while always emphasising their particularly close ties with the other middle-parties, held the door open for the Conservatives as the only realistic way of obtaining a parliamentary majority for a non-socialist coalition.[25] The obstacle lay in the Centre party, where the opposition to co-operating with the Conservatives appeared to be as strong as ever.[26]

One other obstacle had been removed in the two years since the referendum. The Conservatives had given up their efforts to reverse the result. They had started to do this even before the 1973 election by means of a series of clarifications of party policy which had the effect of changing it. First they said they would not expect a non-socialist government to include membership in its programme. They asked only that it recognise the Conservatives' right to maintain their support for membership in principle and call for another referendum if there was evidence of a 'permanent and unmistakable change in public opinion'. In this referendum the voters would be asked to choose between keeping the free trade agreement and a new application for membership.[27] This clarification was then further clarified. It was pointed out that there was no reason to expect the question of reviewing Norway's relations with the EEC to arise before the early

1980s at the earliest, because it would not be possible to assess the working of the free trade agreement until free trade had been fully established.[28] By this the Conservatives ruled out raising the issue for eight or nine years, in other words for the life of the next two parliaments. In early 1975 the process of changing Conservative policy was completed by the Oslo newspaper closest to the party, *Aftenposten,* when it took the clarification process to its logical conclusion. It described the aim of EEC membership as a minority one with no hope of being realised in the foreseeable future. As such it was one which could well be dropped from the party's programme for 1977-81 in the interests of non-socialist co-operation.[29] Two years later, when that programme was being drawn up, it was.[30] So by the beginning of 1975 European policy was no longer a barrier to a coalition between the Conservatives and middle-parties. Although more slowly, and with more obvious reluctance, the Conservatives had finally reached the position Labour had adopted immediately after the referendum, and they had done so for much the same reasons of party interest. The Conservatives had had to abandon any idea of continuing the campaign for membership if they wanted to end their political isolation and reconstruct an alliance to replace Labour in 1977.

That objective seemed far off in December 1974, during the Alcan crisis. In retrospect however the events of that month marked an important turning point on the way towards re-establishing a non-socialist alternative to Labour and with it the pre-referendum pattern of politics. Moreover the initiative came from the Centre party's chairman, Dagfinn Vårvik. Some regarded his move as an attempt to rectify the impression of a *volte face* which had kept Labour in office, others as an opportunity well taken to outflank his own internal party opposition. Arguing that the lesson of the crisis was how politically unprepared the non-socialists would be to take over if the Labour government fell, Vårvik proposed that he open talks with the chairmen of the Conservative and Christian People's parties in order to establish whether there was a basis for co-operation between them.[31] In April 1975 he won a mandate for talks from the party's national congress.[32] The party's approval was less than enthusiastic and unambiguous, but public opinion polls showed that three-quarters of the party's voters wanted to include the Conservatives in the talks[33] — a result which proved that, contrary to what the party's 'green' wing was claiming, most Centrist voters now wanted to return to the situation prevailing before the referendum campaign began.

The mid-term local elections in September 1975 confirmed the evidence of a gradual return to a modified version of the pre-1971 political pattern. The Socialist Left and Anders Lange's party lost heavily. Both had owed their success in 1973 to the direct and indirect results of the referendum. Now Anders Lange's party lost two-thirds of its voters, the Socialist Left half. Labour and the Conservatives recovered ground, in the Conservatives' case doing even better than in 1969. Labour was still some 8 per cent below its 1969 level, but above that of October 1973. Compared with Labour performances before 1970, the party had done badly, losing control of nearly all the larger towns and falling back even further among first-time voters and white-collar workers, but there were several bright spots for the party in the result. The EEC issue was clearly beginning to lose much of its impact, because the party had regained some of its losses in the north. The party had succeeded in casting the Conservatives in the role of its main opponent by stressing such questions as taxation, socialisation of commercial banks, and the control of private property ownership. Moreover Labour still had relatively large reserves of support which it could hope to mobilise in time for the 1977 election. This was because the main legacy of the referendum in this local election appeared to be a notably low turn-out from which Labour was regarded as being the main loser.[34]

The 'return to normal' continued throughout 1976. Labour's climb in the polls took it from 38 per cent in the 1975 local elections to 45 per cent just over a year later.[35] Odvar Nordli succeeded Trygve Bratteli as prime minister in January 1976 and proved a widely popular, reassuring figure. The economy was still performing relatively better than those of most other industrialised countries. Real living standards had risen. Tax rates had at last been cut, and by a socialist government. With the pressure on Labour's left flank reduced, the leadership was able to move closer to the political centre. While regaining supporters from the Socialist Left and enjoying more success in mobilising its own voters, the party was thus also recovering some of its losses to the middle-parties and Conservatives. There was evidence too that it was attracting more young voters.[36] All the signs pointed to the 1977 election being a very close race, but to Labour at least being in it with a real chance of winning enough seats to continue in government. Its concentration on removing the EEC issue from Norwegian politics seemed to have had the desired result.

On the non-socialist side too, progress had been made towards restoring the state of affairs which had existed before the referendum, even if it had been less strikingly successful. In April 1976 the chairmen and vice-chairmen of the Centre, Conservative and Christian People's parties — the three parties engaged in the exploratory talks started on the Centre party chairman's initiative in 1975 — issued a formal, binding declaration committing themselves to negotiate about the formation of a coalition after the 1977 election if it produced a parliamentary majority for one.[37] The declaration did not specify which parties would actually participate in such a coalition, an ambiguity designed to avoid a confrontation with the opposition which still existed in the Centre party towards including the Conservatives. Nor did it say what such a coalition's programme would be: each party would fight the election on its own. The April declaration did not immediately usher in a period of better co-operation either inside or outside parliament, which exposed the parties concerned to Labour's charge of providing no more of an alternative after April 1976 than before it. The pattern of independent parties fighting on their own programmes had however been characteristic of the 1960s too. It was modified anyway by their presentation of a joint counter-proposal to Labour's long-term programme for the 1977-81 period.[38] The reluctance of some groups in the middle-parties to coalesce with the Conservatives was also nothing new, and as in the 1960s there was one very powerful argument for ignoring it: that only a coalition which included the Conservatives offered any of them the prospect of returning to office.

The election took place on 12 and 13 September 1977. When the result was known several conclusions could be drawn from it.[39] Five years after the referendum the EEC had ceased to be a significant factor in voting behaviour. Several events which in 1973 had seemed to usher in a new period in Norwegian politics were seen to have been merely transitory phenomena thrown up by the abnormal political circumstances prevailing immediately after the referendum. The 'no' to the EEC had been neither a vote for radical change in Norway itself nor a long-term rejection of the parties which had campaigned for membership. The winners of the 1977 election were Labour and the Conservatives, especially the latter — the two parties which had tried to take Norway into the EEC in 1972, paid the electoral price for it in 1973, and spent the intervening period working to recover the voters' confidence. Labour had won over 42 per cent of the votes and seventy-six seats, fifteen more than in 1973. The Conservatives had gained twelve more seats to give them forty-two. These moreover were the parties identified with policies aiming at high growth rates, modernisation and industrialisation, the very objectives criticised by many of those who had organised the campaign which defeated them in 1972. It looked as though the latter had won the referendum, only to lose the subsequent struggle for control of the country's economic and political development. Indeed apart from the Christians, the parties which had campaigned against membership had lost ground in 1977. The Socialist Left had held onto only two of its sixteen seats. The Liberals had managed to retain the two they won in 1973, but had lost votes. The Centre party had lost nine of its twenty-one seats, its bad performance appearing to be due principally to its continuing internal disputes over co-operation with the Conservatives. Vårvik had resigned in the spring of 1977, partly because of this, and his successor, a compromise candidate relatively unknown outside the party, had been unable to impose a truce or restore the party's position with the voters in the short time before the election. The two small parties established in the aftermath of the referendum — the New People's party and Anders Lange's party (renamed the Progress party after his death) failed to win any seats in the new parliament.

Despite the Socialist Left's losses, the election again gave the two socialist parties a small overall majority. Together they had seventy-eight seats. The Conservatives, Centrists and Christians had seventy-five. Labour was able to stay in office, though now it would be heavily dependent on the tiny Socialist Left and Liberal parties unless the co-operation between the three large non-socialist parties were to break down. They on their side faced a further four years in opposition, which would be a hard test of their ability and will to co-operate and to challenge Labour again in 1981.

The implications of this situation for Norway's relations with the EEC seemed clear. Barring unforeseen developments producing an overwhelming movement in favour of membership, it seemed extremely unlikely that either Labour or the Conservative party would themselves re-open the question. The two parties whose votes Labour would need in parliament, the Socialist Left and the Liberals, were as strongly anti-market as ever. So were the only two parties whose co-operation offered the Conservatives a hope of returning to government. Individual Labour and Conservative politicians might occasionally touch on the subject, even tentatively suggest that after five years the Norwegians put the referendum behind them and start discussing calmly some of the problems which experience had shown to be connected with a free trade agreement. But they were unlikely to broach the fundamental question of whether or not the free trade relationship was really in Norway's long-term interests: whether, despite the fact that so far the country had managed quite well economically outside the EEC, membership might not be a more advantageous position for Norway seen in a broader foreign and security policy perspective. As far as former supporters of membership were concerned, the question of relations with the EEC was not just 'on ice', it was politically dead, and exceptional events or the passing of a considerable period of time would be needed to resurrect it.

9. Labour's European policy

Aims and achievements

When Labour returned to office in October 1973 it promised to pursue an 'active' policy towards the EEC.[1] In the event it was scarcely more active than its predecessor, and by the time of the 1977 election it had no more than partially fulfilled the aims which it had set for this policy. Indeed by then the deficiencies of Labour's European policy and the need to re-think the problems and means of solving them had become obvious. At the same time however, and partly as a result of the party's own handling of the question of relations with the EEC, the likelihood of the Labour government or any successor seriously doing this seemed as distant as ever.

Labour did not coin the phrase 'active European policy', but by elevating it into something like a solemn policy declaration it managed both to obscure this fact and to arouse unrealistic expectations which dogged it for some time afterwards.[2] In large measure 'active' was simply intended to convey the vigour with which Labour would defend Norwegian interests. As such it said nothing that most people did not already take for granted that it should and would do. 'Active' also had another implication however. This was that although the free trade agreement had solved some problems in Norway's relations with the EEC, it had created others which it must be the aim of Norwegian policy to overcome.[3] By contrast with just a few years later, this was an implication which in 1973 those responsible for the country's foreign policy still seemed anxious should not be forgotten.

In 1973 they were also still ready to discuss publicly what these problems were and how to meet them.[4] The problems were those which they had so often drawn attention to during the referendum campaign. There was their exclusion from the many institutions and areas of co-operation within the EEC, their lack of influence on EEC policies which would affect Norway, and their exclusion from the Nine's foreign policy consultations. In a broader context, there was the danger that even if the referendum did not turn out to be the first step in that loosening of Norway's ties with the West which many pro-marketeers had predicted, they could gradually lose whatever influence they had within the traditional organisations of Atlantic co-operation. The objectives of the government's policy followed from the problems. The Norwegians had to try to extend their economic co-operation with the EEC to areas beyond the free trade agreement. They had to expand their channels of communication with the Nine in order to keep informed about EEC affairs and feed Norwegian views into EEC policy discussions at an early stage. Within the Atlantic alliance they had to remove any doubts that might have emerged about Norway's position as a result of the referendum. They had also to counter any tendency for the real alliance decisions to be taken outside its formal procedures, in prior consultations between its EEC members and the United States.

As for the principles underlying the government's policy towards the EEC, Trygve Bratteli summed them up in 1973 shortly before taking office. They were the need for co-operation, but the primacy of domestic contraints on the type of co-operation. He pointed out that the referendum had not altered the fundamental facts of geographical proximity, economic dependence, and political solidarity underlying the development of close, binding ties between Norway and the countries of Western Europe since the second world war. They would make a continuation of those close relations as vital as they had ever been, indeed more so now that Norway was outside the EEC. Bratteli stressed, however, that Norway's co-operation with the Nine had to take a form on which the Norwegians could agree among themselves. First and foremost his government's European policy had to be one which would heal the divisions opened up by this question after 1970.

Measured against these objectives, the government could point to some success in 1977, after four years in office. Not only had the conflicts over European policy ceased, or at least been successfully covered over. So had even discussion of the subject. On the whole Norway's relations with the EEC were good. And economic co-operation with some of its members was closer than ever before. Within the Atlantic alliance there were no doubts about Norway's membership being the foundation of the country's foreign policy, or about Norway being firmly integrated into the alliance's political and defence co-operation.

In other respects, however, the results fell short of the aims Trygve Bratteli had set for his government in 1973. An essential part of the European policy he had outlined had been the task of fostering the Norwegians' traditionally weak sense of being part of Western Europe, politically as well as economically, and with it their sense of responsibility for Western Europe's problems and future. Yet inso-

far as it was possible to measure such a thing, the Norwegians' identification with the countries to the south of them seemed even weaker
in 1977. Again, while economic co-operation had increased, the Norwegians' ability to influence EEC policies of importance to themselves
had not kept step with it. The consultation arrangements established
on some economic questions had helped to ameliorate their position
as outsiders, but had scarcely solved all the problems created by it.
In the diplomatic field Norway was not benefiting from the opportunities for influence and information opened up by the increasingly
intensive web of political and diplomatic exchanges within the EEC.
In the long term there was the danger that if the EEC was enlarged
and its foreign policy co-operation widened to include even more
European members of the Atlantic alliance, Norway would find its
position in the alliance's political activities undermined even if it
remained unaffected as regards defence co-operation.

Even more serious were the formidable obstacles which had been
erected against discussing these problems, let alone solving them. Not
only did the self-interest of the largest political parties stand in the
way of this. The subject of relations with the EEC had become
surrounded by taboos which scarcely anyone in active political life
seemed to dare to defy. Not that many even saw a need to do so, for
the intellectual obstacles seemed almost as great as the political ones.
With a few notable exceptions, most Norwegians appeared to have
stopped thinking seriously about what was happening in the EEC or
the long-term implications of alternative developments there for
themselves. Much of the responsibility for this lay with the Labour
party and the Labour government of these years. Ever since the referendum Labour's European policy had been subordinated to its
party interests at home. This had required that all genuine and open
debate be avoided and policy expressed in standardised, almost rit-
ualised, formulas on which the party could unite. After four years of
this most public pronouncements on the subject had accommodated
themselves to the acceptable formulas. So too, it appeared, had most
thinking — which was one reason why it seemed to have all but
ceased.

Distractions from Europe

So party interests and domestic politics had clearly been one major
factor producing this net balance for Labour's European policy. Another had been Norway's position in the Atlantic alliance after the
referendum. The complex of foreign policy issues thrown up by developments in the seas around Norway had been a third. Events in
the EEC itself had been a fourth. Between them they had largely

determined what those conducting Norway's relations with Europe were able to do politically, had the diplomatic resources and time to do, and considered it necessary to do.

Domestic politics required an end to the debate about Norway's relations with the EEC. They also contributed to the shift of emphasis away from Europe to other issues and other geographical areas which was such a notable feature of Norwegian foreign policy in these years. In 1973 Trygve Bratteli had assured a European audience that despite the rejection of EEC membership Norway belonged to Western Europe politically and wanted to maintain its close ties with the countries there. By then however he was no longer stating self-evident principles of Norwegian foreign policy called in question by a mere tiny minority on the far left. They were rejected by a vocal section of his own party which, although a minority, had gained in political influence as a result of the referendum. They were rejected too by many politically active young people, some well-known academics, and the more radical members of the middle-parties.[5] For these groups, opposition to EEC membership had been closely bound up with precisely this question of which countries Norway should identify and co-operate with. Their answer then had been the Nordic neutrals and developing countries, not the industrialised countries of Western Europe, and especially not the 'rich man's' EEC. And they regarded their referendum victory as merely a first step in the campaign for a radical re-orientation of Norwegian foreign policy to bring it into line with these priorities.

Bratteli and the Labour leadership knew this and had no intention of allowing such a campaign to succeed. In this the new government had strong forces on its side. There were the undeniable facts of Norway's vital economic links with Western Europe, especially the EEC, to which the prime minister had pointed. Most establishment anti-marketeers had no wish to change the main lines of Norway's foreign policy.[6] Nor, according to the public opinion polls, did most of the electorate.[7] However, the advocates of a new foreign policy also had some important advantages after September 1972, and it was these which partly explained why, although their influence was by no means as great as they had hoped, it was far from negligible. They had the advantage of having been on the winning side in the referendum. Although most 'no' votes had been cast for essentially conservative reasons, not out of a desire for change, the aura of victory gave their views a weight they had not possessed in 1970. Then there was the fact that their views had genuine roots in Norwegian foreign policy thinking. The pre-war tradition of moralistic neutrality and co-operation with fellow Nordic neutrals had been overshadowed by the pro-Western, Atlantic one after 1949, but it had never disappeared.

Rather it had co-existed alongside the new policy, providing one of the most obvious sources of tension in Norwegian foreign policy during the 1950s and 1960s. The reaction of Labour's leaders to two heavy defeats in a row also made things easier for those who were working for a new foreign policy. After the referendum and 1973 election the party leadership was cautious and uncertain, its self-confidence and authority weakened. It was also acutely sensitive and responsive to the views of those on the left of the party, both those who had remained with the party and those who had deserted to the Socialist Electoral Alliance but whom it was hoped to win back. Finally, the referendum debate had given the opponents of Norway's Western and Atlantic orientation a unique opportunity to campaign for their ideas, and this had not been without its effect. Even if their ultimate objectives were still unacceptable to most Norwegians, their outlook and terminology turned out to have gained a larger place in political and even official thinking. Even a politician of Bratteli's stature could not afford to ignore this when his government took office.

Rather accommodation and concessions seemed as necessary in foreign policy as they were at home if Labour was to recover from the events of the previous three years. The consequences were seen in several areas. One was the government's handling of international energy questions, where the most striking example was its decision not to seek full membership of the International Energy Agency when this was set up in November 1974.[8] Norway had participated from the beginning in the negotiations started after the Washington conference in February 1974 to establish a semi-automatic oil-sharing scheme which would come into effect in the event of an embargo like that imposed by OPEC in the previous winter. The government's decision to limit Norway's participation to an association agreement was influenced by other factors as well. The economic ministries wanted to retain sole control over oil policy, and there was the argument that as an oil producer and exporter Norway's interests would not be identical with those of the industrialised oil-importing countries. The primary consideration, however, was the government's fear of starting up another debate about national sovereignty and opening itself to left-wing charges of trying to bind Norway to the EEC by indirect means after having failed to take it in as a full member. The IEA issue saw the Labour government caught between strong pressures from its NATO allies, especially the United States, and domestic and party pressures which those ministers who wanted full membership (and they included the prime minister and foreign minister)[9] lacked the political authority or will to override. Before the referendum a Labour prime minister wielding the argument of solidarity with Norway's Western allies would almost certainly have carried the party. After it he did not even attempt to do so. The retreat to an association agreement illustrated the effect of their referendum and election defeats on the self-confidence and standing of the party's leaders, the primacy of party interests at a time when Labour was at its lowest point in the polls, and the greater influence which the party's left-wingers and anti-marketeers had gained on foreign policy.

It also demonstrated the greater attention now paid to one of the main themes of these two groups: relations with the developing countries. For one of their objections to IEA membership had been that the oil-sharing scheme was a weapon to be used by the industrialised oil-importing countries against the oil-exporting developing ones. Left-wing and anti-market influence was not the only pressure bringing this question to the fore after 1973. North-south questions would have required more attention anyway because of their more prominent place in international politics. Nor did the influence of these groups alone explain Labour's increasingly radical position on these questions. Support for the claims of colonial and developing countries had been a feature of Norwegian foreign policy since the 1950s, and as these claims became more radical in the 1970s, so too, almost as a natural progression, did Norwegian policy. Another push in the same direction was exerted by the way the middle-parties' positions on north-south issues shifted under the influence of their left-wings, for Labour could hardly have been found adopting a more conservative stand than they did. However, even if pressure from Labour's left-wing was only one among several, it was still an important one, and it was one which frequently gave an ideological anti-Western tone at variance with the government's real foreign policy priorities to a policy on which there existed a broad consensus within the party.

For none of the accommodations amounted to a fundamental change in these priorities. Indeed the concessions were mainly designed to avoid this by placating the opposition on non-essential issues. The government's priorities remained the traditional ones of national security and economic prosperity, which meant membership of the Atlantic alliance and NATO and good relations with the industrialised countries with which all but a tiny percentage of Norway's trade was conducted. Even the concessions were at times more apparent than real, a matter of presentation rather than substance. In its handling of the IEA question, for example, the government attached great importance to the views of the United States government and the argument that Norway had to demonstrate solidarity with its allies. The formula eventually found to reconcile these considerations with Labour's party interests — the association agreement — involved political commitments on Norway's part which in practice brought its position very close to membership.[10]

But however superficial the changes made in response to domestic and party pressures might have been, they had two consequences for the government's handling of relations with Western Europe, and especially the EEC. The greater concentration on north-south issues entailed a diversion of diplomatic resources and political attention away from Europe, while the government's concern to avoid friction with its left-wing and underline the ideological progressiveness of its foreign policy made it convenient to play down the closeness of Norway's ties with the industrialised countries of Western Europe. Government spokesmen still regularly referred to the need for good relations with Norway's European allies and trading partners. But they equally regularly counteracted this by criticising the latters' positions on north-south issues and international energy questions. When the conflicting pressures from home and abroad became too great, the government fell back on the old notion of Norway as an international 'bridgebuilder'. But it was a bridgebuilder whose expressions of sympathy and support leant more and more towards one side, the developing countries, as the 1977 election approached.

It was thus paradoxical, yet illustrative of the balance of priorities and the tensions in Labour's foreign policy, that the second major factor diverting the government's attention from Europe in these post-referendum years was one entirely within the tradition so disliked by the party's left-wing. This was the even greater importance attached to Norway's membership of the Atlantic alliance. For most of Labour's leaders, after all, EEC membership had always been in large measure a European means to an Atlantic end. They had seen European unification as the means of strengthening the European side of the alliance in accordance with American wishes, and Norwegian membership as the means of consolidating Norway's place in the two-pillared organisation which the alliance would consequently become. After September 1972 this objective of securing Norway's position within a strong Atlantic alliance remained as fundamental as ever for the party's leaders, but now it had to be pursued by other means. The only ones open to them were within the alliance itself, so the years which saw such emphasis on Norway's relations with developing countries, also saw a concentration on the traditional foundations of Labour's post-war foreign policy, namely Norway's relations with the United States and participation in NATO. Here the government made no concessions to its critics, inside or outside the party. Nearly every foreign policy speech, every defence speech, was used to underline Norway's commitment to NATO, its loyalty to the alliance and its vital interest in being anchored safely within the West and to the United States. Not even verbal concessions were permitted.

One effect of this was to relegate relations with Western Europe to the subordinate place in Norwegian and Labour party thinking which they had traditionally occupied. This development was confirmed when it gradually came to seem to the party's leaders that they had been mistaken in their view of the alliance's future development, and hence of the effect on Norway's position within the alliance if it stayed outside the EEC. European unity did not, after all, seem to be a prerequisite for a strong alliance, as they had thought. The American commitment to Europe's defence did not weaken after 1973 when the Nine were at odds with each other as well as the United States. Indeed the United States no longer seemed to regard European unity as an unmixed advantage from its own point of view, especially when the Europeans took an independent line on important international problems, as they did during the Middle East war in 1973.[11] Nor did Norway's path to a safe position in the alliance seem to have to go through Brussels, or even require closer ties with its European members. Norway's allies had not interpreted the referendum result as a sign that the country's ties with the West were in danger of being loosened. When the United States and EEC were locked in disagreements over Atlantic relations and the Middle East in 1973 and 1974, the Norwegians enjoyed the advantage of remaining uninvolved.[12] If proof were required of Norway's place in NATO's defence co-operation, this was reassuringly supplied when the Euro-group chose the Norwegian minister of defence as its chairman for 1974, the first time one of the alliance's smaller countries had held that post.[13]

At home too pro-market fears that the referendum might have signalled a rejection of the Atlantic alliance as well as the EEC were soon proved to have been greatly exaggerated. Such fears were certainly justified as far as some sections of anti-market opinion were concerned. But otherwise they had been largely a reflection of the pro-marketeers' own equation of EEC membership with strengthening the West and Norway's place in it. Most 'no' voters had made a clear distinction between the Atlantic alliance and the EEC. Indeed in many cases they had probably felt able to reject the latter very much because of the security provided by the former. Confirmation of this came from the public opinion polls taken after the referendum, which showed an even larger support for NATO membership than before.[14] For the government the polls were yet further reassurance that the referendum had not endangered the country's Atlantic orientation. Even Labour's left-wing, apart that is from the youth organisation, did not call for an end to Norway's NATO membership, and as the younger members had been calling for that since the late 1960s, it was nothing new. Most left-wingers could read the evidence of the polls and knew the leadership was unshakeable on this issue. They therefore concentrated on preventing the integration in defence matters being repeated in other areas like energy, and on trying to bring about a gradual re-orientation of the country's foreign policy by means of the positions adopted on other international questions like oil and the economic questions at issue between the industrialised and developing countries.

At least in the foreseeable future such a re-orientation away from the Atlantic alliance seemed out of the question. On the contrary, for most Norwegians the importance of NATO membership was being underlined in these years by several developments in the seas around them — developments which, taken together, were the third factor consigning relations with the EEC to a relatively subordinate area of Norwegian foreign policy. One of them was the expansion of the Soviet Union's northern fleet based on Murmansk, close to the Norwegian-Soviet border. By the early 1970s the ice-free waters between northern Norway and the Norwegian archipelago of Svalbard had become the transit route to and from the Atlantic for the major part of the Soviet Union's seaborne nuclear deterrent. At the same time the growing strength of the Soviet navy was threatening the credibility of NATO's ability to reinforce Norway by sea in times of crisis. Norway's strategic position, in other words, had become at once more important and more vulnerable.[15] The vital importance of the Barents Sea for the Soviet Union had also made it more difficult to resolve other issues in Norwegian-Soviet relations, among them the exercise of Norwegian sovereignty on Svalbard (where Soviet citizens outnumbered Norwegians), the extension of the two countries' fishing limits and delineation of their continental shelves, and the exploitation of the petroleum and mineral resources thought to lie on the shallow shelf beneath the Barents Sea. By the middle of the 1970s these questions had produced the most complicated and potentially most dangerous set of negotiations facing the Norwegian government. Together they made Norway's relations with the EEC appear comparatively unimportant.

So too did the resources in the seas around Norway. Like the developments taking place in the north, these had the effect of making NATO more important (because Norway now had more to defend and more potential sources of conflict with other nations) and generally diverting interest away from Western Europe.[16] The negotiations about extending Norway's fishing limits to 200 miles brought Norwegian-EEC relations back to the front pages at regular intervals over these four years. But the EEC was only one element in the complicated jigsaw of international negotiations about sea limits. Just as much attention was devoted to the negotiations going

214

on at UNCLOS and with the Soviet Union and the other North Atlantic littoral states.[17] Oil also placed heavy demands on political and public attention and on the country's diplomatic resources. There were the Norwegians' own debates about oil policy at home, while abroad oil opened up a whole new area of international diplomacy, from Western energy co-operation to establishing relations with other oil-producing countries. For a small nation with limited diplomatic resources this represented a very heavy additional call on its manpower and expertise. Combined with the parallel sea negotiations, the negotiations with the Soviet Union in the north, and the large United Nations conferences on north-south questions in which Norway was fully engaged, it left little time or energy for relatively problem-free areas like Western Europe.

Oil was anyway bringing the EEC to Norway, or at least some of its most important members, interested in oil and gas from the North Sea and offering industrial co-operation in return. Oil began to demonstrate its diplomatic as well as economic value. To many Norwegians it hardly seemed necessary to be particularly active themselves when their energy resources were winning them co-operation without much additional expenditure of diplomatic effort. The growth rates and rising living standards of these years had already convinced many that there were no problems for Norway outside the EEC anyway. So at a time when the government had many other important foreign policy questions to deal with and initiatives towards the EEC always involved the risk of arousing an anti-market outcry, oil came to be regarded as the card which would secure Norway all the co-operation and influence it wanted. There was a tendency to let oil be a substitute for diplomatic activity and for serious thought in Norway's relations with the EEC.

Much of the explanation of why Labour's promised 'active European policy' failed to live up to its description was thus to be found in Norwegian politics and in the general trend of the country's foreign policy under Labour. Too much obvious activity could have embarrassed the government at home. Domestic pressures diverted resources and activity elsewhere. After a year or so relations with the EEC no longer seemed so important nor the problems of being outside so serious as ministers had still thought when they took office. Events in other areas of Norwegian foreign policy soon came to dominate their horizons and the resources at their command. Nevertheless part of the explanation also lay in events in the EEC. During these years the EEC became at once less attractive and less threatening than it had appeared in the early 1970s, while its absorption in its own problems would have left it little time for responding to Norwegian initiatives anyway.

During the referendum campaign many Norwegians had based their arguments on the assumption that the EEC was irreversibly set on the road to economic and even political union, and to a role in international affairs commensurate with its size, trading strength and collective diplomatic experience. Even those who regarded the goal of economic union as unrealistic had expected the EEC's members to establish an ever closer degree of co-operation. It was not long, however, before these expectations were shown to have been unrealistic. Within a year of the Paris summit of October 1972 the Nine's ambitious plans had got bogged down in conflicting national interests and institutional inadequacies. Then came the Middle East war and OPEC oil embargo, which between them severely damaged the EEC's political credibility by demonstrating its disarray, its members' bitter disagreements over relations with the United States and Western energy co-operation, and its inability to influence major international events. What this did to the Nine politically, the subsequent recession did to their economic cohesion. By 1975 different inflation and growth rates and exchange rate instability had led to a widening divergence between its members' economies, which threatened even the existing degree of integration. Between the height of the oil embargo and trough of the recession came the long drawn out re-negotiation of Britain's terms of entry, with uncertainty hanging over Britain's continuation in the EEC until June 1975, when a referendum approved the revised terms. These years saw some progress. There was the EEC's foreign policy co-operation, for example, its trade and aid agreements with developing countries, its institutional developments, and its agreement on an external fisheries policy. But with the exception of the last of these, the progress was not in areas which offered any scope for an extension of Norwegian-EEC co-operation, even if the EEC had been ready to go much beyond the free trade agreement. Indeed the work required to make even this amount of progress only added to the EEC's concentration on its own affairs.

Apart from a few particular issues like fisheries and the working of the free trade agreement, both sides were thus on the whole absorbed by questions other than their relatively good relations with each other. On the Norwegian side moreover the EEC's many problems and failures made it seem a definite advantage to be outside such an organisation. It also seemed less important to be able to influence policy discussions which usually produced little in the way of concrete results. If the government was less active than it had said it would be, then one reason was that Norway's interests seemed less threatened by an EEC whose prospects of ever turning into a union receded with each new failure. Norway, it seemed, could safely afford to turn its attention elsewhere — to its oil, the north, the developing countries — because doing so would hardly endanger its interests to the south.

Government spokesmen continued to express regret about the obstacles to greater co-operation on the EEC's side. And they may well have been sincere. It was nevertheless a fact that these obstacles were very convenient for the government from one point of view. They spared it the political difficulties it would probably have encountered at home if the EEC had positively encouraged closer co-operation, or if its progress in these years had been such that a notable expenditure of diplomatic effort in Brussels had been necessary to protect Norway's interests. They also furnished the government with what became its standard answer to queries about why there was not more to show for its 'active European policy'. The obstacles, it would explain, lay not in Oslo, but in the EEC's many internal problems and its reluctance to enter into that type of formal co-operation on questions of mutual interest which Norway, on its side, had consistently expressed its wish to establish.[18]

Co-operation and communication

The government could point to some results however. In 1973 it had said it would try to expand Norway's co-operation and channels of communication with the Nine. As regards the first, although less progress had been made than the government seems originally to have hoped for, there had been a steady, if slow, increase in co-operation. The currency co-operation in the EEC's 'snake' was not an innovation, having been established before the referendum, but there had been a notable expansion of Norway's bilateral co-operation with EEC members, and towards the end of Labour's term of office there was the agreement to hold talks about shipping questions. The most striking advances, though, had been made in the area of off-shore resources, probably because it was here that Norway had most to offer the EEC, economic and technical developments having made close co-operation as much in the EEC's interest as Norway's. The exploitation of North Sea oil and gas drew Norway and the EEC countries into ever closer contact during these years. The Nine would be the major market and landing site for Norwegian production, and along with Norway's co-operation with other producers like Britain, this involved them in almost continual negotiations on a multitude of practical questions like pipeline laying, associated industrial production, and the defence of off-shore oil installations. The threat to fish stocks from over-fishing combined with the general move to wider national fishing limits in the mid-1970s made co-operation on such questions as conservation and the exchange of fishing rights and quotas another area of frequent contact. In both the energy and fishing sectors close functional co-operation had thus become a prominent feature of Norway's relations with the Nine by 1977.

Until halfway through Labour's term of office this co-operation in off-shore resources was primarily the responsibility of the governments in the individual North Sea states, negotiating with each other bilaterally. Some aspects of trading in fish were an EEC responsibility because fish was included in its free trade agreements with Norway and Iceland. The agreements had also established a link between the EEC's tariff concessions and their fishing limits. But the EEC had neither a common external fisheries policy nor an energy policy, and each government therefore remained responsible for negotiations with third countries about these matters. From the Norwegians' point of view this had certain advantages. It enabled them for example to offer different terms to individual members and to avoid the long delays associated with the EEC's preparation of a joint negotiating position.

In the energy sector this situation had not altered by 1977, but the effect of transferring responsibility for negotiations with third countries to the EEC had been demonstrated in the fisheries sector.[19] There the Nine had made the commission responsible for external negotiations the year before, and simultaneously begun the process of working out an external fisheries policy. The consequence had been to transform Norway's bilateral negotiations with states whose interests varied widely into a single set of negotiations in which Norway faced the EEC as a whole. The importance of Norwegian waters for EEC fishermen was sufficient to give the Norwegian negotiators a fairly strong position, and this would no doubt also be the case in the energy sector. But the EEC was a powerful *interlocuteur*. Not only did it have fish stocks on which some Norwegian fishermen were dependent for their livelihood. Its markets were of vital importance to other Norwegian exports apart from fish, and it was not inconceivable that in certain circumstances the EEC would use this fact as a lever when negotiating about fishing rights and quotas. The EEC was also a frustrating and time-consuming organisation to negotiate with because of its members' difficulties in resolving their own conflicts of interest. This too could adversely affect Norwegian interests because of the uncertainty and long delays it caused.

In the second area where the government had promised action, expanding Norway's channels of communication with the Nine, the situation remained on the whole much the same as before. While most EFTA countries had separate embassies in Brussels accredited to Belgium and the EEC, the one Norwegian embassy continued to be responsible for both. It was not even significantly enlarged after the trade agreement came into force, as was Sweden's for example.[20] The one new permanent representative appointed within the EEC area during this period was to the Council of Europe in Strasbourg in 1975.[21] The many other calls on Norway's diplomatic resources in these years was one reason for this. Another was that access to information about EEC affairs was not generally a problem. Very close contact on EEC questions was established between the Norwegian embassy in Copenhagen and the Danish foreign ministry. And in other EEC capitals information was also relatively easy to obtain, if not on as simple and routine a basis. Any difficulties the Norwegians experienced probably lay more in their own limited capacity for gathering, transmitting and processing all the information available to them.

The appointment of a permanent representative to the Council of Europe was officially described as an attempt to make better use of this forum as a meeting place for parliamentarians from the Nine and those Western European states outside the EEC.[22] It was certainly a safely uncontroversial step because the Council of Europe was exactly the type of international organisation of which anti-marketeers approved. How much the government really expected to achieve by it was another matter. Despite the publicity which attended the appointment, the government must have had few illusions about its value as regards strengthening contacts with the EEC or influencing EEC policies. The main aim was probably the more modest one of preventing any further weakening of the contacts in Strasbourg when the EEC's own assembly was directly elected.[23] However the very fact that the government was concerned about this indicated that it saw a need to keep in touch with EEC opinion and influence it where possible.

EFTA was another organisation which the Norwegians showed an interest in using in this way. The idea was aired occasionally by some of its members after 1973, although after the departure of Britain and Denmark and the conclusion of free trade agreements with the EEC the organisation seemed to have lost much of its *raison d'être*. Spurred on by the recession and by the fact that when free trade was established in July 1977 each EFTA state would still have to deal separately with the much more powerful EEC, the idea of using EFTA as a framework for joint contacts with the EEC was raised again in 1976. It found support from Norway.[24] The idea was to strengthen EFTA's own economic policy consultations and co-operation and then use the organisation to extend its members' co-operation with the EEC to questions beyond the free trade ag-

219

reements, especially to economic and monetary questions bearing on the major problems of inflation and unemployment.[25]

The proposal acquired more interest by coinciding with the launching of similar ideas by the Danes. To a certain extent the Danes were here merely continuing their traditional policy of trying to harmonise their Nordic and continental links by working to make relations between the two areas as close as possible. By 1976, however, the prospect of an enlargement of the EEC to include more Mediterranean countries had given them an additional motive for arguing in favour of an extension of the Nine's co-operation with EFTA, and especially its Nordic members. Such an enlargement would shift the EEC's centre of gravity southwards, a development which from Denmark's point of view would unbalance its economic interests and political character. The balance would be restored to some extent if the Nine simultaneously expanded their economic co-operation with the Nordic countries and strengthened and formalised the institutional base for this co-operation.[26]

From the Norwegian Labour government's point of view these were proposals which could provide an ideal way of bringing Norwegian views to bear on EEC economic policy discussions. Acting together the EFTA countries might hope to carry more weight in Brussels. Being within an EFTA framework the closer institutional links with the EEC would be less likely to arouse opposition at home. In particular the participation of Western Europe's neutrals would reassure any still watchful anti-marketeers that it was not a prelude to taking Norway into the EEC 'through the backdoor'. Norway's own freedom to determine its economic policy would, after all, hardly be circumscribed by what would amount to no more than regular consultations, with co-operation following if there was a coincidence of views and interests.

Norway and political co-operation

These proposals would provide no solution, however, to another problem mentioned by Trygve Bratteli in 1973, which as time passed seemed to be becoming more acute, not less. This was the EEC's political co-operation, in which Norway did not participate. The problem had intensified for two reasons. It was in this area that the Nine had made most progress since enlargement in 1973, despite the many well-publicised setbacks and failures. And the prospect of the EEC being enlarged to include two more NATO members, Greece and Portugal, meant that its foreign policy consultations might in the not too distant future extend to most of the alliance's European members.

It was the prospect of gradual diplomatic isolation that had been one of the pro-marketeers' main fears in 1972 when they stressed the political disadvantages of being outside the EEC. Another had been that the EEC's political co-operation might eventually come to include the security and defence questions inseparable from foreign policy.[27] At worst the pro-marketeers had envisaged this leading to a separate European defence community within the framework of NATO. Not quite as serious, but more likely, had seemed to be the prospect of European discussions about political and security issues being concentrated in the EEC's foreign policy consultations, leaving only the purely military matters to the Euro-group, the European countries' special forum within NATO. This, the pro-marketeers had thought, could eventually lead to political matters of concern to the whole alliance being discussed and decided in bilateral negotiations between the EEC and the United States, with the alliance's institutions merely giving them the formal stamp of approval.[28]

Once the referendum was over, the government of anti-market politicians formed to negotiate a free trade agreement showed that it too took these dangers to Norway's position seriously. The Korvald government devoted just as much effort to averting them as did Labour when it took over in October 1973.[29] After the 'no' to EEC membership there was no question of doing this by retaining Norway's link with the EEC's political co-operation in the way that the kroner stayed within the 'snake'. Even if the EEC had agreed to it, it would have been politically impossible in Oslo. So both governments could only counter these dangers within the alliance itself, where they concentrated on trying to keep Western security discussions within the alliance framework, and specifically European co-operation within the Euro-group. They even hoped to expand the Euro-group's role to include the discussion of general political and security matters in order to lessen the likelihood of a separate EEC-based defence co-operation developing outside it.[30]

Events in the eighteen months or so after the referendum made these anxieties about Norway's diplomatic position appear as exaggerated as the pro-marketeers' fears about the economic consequences of rejecting EEC membership. The Norwegians experienced some disadvantages in internal alliance negotiations. The Conference on Security and Co-operation in Europe provided an example of how they could find themselves left on the sidelines when the EEC managed to act as a bloc, and in the alliance negotiations about a new 'Atlantic declaration' they saw most of the exchanges concentrated between the EEC and United States.[31] But these last negotiations also demonstrated how deeply divided the Nine were over some major issues, and how unless they overcame their disagreements they would set narrow limits for any co-ordination of their foreign policies. Moreover the Middle East war and subsequent Western energy negotiations — two other outstanding examples of the EEC's difficulty in establishing joint positions — strengthened the United States' position of leadership within the alliance. The first demonstrated the Americans' global strategic capability while the European countries were in disarray.[32] In the second case it was the American government which took the initiative and forced the pace. By mid-1974 all the major questions facing the Western countries — defence, economic policy, energy — were thus being discussed and decided within the framework of the Atlantic alliance or the OECD. Any prospect of the EEC developing a separate identity in defence matters seemed to have been decisively checked.

Three years later the situation remained in many respects the same. The alliance appeared as united as it had ever been. American political and military predominance appeared as great as ever. The EEC's political co-operation had not expanded to include the discussion of defence questions. There was not even the beginning of an EEC defence policy, the differences between France and the other members of the alliance being only one of a number of apparently insuperable obstacles to this. Within NATO the Euro-group remained the main forum for European co-operation.

The new feature was the progress that had been made in developing the EEC's political co-operation in areas other than defence. With Britain's entry in 1973 all the large countries of Western Europe were involved. After February 1974 the British Labour government, although unenthusiastic about many other aspects of the EEC, soon came to value the extra weight which joint European action could give the United Kingdom in international affairs. West Germany's entry into the United Nations in September 1973 enabled the Nine to extend their co-operation to that organisation just at the time when north-south issues were bringing the United Nations back into the centre of international politics.[33] French diplomacy under President Giscard was less ostentatiously anti-American, and that in turn made co-operation between the EEC's three big members easier. With the establishment of the European council in 1975 moreover the heads of government were coming together three times a year. Abroad the Nine increasingly tried to act as a group, and although they frequently failed to do so the effort itself involved them in continuous consultations and exchanges of information. The questions brought within the scope of their political co-operation steadily increased as external events and the existence of internal common policies put pressure on them to find joint positions. Already having a common fisheries policy for internal waters, for example, they were forced by the actions of neighbouring states and changes in international law to evolve an external policy too. What had originally been a trade policy for the Mediterranean was turned into a search for a common political approach to the region as a result of the wars in the Middle East and Cyprus and the changes of regime in Greece, Portugal and Spain.

The opening of membership negotiations with Greece in 1976 and the Portuguese and Spanish applications in 1977 meant that Norway, Iccland and Turkey might one day be the only European NATO countries not participating in the EEC's political co-operation (and in Turkey's case, its association agreement held out the prospect of eventual membership). For Norway this underlined the fact that the dangers pointed to by the pro-marketeers in 1972 had not disappeared in the intervening five years. The EEC's political co-operation machinery was already the focal point for much diplomatic communication in Western Europe. After a further enlargement it would be even more so. If most European NATO states were participating in it, there was at least the possibility that at some time in the future the intensive rounds of discussions between EEC foreign ministers and officials would spill over into matters which formally belonged within the framework of the alliance. Important questions like north-south relations and energy would almost certainly continue to be handled in wider international organisations where Norway was represented because of the inadequacy of regional solutions. Even here however the trend towards regional preparations and negotiations between regional groups would make an enlarged EEC's political co-operation machinery the natural forum for such preparatory negotiations in Western Europe.[34]

Since the referendum the Norwegians had been able to counter-act their exclusion from the EEC's political co-operation by a variety of means. Bilateral contacts with individual EEC governments had supplemented the normal contacts in international organisations.[35] With at least one EEC country, Belgium, there were regular meetings between the political directors in the foreign ministries.[36] In Copenhagen political as well as economic information was available to Norway. With some members — Belgium, Denmark and Holland — Norway had established close co-operation on north-south issues. It was also not to be ruled out that the EEC's political co-operation would suffer a serious setback some time in the future if, for example, communist parties entered the governments of large community states like France and Italy. Such a turn of events would almost certainly impose a limitation on the subjects brought within its scope as well as the closeness of the political relations between the member governments. But if the EEC's political co-operation continued to intensify and then expanded to include more NATO states, the long-term outlook for Norway seemed indeed to be one of gradual isolation from the mainstream of diplomatic activity in Western Europe. The process would be slower, less dramatic and less obvious than some pro-marketeers had forecast in 1972, but the general trend would be the same.

In Oslo there did not seem to be any ideas about how to deal with this problem — or if there were, then they were not being openly discussed because the existence of such a problem was not acknowledged.[37] It was even possible that, outside the narrow circle of officials and professional diplomats, it had gone largely unnoticed, because most Norwegians' attention had been turned elsewhere since the referendum. Ideas were being floated in the EEC countries though, where some thought was being given to how their political co-operation might affect relations with allies outside the EEC. Some of these might have provided at least a starting point for any Norwegian discussions about how to minimise the disadvantages for themselves. There was the suggestion, for example, that the Nine develop a procedure for occasionally consulting allies whose interests would be affected by negotiations on which the EEC was about to embark, in order that it had their views available beforehand.[38] Another possibility had been mentioned by the Belgians with reference to Norway. This was that Norway be given some form of association with the EEC's political co-operation, not linked in any way to future membership.[39] The first idea offered only a very partial solution but would probably be acceptable within Norway. The second held out a closer and more continuous link with the EEC's foreign policy consultations, but could well be considered too sensitive politically even if accompanied by specific assurances that there was no question of it leading to membership. It would almost certainly be opposed by Labour's left-wing and anti-market opinion generally. The difficulties would be increased by the EEC's growing tendency to blur the lines between strictly EEC matters and political co-operation between the member states.

Such domestic difficulties would probably not in fact be the main obstacle to finding a solution. This would lie rather in recognising that there was a problem, which would intensify unless events in the EEC itself halted the trend to closer political co-operation and the community's enlargement, and that in their own interests the Norwegians needed to find a solution. The Labour government had already shown in the energy sector that, once it had taken this step and felt its position sufficiently strong at home, it was ready to pursue policies disliked by its left-wing and anti-marketeers. In 1974, when the Socialist Electoral Alliance was doing well in the polls and Labour badly, the government had drawn back from full membership of the IEA. Eighteen months later, the situation having in the meantime been reversed, the government decided to join the IEA's long-term energy programme despite the vocal opposition of these same groups. A change in the political situation could thus widen its freedom of manoeuvre in such controversial questions. So too could the way the government presented its policy. The scope of the energy and industrial co-operation being discussed with West Germany raised important questions about Norway's economic relations with the EEC. Yet the government successfully avoided anti-market opposition by presenting its use of oil and gas to obtain access to German capital and technology as a victory for Norway's new weight in international economic negotiations.

In both cases the government obviously understood the implications of the agreements it was entering into, but considered the agreements necessary if important Norwegian interests were to be protected. It was unclear whether the domestic constraints on its freedom of action would permit the government to establish an association with the EEC's political co-operation if it saw a similar need in the field of foreign policy. Much would depend on the circumstances and the way it was presented. In 1978 though there was still no sign that the government even perceived a long-term threat to Norwegian interests, let alone the need to contemplate such a politically delicate step.

10. Norway, the EEC and fishing limits

The main issue in Norway's relations with the EEC after the free trade negotiations was the question of fishing limits — the same one which had been uppermost in the membership negotiations. Whereas then, however, it had been Norway's exclusive rights within the twelve-mile limit which were at stake, after 1973 it was Norway's right to extend that limit even further out into international waters. The difficulties were caused by the fact that most of the Nine had important interests which would be affected by Norway's action, and they were compounded by the way in which the conflicts of interest ran between the Nine themselves, as well as between them and Norway. The EEC's importance for Norway was that the Labour government needed the EEC's agreement if it was to achieve one of its major objectives: the establishment of a 200-mile exclusive economic zone before the 1977 election.

One of the anti-marketeers' arguments against EEC membership in 1972 had been that Norway would be freer to extend its sea limits if it was outside the EEC. In the event it probably did not make very much difference to the date when the limit was finally established: both Norway and the Nine extended to 200 miles independently of each other on 1 January 1977. But the anti-marketeers' argument was proved right in some respects. In the three years before the Labour government judged an extension to be politically and legally possible, it had more scope for introducing internationally acceptable measures to satisfy its fishermen's demands for protection than it would have done if bound by the EEC's fisheries policy. That in turn helped it to stave off demands for precipitate unilateral action. The government was also able to open negotiations with other countries about an extension at an earlier stage than would have been possible from inside the EEC. And at UNCLOS the Norwegians were able to play an active and not uninfluential role in bringing about those changes in international law which were one of the pressures on the EEC to alter its position on 200-mile limits in time for its extension to coincide with Norway's.

So in a sense the Labour party after September 1973 enjoyed the diplomatic benefits of its defeat in the referendum, while the coastal fishermen who had done so much to defeat it enjoyed the fruits of their victory. Yet even as the new 200-mile limit was being established, some Norwegians were wondering whether there might not also be some disadvantages in playing this lone diplomatic hand in negotiations about sea resources and boundaries. For there were other Norwegian boundaries which remained in dispute: the negotiations about controlling and exploiting sea resources had by no means ended with the coming into force of its 200-mile limit. Whereas, however, time and the trend of international events had been on the Norwegians' side between 1973 and 1977, because their objective coincided with that of a majority of states in the international community, this would not necessarily be the case when the still outstanding issues came to be settled.

Norway and a new international law for the sea

In December 1970, a few months after Norway's negotiations for EEC membership began, the United Nations General Assembly adopted a resolution convening a third conference on the law of the sea.[1] The task of this conference would be to revise and complete the work of the previous two held in Geneva in 1958 and 1960. The preparations were given to a United Nations committee, and there negotiations continued during the three and a half years between the General Assembly's resolution and the conference's opening session at Caracas in June 1974. The pressures for a revision of the law of the sea came from several sources. The two previous conferences had left a number of important questions unresolved. Many of the newly independent developing states had different interests from those of the older maritime nations which had shaped the modern law of the seas. Technology had opened up the international seabed and continental shelves to exploitation, and thereby made the issues of controlling their resources and activity on them one of growing economic and political significance. Technology had also led to an expansion of many industrialised countries' distant water fishing fleets and of the volume of world fishing. These now threatened both the oceans' fish stocks and the livelihood of coastal fishermen throughout the world.

The conflicts of interest were numerous. Industrialised countries, possessing the means of exploiting the seabed and continental shelves and operating the ocean-going fishing fleets, faced developing countries which lacked the means to do either but wanted a share in the wealth of these resources; this the latter now hoped to gain both indirectly through international control and directly by extending their own national sea limits. States with long coastlines, wanting to gain control of the resources in the seas adjacent to them, faced countries which were landlocked or with only small coastlines. Maritime nations, vitally interested in maintaining the freedom of the seas, faced coastal states wanting sovereign jurisdiction over all shipping passing through the extended national zones they were claiming. Coastal fishing nations faced distant water fishers. Countries with wide continental shelves faced those with narrow ones or none at all. Many states, especially the most powerful industrial and maritime ones, had a variety of potentially conflicting national interests which they had to balance against each other. This only further complicated the work of a conference already made unwieldy by the large number of participating states — 147 met at Caracas — and the ambitious objective of creating a new law for the seas which would be acceptable to all these different interest groups.

UNCLOS had essentially three tasks. It had to delimit the areas of international and national jurisdiction; establish an international regime for the former; and define the precise nature of coastal states' rights within the latter. The main trend of the preparatory negotiations was to expand the area of national control and the rights of coastal states, at the expense of the international area and international jurisdiction. The trend was towards a nationalisation of the seas and their resources instead of the orderly international control which some had hoped would emerge. The main instrument of this nationalisation was the exclusive economic zone (EEZ) of 200 nautical miles. The EEZ won favour and finally triumphed over the initial opposition of many industrialised and non-coastal states, because it accommodated the interests of the conference's two strongest groups: the states which wanted a considerable extension of coastal state jurisdiction (many developing countries and some industrialised ones with long coastlines and rich exploitable sea resources) and the industrialised maritime nations (identical in some cases with the first group), which opposed any significant restriction on the freedom of shipping. These two groups were able to unite in support of the economic zone because it was essentially a resource zone. It gave exclusive rights to the living, mineral and petroleum resources in the seas up to 200 miles off a country's coast. But it did not confer the control over shipping inherent in the traditional concept of the territorial sea, which was to be no wider than twelve miles.

That was why by the middle of 1973 the Norwegian government had decided to support the economic zone.[2] As a state with both coastal and maritime interests Norway stood squarely on both sides of this particular divide. The economic zone offered a solution which would give Norway exclusive control over the resources off its own coast and yet protect its shipping from the interference of other coastal states. Neither the Korvald not Bratteli governments adopted the initially more cautious attitude of some other maritime nations towards greater powers for coastal states, and this illustrated the shift of priorities that had taken place as between Norway's coastal and shipping interests over the previous decade. The oil and gas on Norway's continental shelf had been one factor in this. Sovereign rights over these, however, had already been secured by the Geneva convention on the continental shelf of 1958. The main consideration in 1973 was the coastal fishermen, at once economically threatened by the international trawler fleets and politically strengthened by their victory in the referendum.

It was the Korvald government which took the decision to support a 200-mile economic zone at UNCLOS. After October 1973 the Labour government continued a policy which, apart from any other merits, offered an outstanding opportunity to regain the lost confidence of the fishermen before the 1977 election and relieve the immediate pressures on the Labour party's position in the north. For by then the fishermen's demands for protection and wider limits had intensified, especially as the autumn of 1973 had seen serious damage by trawlers to the coastal fishermen's nets.[3] Labour's main rivals in the north, the Socialist Electoral Alliance and Centre party, were both calling for a unilateral extension to fifty miles by January 1975 if the Caracas conference set for summer 1974 failed to provide the necessary basis for this step in international law.[4] The fishermen's organisation had agreed to wait for the outcome of that conference,[5] but it would almost certainly demand unilateral action too if the results failed to live up to its expectations.

Caracas was to show that events had moved much faster at the domestic level than they had internationally, and the government was to find itself balancing between these two levels for the next two and a half years, doing its best to restrain the first and accelerate the second in its effort to meet the fishermen's demands without endangering other Norwegian interests. That it finally succeeded was due to several things. It had luck. Events elsewhere served its purpose. It employed some skilful diplomacy abroad and political management at home. It was on the strongest side internationally. And Norway's rich fish resources gave it strong cards when it came to negotiations with other European countries.

No-trawling zones

Norwegian expectations were high when UNCLOS met at Caracas in June 1974. Many seemed to think it would produce so clear a con-

:sensus in favour of 200-mile exclusive economic zones that Norway would be able to extend its limit soon afterwards. They were disappointed. The trend towards economic zones was clear enough, but even among the states supporting the idea there were still serious disagreements about the precise character of the zones. The United States, the Soviet Union, and Britain, for example, accepted the idea but took a more restrictive view of coastal states' rights within the economic zones than did the developing countries or some industrialised countries like Norway. Most EEC members wanted to restrict the extent of the zones and the rights of coastal states even more.[6] A second conference session was planned for the spring of 1975 in Geneva and negotiations were to continue during the intervening six months. After Caracas, however, the Norwegians realised that their extension would be delayed for some years if they had to wait for an international convention on which to base it.

Some did not want to wait. Demands for a unilateral extension to fifty miles came from the Socialist Electoral Alliance, the Centre and Liberal parties, Labour's youth organisation and the coastal fishermen.[7] For a party as vulnerable as was Labour in the winter of 1974-75 it was very difficult to resist such pressure. Two other events increased it. In August the Icelandic government announced its intention of extending to 200 miles in 1975.[8] Then the Soviet Union withdrew from its 1974 Arctic cod quota agreement with Norway and Britain, setting off a further intensification of foreign trawler fishing in the north.[9] The government had been placing its hopes of damping pressures for unilateral action on Caracas and effective regional limitations on fishing off north Norway. Now both had failed to produce results, at least in the short term. The political and economic arguments for acting to alleviate the pressures on itself, its coastal fishermen and the endangered fish stocks were irresistible. The government's dilemma was that as yet neither international law nor state practice provided the basis for an extension, and the arguments against unilateral action were as overwhelming as was the necessity to do something.

One of these arguments was the EEC's likely reaction. Most of its members had just demonstrated at Caracas the reluctance with which they would agree to any significant extension of limits or coastal states' rights. Britain supported the economic zone and had similar interests to Norway, having at once a long coastline, rich off-shore fish and mineral resources, and major shipping interests.[10] But the way in which Britain had reacted to Iceland's extension to fifty miles in 1972 by providing naval protection for its fishing vessels showed that it would resist a unilateral extension which threatened its distant water fishing interests, and the British government was unlikely to make an exception for Norway, especially as doing so would weaken its negotiating position when Iceland moved to 200 miles in 1975. The EEC's reaction to Iceland's action in 1972 had been to suspend the tariff concessions in that country's free trade agreement — a particularly relevant point for Norway because of the terms of its own agreement. Apart from the dangers of provoking a 'cod war' and losing its tariff advantages in EEC markets, there was the real risk that one or more of the Nine would take Norway to the International Court of Justice, as Britain had done in Iceland's case. In July 1974 the ICJ had found against Iceland. Although it had not considered a fifty-mile limit to be illegal, a majority of the judges had found that in the existing state of international law a coastal state enjoyed only preferential not exclusive rights within this wider limit, and had therefore ruled that Iceland was bound to respect the historic rights of nations like Britain.[11] The Norwegian government interpreted this judgement as ruling out an extension of Norway's limit without the prior consent of the states affected by it, or until the development of international law or state practice had removed any possibility of Norway being taken before the ICJ and ruled against. Unlike Iceland, Norway recognised the jurisdiction of the ICJ. If the court ruled against it, the government would therefore have to choose between ignoring the judgement or obeying it. The first would mean breaking a cardinal principle of Norwegian foreign policy, respect for international law, while the second would be a severe political defeat and could mean postponing a Norwegian extension until after an international convention had been signed.[12] A final consideration was that the Norwegians had to fear retaliatory measures against their trawlers operating in British waters if they acted without at least Britain's prior consent. This was an important argument against unilateralism because Norway's southwest coast fishermen were dependent on the waters between twelve and fifty miles off Britain's coast.[13] They needed a guarantee that these waters would not be closed to them as a result of Norway itself extending to fifty miles.

However, possible EEC reactions were not the only arguments causing the government to resist unilateral action in the wake of the Caracas conference. The Soviet Union's attitude was equally, if not more, decisive. There were two reasons why Norway could not act without the Soviet Union's prior agreement in the Barents Sea. One was the area's strategic importance for the Soviet Union, which meant that Norway had to demonstrate extreme care in exploiting or exercising its claims over the resources there. The other was the unresolved dispute concerning the boundary between their continental shelves, which would in practice be the same as that between their fishing zones. Before extending, Norway had to find a solution to this problem, or at least some provisional arrangement pending a permanent solution. Negotiations on the boundary were due to open in November 1974, but the size, strategic importance and economic value of the area in dispute made rapid agreement unlikely. As for the Soviet Union's likely attitude towards a Norwegian extension, this was far from clear. The Soviets had moved closer to the 200-mile economic zone at Caracas, but with one of the world's largest navies and distant water fishing fleets the Soviet Union had an obvious interest in delaying any international move towards wider limits as long as possible, and then approving them only when an international convention had guaranteed the freedom of the seas so vital for its global naval activity.[14]

Finally, the government had to consider what the effect of unilateral action would be on the prospects for UNCLOS's success and Norway's position in the negotiations. Norway's long-term interests required the orderly development of a universally recognised body of international sea law because in the future, even more than in the past, so much of the country's economic and political activity would be bound up with the seas. Unilateral action could endanger this objective. It could also cost Norway the advantages it derived from its chief delegate's position as chairman of the small unofficial group of heads of delegation — the Evensen group — where many of the key articles for the proposed convention were originating, in particular those on the economic zone.[15] In the opportunities this offered for influencing the course of events lay a surer, safer and perhaps even faster way of gaining what the Norwegians wanted than by a precipitate extension which could provoke retaliation from the EEC and the Soviet Union.

The policy whereby the government hoped to reconcile these international constraints with the domestic pressures for immediate action was announced on 26 September 1974, a month after the Caracas session ended.[16] It had four points. The first three, which were presented as a three-stage plan of action, were the establishment of no-trawling zones off northern Norway before the end of the year, the introduction of a fifty-mile limit for all northern Norway as soon as possible in 1975, and the continuation of the work at UNCLOS for an international agreement on 200-mile economic zones. The fourth point was the principle that Norway would only act on the basis of international law and after consultation with the states affected by its measures. The first two steps were plainly designed to ease the pressing domestic demands, while the last point was intended to make these steps internationally acceptable. The no-trawling zones were essentially a means of meeting the coastal fishermen's demands for protection without being taken to the ICJ or coming into conflict with Norway's neighbours;[17] they would be non-discriminatory and apply only during the dark winter months. The commitment to establish a fifty-mile limit in 1975 was a concession to political necessity: without it the domestic political effect of the government's four-point programme would have been nullified. But it was a gamble on either UNCLOS or state practice moving fast enough to make such an extension possible, or else the pressures at home easing sufficiently to allow the commitment to be dropped when the time came. The government defended its decision to postpone extending to fifty miles on the ground of speed and effectiveness, arguing that whereas a general extension would take a considerable time to negotiate, no-trawling zones could be set up and recognised by 1 January 1975 after just a rapid round of consultations with the countries most concerned. In order to conduct the negotiations, Norway's chief delegate at UNCLOS, Jens Evensen, was transferred from his post as minister of trade to the newly created one of minister with special responsibility for law of the sea questions.

What were announced as mere talks, however, turned into intensive negotiations which delayed the establishment of the no-trawling zones by a month. And the difficulties lay in London, Bonn and Paris, not Moscow. Agreement with the Soviet Union was reached quite quickly, in December. This was partly because the negotiations were purely bilateral: there was none of the time-consuming travel between several capitals and co-ordination of different states' interests involved in dealing with the EEC. The main reason however was the Norwegian government's willingness to meet the Soviet Union's conditions quickly. These included a bilateral agreement on fisheries co-operation,[18] a reduction of one of the four proposed zones, Norwegian support in the North East Atlantic Fisheries Commission for a total catch level for Arctic cod in 1975 which was much higher than the Norwegians had wanted, and a larger share of this total for the Soviet Union.[19] Having secured these concessions, the Soviet Union announced that it would accept any subsequent agreement on no-trawling zones between Norway and the EEC[20] — which it could safely do because by then the EEC had shown it was going to adopt a more restrictive attitude towards the zones than the Soviet Union had done.

The reactions of Britain, France and West Germany were dictated by several factors. The most obvious was their interest in the waters which would be closed by the ban on trawlers. Calculations about the link between the zones and the Norwegians' next objective of a fifty-mile limit were also important however. So were considerations of what effect an agreement with Norway would have on the three countries' interests in other distant water fishing grounds, especially those off Iceland, and each member's view of how the Norwegian negotiations would affect its position when the EEC revised its own 1970 fisheries policy.

The three countries' fishing interests in north Norwegian waters were substantial. Britain took a third of its distant water catch there, France a half, and West Germany's modern fleet had just established itself as the fourth largest in the area.[21] All three governments were under pressure to protect their trawler industries' interests in the rich Norwegian fishing grounds, which Iceland's extensions were making even more valuable. The economic difficulties facing their fishing industries as a result of steeply rising costs combined with falling demand and prices made them even less sympathetic towards the Norwegian case than they would otherwise have been. So did the fact that low-price imports from Norway's heavily subsidised fishing industry were helping to depress profits in the countries Norway was now asking to agree to no-trawling zones.[22]

Moreover the zones were being described by the Norwegian government as the first move towards a fifty-mile limit. This would threaten the position of EEC fishermen in all north Norwegian waters. Here however Britain's position differed from those of France and West Germany. Britain, because of Norway's interest in waters close to its coast, expected little difficulty in negotiating reciprocal fishing rights as long as Norway's extension coincided with its own. The French and Germans, on the other hand, had nothing to offer the Norwegians and were unable to claim even historic rights; they could well find themselves excluded from Norwegian waters altogether. However, although the British would want an agreement on reciprocal rights at some time in the not too distant future, the British government's position in 1974 and 1975 was that Britain was not ready to extend its own limits, or recognise other countries' wider limits, until either a convention had been agreed at UNCLOS or there was a much greater degree of international consensus than existed after Caracas.[23] Nor did Britain want to see a Norwegian fifty-mile limit established until its bargaining position *vis-à-vis* the Norwegians had been strengthened by setting up one of its own. In the winter of 1974-75 therefore Britain was ready to join with France and Germany in insisting that the no-trawling zones should not acquire any features that could subsequently be interpreted as even an implicit acquiescence in the extension of Norwegian jurisdiction beyond twelve miles. If the Norwegians were granted jurisdiction in the zones, it would weaken the case of other countries if they wanted to contest a Norwegian fifty-mile limit. It would also weaken their position in dealing with Iceland, with which the Germans were still in dispute over the fifty-mile limit and Britain was already preparing to re-negotiate its two-year agreement, which would expire at just about the time Iceland planned to move to 200 miles.

This mixture of diverging and coinciding interests on the EEC's side was reflected in the way the negotiations were conducted.[24] The Norwegians wanted to negotiate separately with each of the three large countries and confine their contacts with the commission, representing the EEC, to a brief 'courtesy call'.[25] This was partly to speed matters up. Partly it was merely a correct interpretation of the division of competence at that time. The commission's responsibility was recognised on questions touching the internal common fisheries policy and trade aspects of external fisheries relations, but in their disputes with Iceland each member had negotiated separately before and was preparing to do so again. There seemed no reason why they should not act in the same way in Norway's case. The Norwegians also had a clear interest in retaining the possibility of bargaining directly with each member. It redressed the diplomatic balance, gave them scope to exploit the others' differing interests, and would enable them to negotiate bilaterally later about their extension to fifty or 200 miles. The last point was important because then they would not want to offer the same terms to all the Nine. Only Britain would be offered permanent fishing rights in Norwegian waters, on a reciprocal basis, while France and Germany would be offered merely transitional arrangements for phasing out their fishing altogether. In order to discriminate between the Nine in this way, however, the EEC member governments had to remain free to conclude separate agreements with Norway. If negotiations with third countries became a community matter, the Norwegians would either have to concede fishing rights to the whole EEC or forfeit their interests in British waters.

The British also had their reasons for wanting to keep these negotiations about no-trawling zones bilateral.[26] They would want to secure their position in Norwegian waters when wider limits eventually came, their bargaining position was good, and they also had an interest in reducing fishing off north Norway by relative newcomers like France and West Germany. The referendum on EEC membership was due in the summer of 1975, and any obvious diminution of sovereignty or provocation of the already dissatisfied fishing industry might strengthen opposition to membership. Moreover the government was already looking to the time when Britain would be extending its own limits. Britain would then want to negotiate not only about continued fishing in non-EEC waters, but also about its limits within what would become the community sea. For unless the 1970 common fisheries policy was re-negotiated, Britain, in a world of 200-mile zones, would find the fishing fleets of the other members working up to its shores after 1982. Unless Britain was able to secure a fairly wide exclusive zone, it would be unable to compensate British fishermen for their losses elsewhere or prevent a diversion of members' fleets to the fishing grounds off Britain's coast. The British fishing industry was demanding a 200-mile exclusive zone,[27] but whatever width the government finally settled for, there was a strong argument for not surrendering competence to the EEC in a matter where Britain's interests so clearly diverged from those of most other members.

France and West Germany, on the other hand, had more to gain in the long run from working within a community framework and presenting a common front to Norway.[28] Their bargaining position was not as strong as Britain's, and a co-ordinated policy would lessen the risk of a bilateral Anglo-Norwegian agreement on reciprocal fishing rights which would deprive the other members of the strongest card they had for securing continued access to Norwegian waters, namely Norway's interest in what would be a British 200-mile zone. Moreover the stronger the EEC's competence in the fisheries sector, the stronger would be their position *vis-à-vis* Britain when the same question of limits — which they wanted as narrow as possible — came up within the community context. In other words France and West Germany, like Britain, were negotiating with Norway about no-trawling zones with an eye both to their interests when Norway extended to fifty or 200 miles and to the time when the EEC's own fisheries policy came up for re-negotiation. The other EEC members with fishing interests off Norway — Belgium, Denmark and Holland — had even more reason to seek a strengthening of EEC competence in external fisheries questions. They too had nothing to offer the Norwegians, but they did have locally important fishing industries dependent on waters from which Norway intended to exclude them. Their only hope of avoiding this lay in negotiating as a community, using British waters and EEC markets as the two main means of pressure and insisting on non-discrimination as between the EEC's members.[29]

So British self-interest was the Norwegians' best hope for retaining bilateralism. On the particular issue of no-trawling zones, however, Britain's aims coincided with those of the other EEC states. It wanted to reduce their size and duration as compared with the original Norwegian proposal, and to deny the Norwegians jurisdiction within them. So although much of the negotiations did remain on a bilateral basis, the British government was willing to co-ordinate its position with the French and Germans[30] and to turn the final negotiating session in January into a quadripartite meeting in which the Norwegians faced the three EEC delegations. The Norwegians were also unable to avoid dealing with the EEC institutions. The smaller countries in particular insisted on this,[31] and were able to do so because Norway's trade agreement, with its tariff concessions for fish, had been concluded with the whole EEC. Eventually therefore the Norwegians found themselves negotiating with the three large EEC countries acting together and with the commission acting on behalf of the EEC. They also found themselves facing all the means of pressure, including threats about the ICJ, suspension of tariff cuts, and non-recognition of the zones, which the Nine had at their disposal.[32]

The final agreement reflected the diplomatic imbalance at a time when neither international law nor state practice had shifted decisively in the Norwegians' favour as regards granting greater rights to coastal states.[33] They had to accept the principle of flag state jurisdiction within the zones, reduce the number of zones from four to three, and cut the time they would be in force. Moreover the experience of negotiating this first stage did not augur well for the prospect of negotiating a fifty-mile limit in the near future. It was true that bilateralism had remained the main feature of the negotiations, that Britain was clearly aware of its need for an agreement with Norway, and that the EEC had allowed Norway to close off areas of the high seas for the exclusive use of Norwegian fishermen. But their position on the question of jurisdiction was hardly encouraging, while Britain had demonstrated its readiness to co-operate with its EEC partners on the question of limits if it seemed in its interests to do so, and the others had plainly seen the advantages to themselves of negotiating with Norway as a community. As the government moved on to its second commitment and deadline — a fifty-mile limit off north Norway in 1975 — the international and domestic pressures seemed as difficult to reconcile as they had been in the previous autumn.

Towards 200 miles

Within nine months of the no-trawling agreement the 50-mile commitment had been abandoned and replaced by one of going straight to 200 miles by the end of 1976.[34] The government's gamble of the previous autumn had succeeded. It had counted on either the international situation changing sufficiently to make a 50-mile limit possible, or else the domestic situation changing in a way that enabled it to avoid implementing the second stage when the time came. The first did not happen, but the second did. The government was thus spared the acute embarrassment it would have faced if both the international obstacles to action and the pressures for it at home had remained as strong as they were after Caracas.

A negotiated fifty-mile limit off northern Norway in 1975 was already regarded as an unrealistic aim by many politicians, and probably by the government itself, by the time the no-trawling zones were established in February.[35] The Nine were not ready to negotiate about it so soon after conceding the zones. Britain was in no position to do so until after the referendum had decided whether or not it was going to remain in the EEC. In the north the Soviet Union's attitude remained ambiguous, but the Norwegian government had to expect difficult negotiations in which Norway would not be able to force the pace. All the countries concerned, including the Norwegians themselves, were waiting for the next UNCLOS session at Geneva in the late spring before deciding what to do next.[36]

When the Geneva session was over in May the result represented a significant step forward in the long term but a disappointment as regards achieving the government's immediate objective. Geneva eased the obstacles to an extension slightly, but not sufficiently to undertake it in 1975. The principle of 200-mile economic zones had been incorporated in the single negotiating text which was the product of the session.[37] Partly because the zone's precise character was still in dispute, however, and partly because its final acceptance depended on agreement being reached on other outstanding issues, the economic zone articles remained no more than an informal basis for further negotiations. The result was a stalemate from Norway's point of view. An extension to 200 miles was not yet possible legally, but the idea of a fifty-mile limit had been overtaken by events.

In the meantime, however, the government's position at home had become easier. The fishermen's grievances had been at least partially assuaged by the introduction of the no-trawling zones and agreement on a new Arctic cod quota for 1975 in the North East Atlantic Fisheries Commission. In the middle of 1975 Labour started its climb back in the public opinion polls, and in the autumn local elections the Socialist Electoral Alliance did badly in the north despite its call for a unilaterally imposed fifty-mile limit. The other large parties in parliament could be more or less relied on to support the government in its rejection of unilateral action, even if they criticised its handling of the question in detail. The government had begun preparing public opinion not to expect a fifty-mile limit in 1975 almost as soon as the no-trawling zones were introduced,[38] though it accompanied this by regular assurances that preparations for negotiations about them were in hand.[39] By the summer with the international situation clearer and the government more confident of its ability to stave off the demands for action at home, ministerial statements became even more calculated to dampen expectations. In October, with the local elections behind it, the government felt itself secure enough to drop the fifty-mile commitment officially, despite

238

the fact that Iceland had declared its 200-mile limit on 15 October.[40] Indeed Iceland's action strengthened the arguments for caution by making the situation in the northeast Atlantic even more tense and complicated, as did the Soviet Union's official protest at Iceland's extension[41] and the hard line adopted by Britain.

The Labour government still felt under political pressure however. This was evident from the fact that once again it committed itself to a target date, with all the attendant dangers for its own credibility if it failed to meet the target and to Norway's relations with other countries if the pace of international developments was slower than it hoped. The feeling was understandable. Although the coastal fishermen's demands for wider limits had eased temporarily, the referendum campaign had shown that where fishing limits were concerned the Labour party was on dangerous ground. The Socialist Electoral Alliance had lost half its votes in September, but Labour had also done badly compared with previous local elections and there was a long way to go if it was to recover from 1973. Labour's political deadline for an extension was thus early 1977 at the latest — in time for it to make an impact on the election in September 1977.

The calculation on which the government based its target date was that even if an international convention had not been signed by early 1977, a consensus would have emerged that the legal basis for establishing 200-mile limits was strong enough to do so without waiting for that formality.[42] Pressures were building up for wider fishing limits in all the Atlantic littoral states. Once one or two governments of major fishing nations yielded to them they would immediately provide the precedents and arguments about self-defence with which the other governments could follow suit. This was because if one country's fishing banks were closed to the large trawler fleets, the pressure on resources would build up elsewhere — as Norway had seen after Iceland's extension to fifty miles and as Britain was experiencing in the North Sea as the Soviet and East European fleets moved into it in force. Now Iceland had extended to 200 miles. In the United States a law to establish a 200-mile economic zone was before congress. In Canada similar plans were even further advanced. In Britain the pressures on the government from its fishing industry were stronger than ever. And further south Mexico planned to introduce its 200-mile limit in the summer of 1976. So when the Labour government announced its revised programme in October 1975, there seemed at least a good chance that a general move to 200 miles would soon be underway in the Atlantic, with Norway only one of a number of countries, including the United States, taking that step.

The major uncertainty in this picture was whether the policies of the

Soviet Union and EEC would change fast enough to enable Norway to negotiate the agreements it needed with them before it extended. The Soviet Union had accepted Norway's request to open negotiations about an extension of Norway's fishing limit, but the negotiations about dividing their continental shelves in the north had made no progress in the year since the first meeting in November 1974. The EEC appeared an even greater problem. West Germany, one of the countries with a short coastline and very small continental shelf, was fighting a rearguard action at UNCLOS to prevent the economic zones becoming exclusive.[43] Even more serious, Britain had become involved in yet a third 'cod war' with Iceland in November 1975. As long as that lasted it would be very difficult for the British government to begin serious negotiations about recognising a Norwegian 200-mile limit or provide the basis for a reciprocal rights agreement by extending itself. So both in the north and south the Norwegian government was still essentially gambling on events somehow working in its favour over the coming year.

However, Norway's position at UNCLOS and as one of the major coastal and fishing nations in the Atlantic did give the government some opportunities for pushing events in the desired direction. At UNCLOS the Norwegians continued their efforts to create an international consensus on the outstanding issues and especially the economic zones. The spring 1976 session in New York produced a revised negotiating text for the international convention.[44] The next session, in the autumn, was a disappointment, producing only a renewed attempt by states like West Germany to secure some legal rights to the resources of the areas soon to be nationalised.[45] This lack of progress at UNCLOS was potentially serious for the prospect of achieving that agreed body of international sea law which it was in Norway's long-term interest to see established. It was less important, however, for the Labour government's immediate objective of obtaining a 200-mile limit by the end of 1976. Here state practice increasingly fulfilled its hopes by forging ahead of UNCLOS, with the Norwegians encouraging this with whatever influence they possessed. Announcing their own deadline was one means of pushing the process forward, in that it contributed to the pressures on other governments to extend and to the dangers and examples to which they could appeal in order to support their action. Norway's bilateral agreements with other states — with Canada in December 1975 and Iceland in March 1976[46] — also eased these countries' extensions and thus in turn Norway's own. By spring 1976 Canada and the United States had both announced dates for establishing economic zones, 1 January and 1 March 1977 respectively. The second announcement was the decisive one. Once the United States' law establishing an economic zone had been passed by congress and signed by the president, the Norwegians knew that it was only a matter of time before all the other Atlantic states followed.

Helping to push developments forward in this way was one of the most effective, if indirect, means the Norwegians had of securing an agreement with the Soviet Union. The Soviet Union's interest was to retard extensions as long as possible, but it shared the Norwegians' concern to exclude from the Barents Sea the foreign trawler fleets which would soon be diverted there from other parts of the Atlantic. The negotiations for an agreement to regulate the two countries' fisheries relations after the establishment of 200-mile limits began in October 1975 and were successfully concluded a year later, the gathering momentum of state practice all the time working for the Norwegians.[47] It helped too that, as during the earlier negotiations on no-trawling zones, the government was ready to give the Russians generous terms as regards the division of fish resources in the future Norwegian zone in order to secure a speedy agreement.[48] Even more important was the fact that in order to avoid delays it was ready to separate the immediate issue of a 200-mile economic zone from that of the disputed continental shelf boundary. It was the Norwegian government which proposed temporarily turning the disputed area into a 'grey zone' for fishing purposes, with all those features of bilateralism and imprecisely defined jurisdiction which it was otherwise one of Norway's guiding principles to avoid in its relations with the Soviet Union.[49]

To the south as well Norway's surest means of gaining EEC recognition of its economic zone was to reinforce the pressures building up on the Nine to establish their own. Here Britain was the key country from the Norwegians' point of view. It was continued access to a future British zone that Norway needed to secure, and as the EEC country most vulnerable to the rapidly developing threats to its coastal and distant water interests, Britain was the large member most interested in driving the others the way Norway wanted them to go. Even before Caracas the British government had recognised the country's interest in having a 200-mile economic zone, for defensive and bargaining purposes and in order to be able to compensate its fishing industry in British waters for what it was going to lose elsewhere. In April 1975 the British government had secured the other EEC countries' agreement to a revision of the common fisheries policy, in which Britain's aim was to win acceptance of permanent national coastal zones within EEC waters.[50] But Britain was prevented from forcing the pace of the EEC's extensions until well into 1976 by its conflict with Iceland. Not until spring 1976 — under heavy pressure from NATO allies, with the United States' 200-mile law through congress, its EEC partners having settled with Iceland,[51] and the British fishing industry pressing for an economic zone of its own — did the British government seriously move to end the conflict. It was then that the Norwegian government acted as mediator and host for the Anglo-Icelandic agreement signed in Oslo on 1 June 1976. From the Norwegians' point of view it was as much an act of self-help as help for its NATO allies. For by disentangling the British from the Icelandic conflict, the Oslo agreement at last freed them to press for the rapid establishment of 200-mile limits by the EEC.

By mid-1976 there were thus strong forces within the EEC working for 200-mile limits, including Britain, France, Eire, and the commission. The principle as such had been accepted some months earlier as part of the revision of the common fisheries policy begun in response to British urging in 1975. But there remained formidable obstacles in the way of the agreements Norway wanted with the Nine. As during the negotiations about no-trawling zones, Norway's negotiations had become entangled in the EEC's internal disagreements. The difficulty was that the EEC was having to negotiate as a community with the outside world at the same time as it was revising its own common fisheries policy. This greatly complicated matters for the Norwegians, causing long delays and creating uncertainty about what EEC policy was and where competence to conduct the negotiations lay.

The Norwegians' aim in October 1975 had been to obtain separate agreements with each EEC country, based on the articles of the UNCLOS negotiating text, which gave coastal states the exclusive right to exploit the resources in their zones or grant other countries access to them. Britain was to be offered continued fishing rights in Norway's zone in return for similar guarantees for Norway's trawler fishermen in Britain's zone. The other EEC members would be offered transitional rights for a limited period.[52] As in the winter of 1974-75, the Norwegians wanted to keep the negotiations bilateral, and for much the same reasons: speed, the actual division of competence as between the EEC and member states when Norwegian policy was being drawn up in 1975, and the opportunity bilateralism offered for exploiting the Nine's different interests. In October 1975 moreover it seemed that this might well be possible. The Nine were still negotiating individually with Iceland, and by appealing to British self-interest Norway's offer seemed likely to split the Nine and prevent them from forming a common front.

But this plan was frustrated. The Norwegians' initiative to open bilateral negotiations early in 1976 coincided with a decisive move towards transferring responsibility for negotiations with third countries to the community institutions. Moreover the British government was the prime mover in this, despite the fact that Britain stood to gain most from the Norwegians' proposals. Until January 1976 Britain seemed ready to negotiate with Norway bilaterally. Then its position suddenly altered.[53] The abruptness of the change demonstrated how unclear and poorly co-ordinated British policy was during this transitional period, but the change was in fact the culmination of a gradual development in which the British government had come to see Britain's fishing interests as best served by acting within an EEC framework. This was partly because it was expected to strengthen Britain's position *vis-à-vis* third countries, especially powerful ones like the Soviet Union. It also reflected, however, a shift of priorities as between Britain's distant water fishing interests and the opportunities offered by its own rich coastal waters.[54] In this respect the timing of Britain's decision to break off preparations for bilateral negotiations with Norway and deal through the EEC instead was significant. It coincided with the publication of commission proposals which showed that the latter had moved closer to Britain's position on two important questions, namely support for 200-mile economic zones and coastal belts for member states.[55] This made it easier for Britain to accept a third commission recommendation, that it be given responsibility for negotiations with third countries. Accepting commission competence in external negotiations might also help to bring the commission onto Britain's side in the coming internal EEC battle over the precise width of the coastal belts. Indeed the British government made it clear that it saw a direct connection between its willingness to forgo the obvious advantages of a bilateral agreement with Norway and the extra compensation it was seeking for its fishermen in Britain's own 200-mile zone.[56]

The Nine approved the commission's three proposals in principle early in February 1976.[57] This was a step forward for Norway in one respect, because with the EEC supporting 200-mile zones Norway could hope for its recognition of a Norwegian zone. It had the immediate effect, however, of further delaying and complicating Norway's negotiations with the EEC. For despite the February decision, the location of competence to negotiate with Norway was unclear. In principle the member states had transferred it to the commission, but the commission had no mandate to negotiate with Norway about reciprocal rights and quotas, because the council of ministers had not yet settled the date of the EEC's extension to 200 miles or the details of its revised fisheries policy. Nor would the commission receive such a mandate until these disputed issues had been resolved. They could not be settled, however, until several obstacles had been removed. The British were still locked in their conflict with Iceland. Some EEC members were still waiting to see what came out of the spring 1976 session of UNCLOS. And a compromise would have to be found between the demand of Britain and Eire for wide coastal belts and the other seven members' insistence on narrow ones.[58]

So during the four months between the Nine's decision to allow the commission to negotiate on their behalf in February and the Anglo-Icelandic agreement in June, the Norwegians were in practice unable to negotiate properly with either the commission or the individual member states.[59] They began exploratory technical talks with the commission aimed at speeding up negotiations if or when the commission eventually received a mandate. These talks had to be based on the community principle that any Norwegian offer would be made to the Nine as a whole and could not differentiate as between one member and another.[60] At the same time the Norwegians continued their bilateral contacts with the individual governments and even their attempts to conclude bilateral agreements with them.[61] These made little headway however. Draft agreements were sent to Britain, France, and West Germany, but in each capital the prevailing view was in favour of observing the February 1976 decision to transfer competence for negotiations with third countries to the community.[62]

Any lingering hopes of a separate agreement with Britain appeared to be extinguished after the ending of the Anglo-Icelandic dispute in June. British ministers threatened a unilateral British extension if EEC action was long postponed, but their real purpose in doing so was obviously to speed up EEC policy-making and EEC extensions. On the other hand, Norway's negotiations with the EEC now seemed to have a chance of making progress at last. Besides urging the other members to establish their 200-mile economic zones as soon as possible, Britain was insisting on high priority being given to negotiations with third countries: with Iceland in the first place in order to renew the six-month Oslo agreement due to expire in December, but also with Norway. In order that the EEC could do this, Britain was also pressing harder than ever for those decisions on the EEC's fisheries policy which were a pre-requisite for any agreement with Norway.[63]

Britain's first aim, to get a date fixed for establishing the EEC's 200-mile economic zones, was achieved on 31 October, when the council of ministers set 1 January 1977.[64] By then the Norwegian government had already announced 1 January as the date for Norway's extension too, and had successfully concluded the negotiations with the Soviet Union.[65] The EEC's decision therefore assured the Norwegians that their new limit would be recognised and respected by all the European countries affected by it. With that the major part of their objective had been secured. It had been secured moreover without provoking any of those dangers which had still seemed very real just a year before: without being taken to the ICJ, without the loss of Norway's tariff advantages in EEC markets, and without the confrontations and displays of force which had followed Iceland's extensions. And it was on time to meet both the government's official target date and Labour's political deadline.

But the Norwegians still did not have an agreement regulating their fishing relations with the EEC after 1 January 1977, although by then they had been seeking one for over a year. The EEC was supposed to be giving priority to negotiations with Iceland and Norway, but in Norway's case the Nine's inability to resolve their own disagreements continued to make it impossible for the council of ministers to give the commission a negotiating mandate.[66] While the Norwegians waited, the Nine went on inconclusively debating the claims of Britain and Eire to coastal belts wider than the twelve miles which the commission, to their disappointment, had finally proposed.[67] As long as Britain and Eire maintained their demand and the other members resisted it, there was no basis for discussing an exchange of fishing rights with Norway, because the commission was unable to enter into formal negotiations. The outcome of this internal dispute would determine whether there existed a basis for a Norwegian-EEC deal at all. Norway wanted a guarantee of continued access to the waters between twelve and fifty miles off Britain's coast.[68] But if Britain's demand for a variable exclusive coastal belt of between twelve and fifty miles was granted and this belt were to extend to fifty miles in the traditional areas for Norwegian fishing, the EEC would be unable to offer Norway anything in return for fishing rights in Norway's zone, and there would therefore be no scope for an exchange of rights. The Norwegians' situation in these negotiations was not without its irony. Had they been in the EEC themselves, they would undoubtedly have adopted the same position at Britain and Eire. Outside it, Norway's interests would be best served by an EEC fisheries policy as *communitaire* as possible unless, of course, Britain were to abandon its policy of negotiating with Norway through the EEC, and seek a bilateral agreement after all.

The Nine's disagreements continued to delay negotiations with Norway throughout the remainder of 1976. When 1 January 1977 arrived, they had still not progressed beyond the level of informal preparatory discussions. Each side, however, had a genuine interest in reaching an agreement, so it was not difficult to decide to 'stop the clock' in traditional EEC fashion and allow fishing to proceed on the previous basis for the first few months of 1977 while efforts went on to resolve the outstanding questions between the Nine themselves and between the Nine and Norway.[69] When the new limits came into force, uncertainty about the future of Norwegian fishing in British waters had not been removed, as the government had hoped it would be. But the considerable fishing interests of Britain and the other members in Norwegian waters gave the Norwegians reasonable grounds to hope that a satisfactory agreement from their point of view would eventually be reached, either with the Nine or with Britain alone.

Just four years after the referendum in which much of the debate had turned on exclusive national control within a twelve-mile limit and what would happen after 1982, both the limit and the date had been entirely overtaken by events. At the same time developments in the law of the sea had given the coastal fishermen even more reason to oppose membership if the subject was ever raised again. For after 1 January 1977 they had a permanent, exclusive, and undisputed 200-mile limit, while in the British fishing industry's struggle for a mere fifty-mile coastal belt they saw what their own position would have been if they had lost the referendum. As long as Norway's fishing industry retained its importance for regional settlement, and thus its disproportionate weight in national politics, the slogan of inviolable national fishing limits would probably remain as effective as it had been in 1972.

The coastal fishermen had done well out of the referendum and the subsequent changes in the international law of the sea. The Labour party had also been able to use the extension of Norway's limits to re-establish its political position in the fishing communities. Norway's national position seemed to have been strengthened too insofar as it now possessed greater resources and controlled large areas of sea around its coast. From a long-term point of view, however, the new situation was not without its problems, even for the fishermen themselves. One was that although the new economic zone was legally exclusive, the fishing within it would in practice be influenced by decisions taken by countries with adjacent zones and by Norway's agreements with them. In the North Sea this was the EEC, in the Barents Sea the Soviet Union. Both were powerful negotiating partners. The EEC's decisions about catch levels and quotas, in which politics as well as resource considerations would play a part, would necessarily affect the level of fish stocks and fishing in Norway's part of the North Sea. And although there would of course be almost permanent consultations on these matters, Norway, being outside the EEC, would have only a limited influence on their fisheries policies. In the Barents Sea the concessions which the Norwegian government had felt obliged to make in 1974 and again in 1976 demonstrated how extraneous political and strategic considerations would affect Norway's bargaining position when it came to fisheries questions.

246

Also in the Barents Sea, the Norwegians still had to settle their continental shelf boundary with the Soviet Union. The 200-mile limit had made an agreement even more urgent if Norway was to avoid an indefinite period of uncertainty, tension and blurred jurisdiction.[70] On this particular question, however, neither of Norway's usual means of redressing the diplomatic balance, international law and the backing of its allies, could be counted on. The median line principle which Norway was maintaining against the Soviet Union's sector line principle had been weakened at UNCLOS, and the Norwegians did not appear to have any assurances of support from the United States or Western Europeans. Involving the United States overtly in this boundary dispute — indeed any Norwegian dispute with the Soviet Union in this area — would anyway be highly questionable from the Norwegian point of view, because it could raise the level of tension dangerously in an area where Norway was intent on keeping it as low as possible. It might have been possible to involve the EEC without having this effect because it was not a military organisation, and as an EEC member Norway might have been able to strengthen its bargaining position by calling the EEC into negotiations which after 1 January 1977 would have concerned the limits not only of Norwegian but community jurisdiction. As it was, none of the EEC countries seemed to have any interest in becoming involved in a boundary dispute with the Soviet Union in this faraway northern region.

This was only one issue on which the Norwegians, having opted in 1972 for the maximum possible independence and exclusive control of their own resources, would have to face the Soviet Union alone in an area where their joint land and sea frontier now stretched for several thousand miles. An historic shift in Norway's territorial interests and responsibility had taken place in the 1970s, the effect of which was to bring them into closer and more extensive contact with the Soviet Union than ever before. Yet apart from the overarching protection of the United States' nuclear deterrent the Norwegians were very much on their own in dealing with the many problems this would raise. That was doubtless how many of them preferred it to be, partly out of a wish to retain national control over the policies pursued in the region, partly because it was thought less likely to provoke the Soviet Union. It was nevertheless a situation which opened up new dangers and uncertainties for Norway. It was also likely to draw the Norwegians' attention even further away from Western Europe than the referendum had already done — unless the process was reversed by unforeseen events or by a radical rethinking in Norway itself.

References and notes

PREFACE

1 There are exceptions. See J. J. Holst 'Norway's EEC referendum: lessons and implications' *The World Today* March 1975 p 115; and Nils Peter Gleditsch and Ottar Hellevik *Kampen om EF* (Oslo 1977). The appearance of the second is particularly interesting because the authors opposed EEC membership in 1972. It is the first serious attempt in Norwegian to describe the referendum campaign, and perhaps a sign that the inhibitions of the intervening five years are at last breaking down.

2 See for example *St meld nr 75 (1976—77) Langtidsprogrammet 1978—1981* published by the Labour government prior to the election in 1977

3 The outstanding recent example is the postponement of exploratory drilling for oil off northern Norway, planned for 1978, before the 1977 election. Drilling is opposed by, among others, the coastal fishermen on whose votes the Labour party is dependent in the north.

4 See chapter 9

INTRODUCTION

1 Ottar Hellevik and Nils Petter Gleditsch 'The Common Market decision in Norway: a clash between direct and indirect democracy' *Scandinavian Political Studies* vol 8 1973 p 228

2 Willy Martinussen, author of *Fjerndemokratiet* (Oslo 1973), quoted in *Dagbladet* 31 January 1972

3 This fear of 'loyalty to Bratteli' runs through the diary of a Labour member of parliament who opposed EEC membership, Arne Kielland *All makt? Dagbok fra Stortinget* (Oslo 1972)

4 Henry Valen 'Norway's "no" to EEC' *SPS* vol 8 1973 p 221

5 See for example Håkon Lie 'Hva var det egentlig som skjedde?' *Internasjonal Politikk* no 4B 1972 pp 783—94; Egil Sundar 'Folkeavstemningen og politikernes ansvar' *IP* no 1 1973 pp 123—27

6 Holst, *The World Today* March 1975 p 117; Valen, *SPS* vol 8 1973 p 215

7 Support for this view is found in Willy Brandt *Begegnungen und Einsichten. Die Jahre 1960—1975* (Hamburg 1976) p 332. When Brandt visited Oslo shortly before the referendum, the prime minister Trygve Bratteli, told him that he had never known such a 'schwer erfassbare politische Situation'.

8 Lie, *IP* 4B 1972 pp 788—89; commentary by Arve Solstad in *Dagbladet* 26 September 1972

9 See Björn Björnsen and Geir Övrevik, *Hvem løy? Referat av saken mellom Arne Haugestad og Aftenposten/Erling Norvik* (Oslo 1973); Sundar *IP* no 1 1973 p 126; Lie *IP* 4B 1972 p 790

10 See for example Nils Petter Gleditsch 'Generaler og fotfolk i utakt' *IP* 4B 1972 pp 798, 804; Daniel Heradstveit 'The red/green alliance in Norwegian politics: a strange partnership' *Norway's no to Europe* International Studies Association (United States 1975); Arild Underdal 'Diverging roads to Europe' *Cooperation and Conflict* 1/2 1975 pp 65—76

11 For a later, succint exposition see Jens A Christophersen 'Valget 1975. Tilbake til det normale?' *Samtiden* 1 1976 pp 4—12

12 Sivert Langholm 'On the concepts of center and periphery' *Journal of Peace Research,* 8 no 2-4 1971; Arne Kielland 'Skillelinjer i norsk politikk' *Samtiden* no 6 1971 pp 348—59; Gleditsch *IP* 4B 1972; Ottar Brox 'Hva hendte i Norge 25. sept. 1972' *IP* 4B 1972 pp 771—82; Hellevik and Gle-

ditsch *SPS* vol 8 1973 pp 227—35
13 Valen *SPS* vol 8 1973 pp 215—17
14 *ibid;* for the history and character of this town-country axis in Norwegian politics see Stein Rokkan and Henry Valen 'Regional contrasts in Norwegian politics' pp 190—247 in Allardt, E. and Rokkan, S. (eds.) *Mass Politics. Studies in Political Sociology* (New York 1970); Philip E Converse and Henry Valen 'Dimensions of cleavage and perceived party distances in Norwegian voting' *SPS* vol 6 1971 pp 108—52

CHAPTER 1

1 For descriptions of the Norwegian economy in English see Fritz Hodne *An Economic History of Norway 1815—1970* (Trondheim 1975); T K Derry *A History of Modern Norway 1814—1972* (Oxford 1973); Sigurd Ekelund *Norway in Europe. An Economic Survey* (Oslo 1970); Brian Fullerton and Alan F Williams *Scandinavia* (London 1972); Per Kleppe *Main Aspects of Economic Policy in Norway since the War* (Oslo 1968). In Norwegian useful surveys are contained in *St meld nr 50 (1971—72) Om Norges tilslutning til De Europeiske Fellesskap* and *St meld nr 67 (1974—75) Norsk industris utvikling og framtid*
2 Ekelund *Norway in Europe* p 8
3 Two books which gave impetus to the debate and were influential in circles which later opposed EEC membership were Ottar Brox *Hva skjer i Nord-Norge?* (Oslo 1966) and Hartvig Seatra *Den økopolitiske sosialismen* (Oslo 1973)
4 Eklund *Norway in Europe* p 8
5 Derry *A History of Modern Norway* p 118
6 *St meld nr 50 (1971—72)* p 78
7 *ibid* p 80
8 Kleppe *Main Aspects of Economic Policy* pp 17—18
9 Derry *A History of Modern Norway* pp 191—96
10 *ibid* pp 196—200; *St meld nr 67* (1974—75) p 36
11 Ekelund *Norway in Europe* pp 46—47. The state purchased half of Alcan's shares in 1975
12 *St meld nr 95 (1969—70)* and *St meld nr 76 (1970—71) Undersøkelse etter og utvinning av undersjøiske naturforekomster på den norske kontinentalsokkel m. m.*
13 *St meld nr 50 (1971—72)* p 59; Knut Frydenlund *Norsk utenrikspolitikk i etterkrigstidens internasjonale samarbeid* (Oslo 1966) pp 118—19
14 *St meld nr 92 (1969—70) Om Norges forhold til de nordiske og europeiske markedsdannelser* p 3
15 Kleppe *Main Aspects of Economic Policy* p 17
16 Ekelund *Norway in Europe* p 60
17 *St meld nr 50 (1971—72)* p 11
18 Ekelund *Norway in Europe* pp 45—46; *St meld 50 (1971—72)* pp 59, 69—70
19 *St meld nr 67 (1974—75)* pp 4—6, 48—50; *St meld nr 92 (1969—70)* pp 4—17
20 Ekelund *Norway in Europe* p 65
21 *ibid* p 65; Valter Angell 'Om skandinavisk inntreden i fellesmarkedet uten Storbritannia' *IP* no 5 1968 pp 442—45
22 *St meld nr 50 (1971—72)* pp 67—69
23 Ekelund *Norway in Europe* pp 65, 71
24 *UD-informasjon nr 9* 21 February 1972

25 Ekelund *Norway in Europe* pp 25, 90

26 *UD-informasjon* nr 9 1972; *St meld nr 50 (1971—72)* p 94

27 *ibid* p 62

28 Ekelund *Norway in Europe* pp 20—26; for details of the subsidies to agriculture see *St meld nr 92 (1969—70)* pp 40—41

29 *ibid* p 39

30 See the section on politics in this chapter

31 Ekelund *Norway in Europe* p 25

32 *St meld nr 50 (1971—72)* pp 92—93

33 Ekelund *Norway in Europe* pp 26—32

34 15 per cent on frozen fish fillets and 20—25 per cent on tinned fish, *UD-informasjon* nr 9 1972

35 *Uttalelser vedrørende Norges stilling til de europeiske fellesskap. Særskilt vedlegg 111 til St meld nr 86 for 1966—67* pp 19—20

36 Kleppe *Main Aspects of Economic Policy* pp 6—11

37 The average for the 1960s was 4.75 per cent a year, *St meld nr 50 (1971—72)* p 60

38 Kleppe *Main Aspects of Economic Policy* p 8

39 Henry Valen and Stein Rokkan 'The election to the Norwegian Storting in September 1968' *SPS* vol 5 1970 p 290; see also Rokkan and Valen 'Regional contrasts in Norwegian politics'; Henry Valen and Stein Rokkan 'Cleavage structures and mass politics in a European periphery: Norway' in *Electoral Behaviour: A Comparative Handbook* ed R Rose (New York 1974); Converse and Valen *SPS* vol 6 1971

40 Jahn Otto Johansen 'Norge' pp 15—60 in *Kommunismen i Norden* ed Åke Sparring (Oslo 1965)

41 Ragnar Kvam jr *DNA mot splittelse. Da venstrefløyen ble ekskludert og SF stiftet* (Trondheim 1973)

42 John Lyng *Mellom øst og vest. Erindringer 1965—68* (Oslo 1976) pp 9—50; Arve Solstad 'The Norwegian coalition system' *SPS* vol 4 1969 pp 160—67

43 For an historical account see Derry *A History of Modern Norway* chapters 2, 5—6 and 10; also Henry Valen and D Katz *Political Parties in Norway* (Oslo 1964) pp 12—41

44 Derry *A History of Modern Norway* pp 27—29, 51—59

45 Valen and Katz *Political Parties in Norway* p 25

46 Exceptions were, for example, the alliance between the Conservatives and the 'moderate' Liberals in the 1890s and the 1930 election in which the non-socialist parties campaigned in a common front against the Labour party, *ibid* p 29

47 *ibid* pp 26—28 for the effects of proportional representation on the Norwegian political system

48 For the details see Stein Rokkan and Torstein Hjellum 'The Storting election of September 1965' *SPS* vol 1 1966 pp 237—45

49 After the 1961 election, Labour had seventy-four seats, the four non-socialist parties also had seventy-four, and the SPP had two. Thus the SPP held the balance. Following a serious accident in the state-owned coal mine at Kings Bay on Spitzbergen, the SPP joined with the non-socialists to defeat the minority Labour government on a motion that it had failed to implement parliament's instructions regarding safety measures. The non-socialist parties thereupon formed a minority government with John Lyng as prime minister. After about a month the SPP joined with Labour to defeat it in parliament and Labour returned to office.

50 Valen and Katz *Political Parties in Norway* pp 23, 36

51 *ibid* pp 23—28

52 Rokkan and Valen 'Regional contrasts in Norwegian politics' p 216
53 Olav Brunvand *Fra samspill til sammenbrudd* (Trondheim 1973); Valen and Rokkan *SPS* vol 5 1970 p 288
54 *ibid* p 292. In percentage terms the losses looked less serious, the Liberals falling from 10.5 to 9.38 per cent of the vote. The explanation for the losses in the southwest appeared to lie in the running conflict between 1965 and 1969 between the CPP minister for education and culture and the Liberals' radical wing, in which the latter's position had alienated traditionally-minded Liberal voters in that region.
55 In the 1921 election the Agrarians won 13 per cent of the vote, most of it from the Liberals, Valen and Katz *Political Parties in Norway* p 28
56 Derry *A History of Modern Norway* pp 185—86; Theo Koritzinsky *Velgere, partier og utenrikspolitikk. Analyse av norske holdninger 1945—1970* (Oslo 1970) pp 62, 149
57 Converse and Valen *SPS* vol 6 1971 p 116; Rokkan and Valen 'Regional contrasts in Norwegian politics' pp 199—204
58 Bjørn Hansen 'Foran en oppløsning' *Arbeiderbladet* 10 June 1970
59 Valen and Katz *Political Parties in Norway* pp 27, 31
60 Koritzinsky *Velgere, partier og utenrikspolitikk* pp 62, 145
61 Rokkan and Valen 'Regional contrasts in Norwegian politics' pp 209—10, 214
62 Lyng *Mellom øst og vest* pp 9—50
63 The only change was when the Centre party minister of fisheries was replaced by another member of his party owing to ill-health, Per Vassbotn *Lekkasje og forlis* (Oslo 1971) p 103
64 *ibid* pp 101—07
65 *ibid* pp 103, 109—10
66 For an interesting discussion of Per Borten's character see *ibid* pp 140—46
67 Brunvand *Fra samspill til sammenbrudd* pp 35—36; and the comments by Tor Oftedal (Labour) after the coalition's fall in *St forh* 25 March 1971 p 2365
68 Vassbotn, *Lekkasje og forlis* pp 108—13
69 Brunvand *Fra samspill til sammenbrudd* p 49
70 Converse and Valen *SPS* vol 6 1971 pp 119—23; Derry *A History of Modern Norway* p 327
71 Investigations of the second party preferences of Labour voters in 1965 showed 41 per cent choosing parties to the left of Labour (37 per cent the SPP, 4 per cent the Communist party), 33 per cent the Liberals, 11 per cent the Conservatives, 8 per cent the CPP and 7 per cent the Centre party. The preferences were related to economic views, moral and religious questions and language, Converse and Valen *SPS* vol 6 1971 p 128
72 Rokkan and Hjellum *SPS* vol 1 1966 pp 237—38
73 Rokkan and Valen *SPS* vol 5 1970 p 296
74 *ibid* p 294
75 See Kielland *All makt?* Kielland joined the SPP after the referendum
76 Rokkan and Valen *SPS* vol 5 1970 p 298
77 Derry *A History of Modern Norway* p 201; Rokkan and Valen 'Regional contrasts in Norwegian politics' pp 197, 201
78 Rokkan and Valen *SPS* vol 5 1970 p 293
79 *ibid* pp 288—89
80 Ottar Hellevik, Tord Høivik and Nils Petter Gleditsch 'Folkemeininga om EEC i 1971' *Syn og Segn* nr 2 1972 p 112: 'It is clear from the public opinion polls that many regard the EEC issue as a difficult one to make up their minds about' (author's translation from the Norwegian).
81 There are few sources in English on Norwegian foreign policy. The best books

deal with earlier periods, for example, Olav Riste *The Neutral Ally* (Oslo 1965); and Nils Morten Udgaard *Great Power Politics and Norwegian Foreign Policy* (Oslo 1973), which covers the years 1940 to 1948. Other English sources include Helge Hveem *International Relations and World Images: A Study of Norwegian Foreign Policy Elites* (Oslo 1972); Chris Prebensen *Norway and NATO* (Oslo 1974); Nils Ørvik 'Norwegian foreign policy. The impact of special relationships' in *The Other Powers* ed R P Barston (London 1973); Jens A. Christophersen 'The making of foreign policy in Norway' *Cooperation and Conflict* no 1 1968, pp 52—74. The only book which provides a comprehensive survey is in Norwegian and over ten years old, but it is still useful: Knut Frydenlund *Norsk Utenrikspolitikk i etterkrigstidens internasjonale samarbeid* (Oslo 1966)

82 For the full range of Norwegian views on NATO in the late 1960s see *Ja eller nei til NATO* ed Herbjørn Sørebø (Oslo 1968)

83 *Norsk Utenrikspolitisk Årbok 1973* (Oslo 1974) p 397

84 Trygve Bratteli, chairman of the Labour party and prime minister at the time of the referendum in September 1972, expressed this point of view as follows: 'For Norway [EEC membership] is a question of whether or not we continue the foreign policy line we have followed since the second world war. It has been a policy of participating in international organisations and international co-operation. We have joined in. In many areas we would have been worse off if we had not done so. Are we now going to break with that policy and take a neutral, isolationist course?' (author's translation), quoted in Sundar *IP* no 1 1973 p 126

CHAPTER 2

1 Halle Jørn Hanssen and Kåre Sandegren 'Norway and Western European economic integration' *Cooperation and Conflict* no 1 1969 p 59

2 Tord Høivik, Ottar Hellevik and Nils Petter Gleditsch 'Folkeopinionen og EEC' *Samtiden* no 4 1971 p 253

3 *Dagbladet* 18 June 1971 maintained that the proposal was launched by Helge Seip as editor of that newspaper when the question of EEC membership first arose in the early 1960s. At that time Seip opposed membership.

4 Nils Petter Gleditsch 'Generaler og fotfolk i utakt' *IP* 4B 1972 p 797

5 Høivik, Hellevik and Gleditsch *Samtiden* no 4 1971 pp 243—44

6 See Brox *IP* 4B 1972

7 Ørvik 'Norwegian foreign policy' in *The Other Powers* p 32

8 Halvard Lange *Retningslinjer i norsk utenrikspolitikk* (Den norske Atlanterhavskomité Oslo 1960) pp 8—9; Frydenlund *Norsk utenrikspolitikk* pp 75—80

9 Hanssen and Sandegren *Cooperation and Conflict* no 1 1969 pp 47—48

10 In article 93

11 Frydenlund *Norsk utenrikspolitikk* pp 5—12

12 See Udgaard *Great Power Politics and Norwegian Foreign Policy* for the impact of the wartime experience on Norwegian foreign policy thinking

13 For the ten year debate about amending article 93 see Trygve Ramberg 'Sovereignty and cooperation' in *Fears and Expectations. Norwegian Attitudes towards European Integration* (Oslo 1972) pp 49—133

14 *ibid* pp 55—56

15 *ibid* p 57

16 *ibid* pp 85—86

17 *ibid* pp 57—58

18 Hanssen and Sandegren *Cooperation and Conflict* no 1 1969 p 48

19 See the memoirs of Håkon Lie, at that time general secretary of the

Labour party, ... *slik jeg ser det* (Oslo 1975) pp 223—38

20 For the considerations determining Norwegian policy at this juncture see *ibid;* Hanssen and Sandegren *Cooperation and Conflict* no 1 1969 pp 48—50; Frydenlund *Norsk utenrikspolitikk* pp 81—83
21 Hanssen and Sandegren *Cooperation and Conflict* no 1 1969 p 52
22 For the arguments of the various political parties and groups as expressed in parliament see Daniel Heradstveit 'The Norwegian EEC debate' in *Fears and Expectations* pp 177—206
23 The exceptions were the self-employed and employers in the rural areas, Rokkan and Valen 'Regional contrasts in Norwegian politics' pp 219—20
24 *ibid* p 219
25 *ibid* p 216
26 *ibid* p 219
27 Høivik, Hellevik and Gleditsch *Samtiden* no 4 1971 p 243
28 Ramberg *Fears and Expectations* pp 58—59; James A Storing *Norwegian Democracy* (Oslo 1963) p 237
29 Heradsveit *Fears and Expectations* p 180
30 Høivik, Hellevik and Gleditsch *Samtiden* no 4 1971 p 240
31 *ibid* p 243
32 Hanssen and Sandegren *Cooperation and Conflict* no 1 1969 p 52
33 Richard Mayne *The Recovery of Europe from Devastation to Unity* (London 1970) pp 260—62
34 Hanssen and Sandegren *Cooperation and Conflict* no 1 1969 p 57
35 For foreign minister Lyng's view of the situation at that time see *Mellom øst og vest* pp 209—33
36 Hanssen and Sandegren *Cooperation and Conflict* no 1 1969 p 57
37 Lyng *Mellom øst og vest* pp 213, 233
38 For events and calculations in the Centre party see the account by Dagfinn Vårvik in *Nationen* 17 August 1970
39 Lyng *Mellom øst og vest* p 232
40 *Innstilling S nr 332 (1969—70) Innstilling fra utenriks- og konstitusjonskomitéen om Norges forhold til de nordiske og europeiske markedsdannelser (St meld nr 92 for 1969—70)* p 593
41 *St meld nr 92 (1969—70)* p 29
42 For an analysis of the 1967 debate see Olav Vefeld 'The 1967 EEC debate' in *Fears and Expectations* pp 207—79
43 *ibid* p 211
44 Høivik, Hellevik and Gleditsch *Samtiden* no 4 1971 pp 243—44
45 Hanssen and Sandegren *Cooperation and Conflict* no 1 1969 p 58
46 *Uttalelser vedrørende Norges stilling til de europeiske fellesskap (St meld nr 86 for 1966—67)* pp 21—23
47 Ian Davidson *Britain and the Making of Europe* (London 1971) pp 110—11
48 Erling Engen (Centre) in *St forh 24 November 1969* p 277
49 Hanssen and Sandegren *Cooperation and Conflict* no 1 1969 p 55; *Uttalelser vedrørende Norges stilling til de europeiske fellesskap (St meld nr 86 for 1966—67)* pp 19—20
50 *Rapport om De Europeiske Fellesskap fra et utvalg nedsatt av Regjeringen 29. mars 1966 (Markedsutvalgets rapport vi)* avgitt 21. april 1971 pp 93—94
51 Vefeld *Fears and Expectations* p 227
52 See the comments by Tor Oftedal (Labour) in *St forh 3 February 1970* pp 1742—43
53 *St meld nr 92 (1969—70)* pp 8—9
54 Davidson *Britain and the Making of Europe* pp 123—29
55 *ibid* pp 76—96, 107—24

56 See for example Johan Østby (Centre) in *St forh* 24 November 1969 p 749
57 See the exchange between Erling Engen (Centre) and Bent Røiseland (Liberal) in *St forh* 3 February 1969 pp 1740—41

CHAPTER 3

1 *St forh* 12 June 1969 pp 3817, 3819
2 Uwe Kitzinger *Diplomacy and Persuasion. How Britain Joined the Common Market* (London 1973) pp 45—58
3 *ibid* p 70; *St forh* 12 June 1969 pp 3791, 3824; *St forh* 24 November 1969 p 715
4 *St forh* 12 June 1969 pp 3816—18
5 See *St meld nr 92 (1969—70)* pp 17—29; the treaty text published by the foreign ministry in 1970; Claes Wicklund 'The zig-zag course of the Nordek negotiations' *SPS* vol 5 1970 pp 307—36
6 *St forh* 7 May 1968 pp 3447—48
7 *ibid* pp 3449—51; *St forh* 13 May 1968 pp 3626—29; *Dagbladet* 20 April 1968; Protocol of the *Nordic Council* session on 8 February 1970 p 65
8 Lie ... *slik jeg ser det* pp 214—22
9 *St forh* 13 May 1968 pp 3594, 3623, 3628
10 *ibid* p 3590; *St forh* 12 June 1969 p 3792
11 *ibid* p 3795
12 *ibid* pp 3808—10; 3790—91
13 *St meld nr 92 (1969—70)* p 17
14 *ibid* pp 28—29
15 *Nordic Council* 8 February 1970 p 74
16 *ibid* p 66
17 For the comments of Norway's chief negotiator regarding the limited character of Nordek, see Emil Vindsetmo 'Norsk markedspolitikks både/og — enkelte hovedsynspunkter' in *Norge i Europa. Norge i forhandlingsposisjon* vol 1 (Oslo 1970) pp 15—16
18 There are various conjectures about the reasons for the Finnish government's decision. Some see Soviet influence as the main factor, others stress the Finnish government's possible calculation that membership of Nordek would make it harder for Finland to negotiate a trade agreement with the EEC.
19 Vindesetmo *Norge i Europe* vol 1 pp 16—20; Lie ... *slik jeg ser det* pp 375—77
20 As it was, Labour criticised the government's unwillingness to commit itself in principle to a Nordek treaty in April 1968, *St forh* 13 May 1968 pp 3594—95, 3624—25
21 *ibid* pp 3626—29, 3632—33
22 *St forh* 12 June 1969 pp 3808—10; Vindsetmo *Norge i Europe* vol 1 p 11
23 *St forh* 12 June 1969 pp 3803—04, 3819; *St forh* 3 February 1970 p 1756
24 See for example *St forh* 12 June 1969 p 3791
25 Lie ... *slik jeg ser det* p 221
26 *St forh* 13 May 1968 pp 3221—24; *St forh* 12 June 1969 pp 3820—22
27 *ibid* p 3824
28 *ibid* pp 3816—18
29 *UD-informasjon* no 13 10 April 1970, speech by Kåre Willoch on 'Nordic cooperation — European integration'.
30 See the statement by the Norwegian federation of industries in Per Kleppe *EFTA-Nordek-EEC. Analyse av de nordiske ländernas integrationsproblem* (Stockholm 1970) pp 97—98; *St forh* 3 February 1970 pp 1721—22
31 The dilemma for some Centre party members at this stage was that they saw and welcomed the opportunity of creating a Nordic alternative to EEC

membership, but disliked the Danish proposals for agriculture. Their aim was therefore to encourage Nordek in principle while adopting a hard line in the negotiations, see *St forh* 13 May 1968 pp 3621—24; *St forh* 12 June 1969 pp 3820—22

32 *Nordic Council* 8 February 1970 p 67
33 By mid-1969 a Centre party speaker could say that there was nothing in Nordek which required Norway to give up its independent national agricultural policy, *St forh* 12 June 1969 p 3828
34 *ibid* pp 3794—96
35 Though some members of the Liberal party and CPP also seemed to harbour doubts about Nordek, see *ibid* p 3791; *Nordic Council* 8 February 1970 p 144. For Conservative views see *St forh* 13 May 1968 pp 3590—91, 3609—11, 3626—29, 3636—37, *St forh* 12 June 1969 pp 3825—27; *St forh* 3 February 1970 pp 1725—26, 1751—53
36 *Nordic Council* 8 February 1970 p 103
37 *ibid* p 113
38 *St forh* 12 June 1969 p 3791
39 *Nordic Council* 8 February 1970 p 144
40 *St forh* 3 February 1970 p 1758
41 *St forh* 12 June 1969 pp 3791, 3804
42 *St forh* 13 May 1969 p 3581
43 *St forh* 12 June 1969 pp 3791—92
44 *St forh* 3 February 1970 pp 1728—30
45 *ibid* p 1741
46 *ibid* p 1733
47 *Nordic Council* 8 February 1970 p 67
48 *St meld 92 (1969—70)* p 27
49 *Nordic Council* 8 February 1970 p 66
50 *St forh* 13 May 1968 p 3620; *St forh* 3 February 1970 pp 1744—45; *Nordic Council* 8 February 1970 pp 134—36
51 *St forh* 12 June 1969 pp 3792—94; *St forh* 3 February 1970 pp 1726—28
52 Knut Frydenlund 'Et nordisk alternativ?' *IP* no 1 1968 p 49
53 For a Swedish social democratic view of Nordek see Olaf Palme's speech to the *Nordic Council* 8 February 1970 pp 80—83
54 *St forh* 12 June 1969 p 3792; *St forh* 3 February 1970 p 1759
55 *St forh* 12 June 1969 pp 3798—3800, 3807—08; Frydenlund *IP* no 1 1968 p 50
56 *St forh* 12 June 1969 pp 3803—04
57 *ibid* pp 3813—14
58 See *St forh* 13 May 1968 p 3617, in which one speaker quotes a newspaper report according to which Guttorm Hansen, a prominent Labour party spokesman on foreign affairs, commented unfavourably in February 1968 on the economic and political consequences of a Nordic customs union.
59 *St forh* 3 February 1970 pp 1755—56
60 *St forh* 12 June 1969 pp 3810—13; *St forh* 13 May 1968 pp 3603—07
61 *St forh* 24 November 1969 p 760
62 *St forh* 12 June 1969 pp 3795—96
63 *ibid* pp 3793, 3798—99, 3801—02, 3816—17, 3827—28
64 *Nordic Council* 8 February 1970 p 104
65 *ibid* pp 78—80, 129—30, 136

CHAPTER 4

1 *St meld nr 92 (1969—70)* p 56
2 *ibid* p 42

3 *St forh* 25 June 1970 p 3933
4 Kitzinger *Diplomacy and Persuasion* pp 126—27; *St forh* 24 June 1970 pp 3801, 3820—21
5 *ibid* p 3803
6 *ibid* p 3806; 25 June 1970 pp 3895, 3923
7 Simon Z Young *Terms of Entry. Britain's Negotiations with the European Community 1970—1972* (London 1973) p 1
8 *Innst S nr. 332 (1969—70)* p 592
9 *St forh* 24 June 1970 pp 3799, 3848; *St forh* 23 November 1970 pp 991—92, 1001—02, 1006, 1065
10 *ibid* p 1068; *Dagbladet* 21 January 1971
11 For the debate see *St forh* 24 and 25 June 1970
12 *ibid* p 3792; *Innst S nr 332 (1969—70)* p 596
13 *ibid* pp 596—97; *St forh* 24 June 1970 p 3794
14 *St forh* 25 June 1970 pp 3865—67, 3872—73, 3900—02, 3905, 3918—19
15 *Innst S nr 332 (1969—70)* pp 598—99
16 *Dagbladet* 11 July 1970
17 Brunvand *Fra samspill til sammenbrudd* pp 50—53, 60—63
18 *Dagbladet* 19 August 1970
19 *Innst S nr 332 (1969—70)* pp 597—98; *St forh* 24 June 1970 p 3804
20 *Arbeiderbladet* 5 September 1970; *Dagbladet* 19 August 1970 and 9 January 1971
21 See for example *St forh* 24 June 1970 pp 3847—50
22 *Innst S nr 332 (1969—70)* p 598; *St forh* 24 June 1970 pp 3815—18
23 *UD-informasjon* nr 7 15 February 1971
24 *St forh* 23 November 1970 p 1026
25 Høivik, Hellevik and Gleditsch *Samtiden* no 4 1971 p 245
26 *Dagbladet* 12 January 1971
27 *St forh* 23 November 1970 p 991
28 *Dagbladet* 18 January 1971; *St forh* 24 March 1971 p 2303
29 *Dagbladet* 12, 14 and 15 January 1971
30 *ibid* 16 and 18 January 1971
31 *ibid* 14 January 1971
32 *ibid* 16 January 1971
33 Brunvand *Fra samspill til sammenbrudd* pp 88—90
34 *ibid* pp 52—53
35 Kielland *All makt?* p 45
36 See Per Vassbotn's comments in *Dagbladet* 15 April 1971 and Arne Haugestad's in *Arbeiderbladet* 28 October 1977
37 Brunvand *Fra samspill til sammenbrudd* pp 53—63
38 *St meld nr 92 (1969—70)* pp 33—34
39 See for example Bent Røiseland's description of Borten's behaviour as 'unjust and disloyal (ukollegial)' (author's translation), *St forh* 24 June 1970 p 3821
40 *Arbeiderbladet* 24 and 29 July 1970; *Dagbladet* 3 August 1970
41 *Arbeiderbladet* 1 August 1970
42 *ibid* 29 July 1970; *Dagbladet* 18 July 1970
43 *ibid* 7 August 1970
44 *Arbeiderbladet* 28 September 1970
45 Protocol of the *Nordic Council* session on 14 February 1971 pp 124—26
46 See for example Dagfinn Vårvik in *Arbeiderbladet* 1 June 1970 and Per Magne Arnsted, the Centre party's assistant general secretary, in *Dagbladet* 22 August 1970
47 See the section on the negotiations in this chapter.
48 *St forh* 23 November 1970 pp 1016—19

49 *ibid* pp 1060—62
50 *ibid* p 1019
51 *ibid* p 1018
52 See for example Kåre Willoch in *Arbeiderbladet* 25 July 1970 and the Centre party's reply, reported in the same newspaper on 7 October 1970
53 *Dagbladet* 9 January 1971; Bruvand *Fra samspill til sammenbrudd* p 61
54 *ibid* pp 78—85
55 *Nationen* 25 June 1970
56 *Arbeiderbladet* 22 September 1970
57 For the text see *Markedsutvalgets rapport vi* pp 205—08
58 *Arbeiderbladet* 24 September 1970
59 Contrast it with for example the foreign minister's speech in parliament on 24 June 1970, *St forh* pp 3838—42
60 *UD-informasjon* no 37 10 October 1970
61 For their comments see *Arbeiderbladet* 24 September 1970
62 *UD-informasjon* no 41 3 November 1970
63 *Innst S nr 332 (1969—70)* p 593
64 *St forh* 27 October 1970 pp 356—57; *St forh* 23 November 1970 p 989
65 *ibid* pp 1016—17
66 Young *Terms of Entry* pp 98—99
67 See for example *St meld nr 92 (1969—70)* p 55; *St forh* 24 June 1972 pp 3792, 3841—42
68 *St forh* 27 October 1970 pp 354—55
69 *St forh* 23 November 1970 p 1013
70 *ibid* pp 1007—08, 1043
71 *St forh* 27 October 1970 pp 354—55
72 *Arbeiderbladet* 27 October 1970
73 *St forh* 23—24 November 1970 pp 1018, 1061, 1072—73
74 *Arbeiderbladet* 3 July 1970
75 *ibid* 31 October 1970
76 *St forh* 23 November 1970 p 1018
77 Torbjørn Frøysnes 'Jordbruksforhandlingen med EF' in *EF — Norges vei? Forhandlingsresultatet satt i perspektiv* ed Valter Angell and Johan Jørgen Holst (Oslo 1972) p 51; *St forh* 24 June 1970 p 3805
78 Frøysnes *EF — Norges vei?* pp 51—52
79 *Dagbladet* 9 and 18 February 1971
80 *ibid* 9 February 1971
81 *Innst S nr 332 (1969—70)* p 595
82 *Dagbladet* 12 January 1971
83 Høivik, Hellevik and Gleditsch *Samtiden* no 4 1971 pp 242—45
84 Hellevik and Gleditsch *SPS* vol 8 1973 p 232
85 *Dagbladet* 27 January 1971
86 *Arbeiderbladet* 25 June and 3 September 1970
87 See Trygve Bratteli in *Arbeiderbladet* 30 June 1970, Knut Frydenlund *St forh* 24 June 1970 p 3797, and *Arbeiderbladet* editorials of 17 and 19 August 1970
88 *ibid* 26 June 1970
89 For example between Reiulf Steen, Einar Førde and Thorbjørn Berntsen, *ibid* 30 October 1970
90 *ibid* 23 September 1970
91 *ibid* editorial 25 June 1970
92 Kielland *All makt?* p 11
93 *Dagbladet* 27 January 1971 reported Trygve Bratteli as saying that internal party difficulties were usually caused more by the way issues were handled than by differences over the actual issues themselves. On 30 January

1971 it reported him as being prepared to sanction opposition to membership inside the party in return for Labour's anti-marketeers not campaigning outside the party framework in alliance with other anti-market groups.

94 *Innst S nr 332 (1969—70)* p 595; *Arbeiderbladet* 17 August and 23 September 1970

95 For the decision to emphasise this argument see Lie ... *slik jeg ser det* pp 378—79; *Innst S nr 332 (1969—70)* pp 595; *St forh* 23 November 1970 p 1003; articles by Per Kleppe in *Arbeiderbladet* 27 May 1970 ('Markedspolitikken i Norge og EF må bli politisert') and *Dagbladet* 25 July 1970; Reiulf Steen in *Arbeiderbladet* 8 June and 30 October 1970

95 *St forh* 23 November 1970 p 1069

97 *Dagbladet* 27 May 1970

98 According to a poll published in *Dagbladet* on 12 January 1971 37 per cent of those respondents claiming to vote for the Labour party wanted the membership negotiations broken off

99 *St forh* 24 June 1970 p 3855; *Arbeiderbladet* 30 October 1970

100 *St forh* 24 and 25 June 1970 pp 3825—31, 3855—57, 3895

101 Indeed they stressed their loyalty to the party and disclaimed any intention of weakening it, see Rune Gerhardsen in *Dagbladet* 25 February 1970

102 *Dagbladet* 3, 4 and 6 February 1971

103 Høivik, Hellevik and Gleditsch *Samtiden* no 4 1971 p 244

104 *ibid* p 242

105 See the joint declaration in *Arbeiderbladet* 19 June 1970

106 *ibid* 12 August 1970

107 *ibid* 31 August 1970; *Dagbladet* 21 January 1971

108 According to Arne Haugestand in *ibid* 30 January 1973 the People's Movement's campaign expenses amounted to ten million kroner, of which 3.4 million came from the central agricultural organisations.

109 *Folkebevegelsens melding om Norges forhold til De Europeiske Fellesskap (EF)* (Motmelding til Regjeringens Stortingsmelding nr 50, 1971—72) April 1972

110 See for example *Dette bør du vite om EF. Argumentbok for motstandsbevegelsen* (Oslo 1972)

111 See for example *Dagbladet* editorials on 28 January and 12 February 1971. The pro-marketeers recognised the danger of this word 'union' and tried to counter it by stressing that in the EEC context it meant merely close co-operation, not the type of union Norway had been forced into with Sweden in the nineteenth century, see *St forh* 23 November 1970 pp 1066, 1074 and *St forh* 16 June 1971 p 3355

112 Knut Frydenlund *St forh* 23 November 1970 p 1015

113 Henry Valen 'Local elections in the shadow of the Common Market' *SPS* vol 7 1972 pp 278—79; Høivik, Hellevik and Gleditsch *Samtiden* no 4 1971 p 244

114 Valen *SPS* vol 7 1972 p 277

115 A FAKTA public opinion poll taken in January 1971 recorded that 39 per cent of those interviewed were 'not interested' in the EEC issue, *Dagbladet* 13 March 1971

116 Valen *SPS* vol 7 1972 p 277

117 *ibid* p 278

118 The best accounts of these events are in *Dagbladet's* daily coverage between 19 February and 11 March, and in the book written shortly afterwards by the journalist at the centre of the affair, Per Vassbotn *Lekkasje og forlis*. For an account by a journalist close to the Labour party see Brunvand *Fra samspill til sammenbrudd* pp 11—33, 98—122

259

119 Kielland *All makt?* p 45; Arne Haugestad in *Arbeiderbladet* 28 October 1977
120 *ibid;* and *Dagbladet's* editorial 1 March 1971 entitled 'Tid for Bratteli'
121 *ibid* 6 March 1971
122 *ibid* 12 March 1971
123 Almost two months before these events, *Dagbladet* had reported on 2 January 1971 anti-market fears that Norway's membership negotiations might suddenly be brought to a successful conclusion before they could extricate the Centre party from the coalition. They felt that time was running out and decisive action had to be taken as soon as possible.
124 During the crisis the 'young turks' in the Centre party's youth movement and party bureaucracy wrested control of events from the leaders of the parliamentary group, *ibid* 19 April 1971
125 Kielland *All makt?* p 45; Reidar T Larsen (Communist party) in *Dagbladet* 15 February 1971

CHAPTER 5

1 Text in *Markedsutvalgets rapport vi* pp 208—09
2 *Dagbladet* 31 March 1971
3 For the negotiations see *St meld nr 50 (1971—72)* Appendix 1 pp 13—19; Frøysnes *EF — Norges vei?* pp 50—66
4 *St forh* 20 January 1972 p 1963
5 Text in *UD-informasjon* no 25 22 June 1971
6 *Dagbladet* 22 June 1971
7 Frøysnes *EF — Norges vei?* pp 57—58
8 *ibid* pp 58—59
9 *St meld nr 50 (1971—72)* Appendix 1 p 16
10 *ibid* p 16
11 *ibid* pp 17—19
12 Foreign minister Cappelen, *St forh* 14 January 1972 p 1844; *St meld nr 50 (1971—72)* pp 34—35
13 *Folkebevegelsens melding . . . til St meld nr 50, 1971—72* pp 110—23
14 See Bjørn Dynna 'Fiskerisektoren i EF-forhandlingene' in *EF — Norges vei?* pp 31—49
15 *UD-informasjon* no 19 11 May 1971; *ibid* no 25 22 June 1971; *St meld nr 50 (1971—72)* Appendix 1 pp 22—23
16 *Innst S nr 333 (1970—71)* pp 706—07
17 *ibid*
18 Young *Terms of Entry* pp 98—102
19 Per Kleppe quoted in *Dagbladet* 13 December 1971
20 *St forh* 14 January 1972 p 1845
21 *ibid* 20 January 1972 p 1890
22 Ambassador Sommerfelt in *Dagbladet* 15 January 1972 and *UD-informasjon* no 9 21 February 1972
23 Text in *St meld nr 50 (1971—72)* Appendix 1 pp 24—25
24 *ibid* p 25
25 *St forh* 20 January 1972 p 1889
26 The arguments are summarised in *Folkebevegelsens melding . . . til St meld nr 50, 1971—72* pp 123—27
27 *St forh* 20 January 1972 pp 1916—17
28 *Dagbladet* 15 January 1972
29 Berge Furre (SPP) *ibid* 11 November 1971
30 *UD-informasjon* no 3 17 January 1972

31 *Folkebevegelsens melding* ... *til St meld nr 50, 1971—72* pp 127—32;
St forh 20 January 1972 pp 1951—53

32 *St meld nr 50 (1971—72)* pp 36—37, Appendix 1 pp 30—33

33 *Folkebevegelsens melding* ... *til St meld nr 50, 1971—72* Appendix 1 pp
47—62

34 *Dagbladet* 18 January 1972

35 *St forh* 21 January 1972 pp 2017—18

36 *Dagbladet* 20 January 1972

37 *UD-informasjon* no 5 24 January 1972

CHAPTER 6

1 *Innst S nr 332 (1969—70)* p 59; *St forh* 24 June 1970 pp 3796—97

2 *Dagbladet* 12 May 1972

3 Nils Ørvik 'The Norwegian Labour party (NLP) and the 1972 referendum'
in *Norway's no to Europe* p 34

4 Rune Gerhardsen in *Dagbladet* 22 May 1971

5 Text in *Innst S nr 333 (1970—71) Innstilling fra utenriks- og konstitusjonskomitéen om Norges forhold til De europeiske fellesskap (St meld nr 90)*
pp 701—02

6 Kielland *All makt?* p 63

7 *St meld nr 90 (1970—71) Om Norges forhold til De Europeiske Fellesskap*

8 See chapter 4

9 *St forh* 24 March 1971 pp 2281—82, 2326, 2401, 2399

10 *St meld nr 90 (1970—71)* pp 67—68, 101

11 *ibid* pp 89—94, 101

12 *ibid* pp 101—02

13 St forh 16 June 1971 p 3349

14 *Dagbladet* 21 May 1971

15 *ibid* 26, 27 and 30 May 1971

16 *Innst S nr 333 (1970—71)* pp 706—07

17 *ibid* p 705

18 *ibid* pp 706—07

19 See for example *St forh* 17 June 1971 p 3495

20 Kielland *All makt?* p 63

21 *St forh* 16 June 1971 pp 3348, 3368

22 *ibid* 16 June 1971 p 3368

23 *ibid* 16 June 1971 p 3420

24 *Dagbladet* 13 September 1971

25 Kielland *All makt?* p 83

26 *St fork* 16 June 1971 p 3418

27 Valen *SPS* vol 7 1972 p 279

28 *Dagbladet* 1, 3, 16 and 18 September 1971

29 Valen *SPS* vol 7 1972 pp 273—82

30 *Dagbladet* 19 August 1971

31 See for example *ibid* 1 December 1971 'Norsk glideflukt' (Norwegian retreat)
and 14 January 1971 'Regjeringen godtar EEC's fiskeridiktat' (Government
accepts terms dictated by EEC) (author's translations)

32 *ibid* 19 and 20 January 1972; *Arbeiderbladet* 8 March 1972

33 Rune Gerhardsen in *Dagbladet* 4 November 1972

34 *Norge og EEC. Innstilling fra Venstres EEC-utvalg* (Oslo 1971) pp 317—18

35 *Folkebevegelsens melding* ... *til St meld nr 50, 1971—72* p 257

36 Kielland *All makt?* p 44

37 *ibid* p 90

38 *ibid* pp 100—01

39 Quoted in *Dette bør du vite om EF, Argumentbok for motstandsbevegelsen*
p 2
40 The referendum campaign produced many books and articles. Most of the
arguments advanced by each side can be found, however, in the parliamentary
debates and various official and non-official reports of these years. See *St
meld nr 92 (1969—70), nr 90 (1970—71)* and *nr 50 (1971—72); Folkebevegelsens melding ... til St meld nr 50, 1971—72; Innst S nr 332 (1969—
70), nr 333 (1970—71)* and *nr 277 (1971—72); St forh* 24 and 25 June
1970, 16 and 17 June 1971, and 6, 7 and 8 June 1972. For the simplified
campaign arguments see the Peoples' Movement's *Hva er EEC?* (Oslo 1971)
and *Dette bør du vite om EF. Argumentbok for motstandsbevegelsen*, the
Labour party's *De sier — vi svarer om EF*, and *Ditt valg. Hva betyr JA?
Hva betyr NEI?* published by the Youth Campaign for EEC Membership
(Ungdomskampanjen for EF). For the more sophisticated debate between
academics see *10 innlegg om EEC* ed Susan Høivik (Oslo 1971) and
Johan Galtung *EF — en supermakt i verdenssamfunnet* (Oslo 1972)
41 Knut Frydenlund *St forh* 16 June 1971 p 3349
42 *Ditt valg. Hva betyr JA? Hva betyr NEI?*
43 'Felles mål' (Common aims, author's translation) a declaration issued in
November 1971 by ten national organisations and thirty-seven members of
parliament opposed to EEC membership. Text in *Dette bør du vite om EF.
Augumentbok for motstandsbevegelsen* pp 2—3
44 On 15 March 1972 Kielland wrote in *All makt?* p 148 'The government
and party leadership are sure they will win the referendum and I think they
will.' (author's translation).
45 Hellevik and Gleditsch *SPS* vol 8 1973 p 233
46 Arne Haugestad in *Dagbladet* 16 January 1972
47 *St forh* 14 April 1972 pp 320—59
48 See the memorandum from Labour party general secretary Bye to local party
organisers outlining the party's campaign strategy published in *Dagbladet* 7
March 1972
49 Nikolaj Petersen and Jørgen Elklit 'Denmark enters the European Communities' *SPS* vol 8 1973 pp 201—02
50 Kielland *All makt?* pp 127—29, 144
51 ibid p 103
52 *Dagbladet* 3 and 6 March 1972
53 *ibid* 7 and 8 April 1972
54 *Innst S nr 277 (1971—72)* pp 520—32; *St forh* 6 June 1972 pp 3261—63
55 Kielland *All makt?* p 214
56 *Innst S nr 277 (1971—72)* pp 505—19
57 In Baerum, a suburb of Oslo, for example, it was supported by Inger Louise
Valle (Labour), Jo Benkow (Conservative) and Halfdan Hegtun (Venstre)
Dagbladet 19 April 1972
58 *ibid* 3 and 6 May 1972
59 Kielland *All makt?* pp 131—33
60 *ibid* p 148
61 *Dagbladet* 6 April 1972
62 Kielland *All makt?* p 128
63 *Dagbladet* 7 and 10 February and 21 April 1972
64 *ibid* 21 and 22 April 1972
65 Hellevik and Gleditsch *SPS* vol 8 1973 p 233
66 *Arbeiderbladet* 21, 22 and 24 April 1972
67 Kielland *All makt?* pp 173—74
68 Quoted in the Labour Information Committee's pamphlet *Til Arbeiderpartiets
velgere*

69 *Dagbladet* 13 May 1972
70 *ibid* 1 August and 21 September 1972
71 *Arbeiderbladet* 4 September 1972
72 *St forh* 6 June 1972 p 3228
73 *Dagbladet* 22 September 1972
74 *Arbeiderbladet* 22 August 1972
75 Thorbjørn Berntsen in *Dagbladet* 26 August 1972
76 *ibid* 16 August 1972
77 For an analysis of the result see Henry Valen 'Norway: "no" to EEC' *SPS* no 8 1973 pp 214—26
78 Holst *The World Today* March 1975 p 118
79 *ibid* p 117

CHAPTER 7

1 Brandt *Begegnungen und Einsichten* p 333
2 Knut Getz Wold 'Den økonomiske situasjon' *Penger og Kreditt* no 1 1973 p 9
3 *St forh* 30 October 1972 p 79
4 *ibid* p 120; *Aftenposten* 17 March 1973; *St forh* 24 May 1973 p 3244
5 Except Finland; Finland's free trade agreement was not ratified until November 1973, F Singleton 'Finland, Comecon, and the EEC' *The World Today* February 1974 p 65
6 *St prp nr 126 (1972—73) Om samtykke til ratifikasjon av Avtale mellom Norge og Det Europeiske Økonomiske Fellesskap og Avtale mellom Norge og medlemsstatene i Det Europeiske Kull- og Stålfellesskap og Det Europeiske Kull- og Stålfellesskap* pp 3—7
7 Rune Gerhardsen in *Dagbladet* 5 October 1972
8 For the events and negotiations leading to the formation of the Korvald government see *ibid* 26 September to 5 October 1972
9 See chapter 8
10 *St forh* 30 October 1972 pp 78, 120
11 *ibid* 29 November 1972 p 822; *ibid* 24 May 1973 pp 3212, 3243
12 *ibid* 24 May 1973 p 3212
13 *ibid* 29 November 1972 pp 824—25, 848—49
14 *ibid* 24 November 1972 p 663
15 *St prp nr 126 (1972—73)* pp 1—2, 7—15
16 *Norway Information* no 111 1973
17 For the details see *St prp nr 126 (1972—73)* pp 3—7
18 *St forh* 24 November 1972 p 665
19 *ibid* 29 November 1972 p 822
20 For the EEC's initial demands in this sector see *Aftenposten* 24 February 1973
21 Brandt *Begegnungen und Einsichten* p 338
22 *St forh* 30 October 1972 pp 86, 148—49
23 *ibid* 29 November 1972 p 824
24 Brandt *Begegnungen und Einsichten* p 333
25 *St forh* 29 March 1973 pp 2439—40; 4 April 1973 pp 2458—59; 8 June 1973 pp 3721—3821
26 *Aftenposten* 3 and 6 April 1973
27 For the Norwegian aims in the negotiations, and the arguments with which they supported them, see *St prp nr 126 (1972—73)* pp 50—62
28 Foreign minister Vårvik, *St forh* 24 November 1972 pp 667—68
29 *ibid* 30 October 1972 pp 72, 143, 153
30 *St prp nr 126 (1972—73)* p 53
31 *St forh* 24 May 1972 p 3211
32 *St prp 126 (1972—73)* pp 15—40
33 *St forh* 24 May 1973 pp 3210, 3220, 3222, 3241

34 *ibid* pp 3215, 3221—22, 3239
35 *St prp nr 126 (1972—73)* p 38
36 *Innst S nr 296 (1972—73) Innstilling fra utenriks- og konstitusjonskomitéen om ratifikasjon av Avtale mellom Norge og Det Europeiske Økonomiske Fellesskap og Avtale mellom Norge og medlemsstatene i Det Europeiske Kull- og Stålfellesskap og Det Europeiske Kull- og Stålfellesskap* p 961
37 *ibid* p 967
38 *St forh* 24 May 1973 pp 3221—22, 3239, 3241
39 *Innst S nr 296 (1972—73)* p 961
40 See chapter 8
41 *St forh* 24 May 1973 p 3210
42 *Norsk Utenrikspolitisk Årbok* p 347
43 *ibid* pp 349, 351, 379
44 *St forh* 24 May 1973 pp 3221, 3239
45 See chapter 8
46 *Uttalelser vedrørende Norges avtaler med De Europeiske Fellesskap. Særskilt vedlegg 2 til St prp nr 126 for 1972—73* pp 3—8, 10—34
47 Knut Getz Wold 'Den økonomiske situasjon' *Penger og Kreditt* no 1 1977 pp 1—5
48 Wold 'Den økonomiske situasjon' *Penger og Kreditt* no 1 1974
49 *Aftenposten* 27 May 1974; Valter Angell 'Norsk utenriksøkonomi under endrede forutsetninger' *Norsk Utenrikspolitisk Årbok 1974* p 58
50 Wold 'Den økonomiske situasjon' *Penger og Kreditt* no 1 1976 pp 3—4
51 *Aftenposten* 23 August 1974
52 Wold *Penger og Kreditt* no 1 1976 pp 1, 3—4, 10—11
53 *Norsk Utenrikspolitisk Årbok 1974* p 338
54 Angell *ibid* p 63
55 *St meld nr 30 (1973—74) Virksomheten på den norske kontinentalsokkel m v* p 15
56 *Norges Handels- og Sjøfartstidende* 28 January 1977
57 'The tanker crisis . . . and its effect on Norway' in *The OECD Observer* no 79 January—February 1976 p 27
58 Wold *Penger og Kreditt* no 1 1976 p 3
59 These debates centred around the Labour government's three major reports to parliament on oil and energy policy in the first half of 1974: *St meld nr 25 (1973—74) Petroleumsvirksomhetens plass i det norske samfunn; St meld nr 30 (1973—74);* and *St meld nr 100 (1973—74) Energiforsyningen i Norge i fremtiden*
60 Wold *Penger og Kreditt* no 1 1976 p 13
61 Arild Holland 'Norges handelsavtale med EF og norsk papirindustri' *Aktuelle Økonomiske og Handelspolitiske Spørsmål* no 3 1976 pp 32—38
62 Information from the Norwegian federation of industries
63 *Aftenposten* 28 November 1975
64 Alice Rostoft 'Valutauro og valutapolitikk' *Penger og Kreditt* no 1 1973 p 25
65 *ibid* p 24
66 Information from the Norwegian federation of industries
67 *Aftenposten* 30 March 1977
68 *ibid* 3 and 5 June 1975; 'Oslo—Bonn' *Noroil* June 1976 pp 25—32

CHAPTER 8

1 See for example *St forh* 30 October 1972 pp 153—54; Bjørn Unneberg 'Grønt valg' *Samtiden* no 8 1973 pp 477—83
2 *Dagbladet* 21 October, 11 and 13 November 1972
3 *ibid* 30 September 1972

4 *ibid* 27 March 1973
5 A process well documented in Kielland *All makt?*
6 Lie ... *slik jeg ser det* pp 399—400
7 *Dagbladet* 30 April, 2 and 3 May 1973
8 The result is described and analysed by Henry Valen and Stein Rokkan in 'The election to the Storting in September 1973' *SPS* vol 9 pp 205—18
9 *Aftenposten* 2 July 1974
10 For a discussion of these see Henry Valen 'The local elections of September. 1975' *SPS* vol 11 1976 pp 181—82
11 See Ronald Bye in *Aftenposten* 21 December 1973
12 Lie ... *slik jeg ser det* p 403
13 *ibid* pp 406—07; Bratteli in *Arbeiderbladet* 6 June 1974
14 Guttorm Hansen in *Aftenposten* 29 July 1974
15 *Arbeiderbladet* 30 May 1974
16 See chapters 9 and 10
17 *Aftenposten* 11 February 1975
18 *Arbeiderbladet* 8 June 1974
19 Lie ... *slik jeg ser det* pp 411—14
20 *Aftenposten* 16 March 1975
21 *ibid* 22 April 1974
22 *ibid* 23 March 1975
23 For the debate and vote on the Alcan issue see *St forh* 13 December 1974 pp 2079—3156
24 *Aftenposten* 14 and 18 June 1974
25 *ibid* 24 April and 23 November 1974
26 *ibid* 27 June 1974 and 17 February 1975
27 *Dagbladet* 22 June and 2 August 1973
28 *ibid* 22 August 1973
29 *Aftenposten* 4 January 1975
30 *Høyres program for perioden 1978—81 vedtatt av Høyres Landsmøte* (Oslo 1977)
31 *Aftenposten* 3 February 1975
32 *Dagbladet* 7 April 1975
33 *Aftenposten* 8 June 1974 and 28 June 1975
34 Valen *SPS* vol 11 1976; *Aftenposten* 17 September 1975; *Arbeiderbladet* 17 September and 11 October 1975
35 *Aftenposten* 11 December 1976
36 *Arbeiderbladet* 12 August 1976
37 Text in *Nationen* 29 April 1976
38 *Innst S nr 440 (1976—77)*
39 *Stortingsvalget 1977,* Statistisk Sentralbyrå (Oslo 1977)

CHAPTER 9

1 *UD-informasjon* no 44 1973
2 See chapter 7; for a discussion of what it ought to mean in practice see J J Holst 'Aktiv norsk Europapolitikk' *NUPI-Notat* no 92 1975
3 *UD-informasjon* no 44 1973 and *Aftenposten* 14 May 1974
4 See the speech by Trygve Bratteli to the 'Gesellschaft für Auslandskunde' in Munich on 20 September 1973, *UD-informasjon* no 30 1973
5 This was well illustrated by the debate over Norway's relationship with the International Energy Agency in the winter of 1974—75. See for example *Arbeiderbladet* 2 November 1974; *Dagbladet* 19 March 1975; *Aftenposten* 15 April 1975; *Cultura* no 2 March 1975 and no 3 April 1975

6 See the Korvald government's policy declaration, *St forh* 24 October 1972 pp 71—72

7 *Norsk Utenrikspolitisk Årbok 1973* p 397

8 J J Holst 'Norge og forhandlingene om det internasjonale energibyrået, IEA' *Norsk Utenrikspolitisk Årbok* 1974 pp 67—79

9 Lie . . . *slik jeg ser det* p 410

10 *Aftenposten* 20 December 1974 and 22 September 1975

11 Anders C Sjaastad 'Økonomi og politikk i Atlanterhavssamarbeidet' *IP* no 2B 1974 pp 597—618

12 Indeed some Norwegian politicians began to see a bridgebuilding role for Norway in Atlantic relations too, this time between the United States and EEC, *Aftenposten* 9 December 1973 and 13 February 1974

13 Anders C Sjaastad 'Norge i Euro-gruppen' *Norsk Utenrikspolitisk Årbok 1974* pp 26—27

14 *Norsk Utenrikspolitisk Årbok 1973* p 397

15 In its long-term programme for the years 1978—81, *St meld nr 75 (1976— 77)*, the Labour government put the northern region at the top of the list of tasks for Norwegian foreign policy; see also Nils Morten Udgaard 'Stor-Norges nye dobbelte dilemma' *Aftenposten* 29 December 1976

16 Except, of course, in areas where Norway's oil brought it into close contact with Western European countries as either consumers or producers.

17 See chapter 10

18 Knut Frydenlund in *UD-informasjon* no 10 1975 and *Aftenposten* 14 May 1975

19 See chapter 10

20 *Aftenposten* 21 December 1973

21 *St forh* 2 June 1975 p 4480

22 The Korvald government had used a similar argument, and indicated that it too was considering appointing a permanent representative, *UD-informasjon* no 17 1973

23 *Aftenposten* 10 October 1975

24 *ibid* 15 and 16 February 1976

25 See *UD-informasjon* no 21 1975 for the Norwegian prime minister's speech at the EFTA heads of government meeting in Vienna on 13 May 1977, and the declaration issued at the end of the meeting.

26 Interview with the Danish foreign minister, K B Andersen, in *Europa* no 10 December 1976 p 8, and the article by the Danish member of the commission, Finn O Gundelach 'En sydvendt EF-politik må afbalanceres af en mere nordvendt' in the same number of the magazine, pp 4—5

27 This fear was still being expressed a year or more after the referendum, for example in Holst *NUPI-Notat* no 92 1975 pp 6—7; even the Korvald government, in its long-term defence programme, had considered it possible that the EEC would eventually extend its co-operation to defence matters too, J J Holst 'Langtidsplanen for forsvaret 1974—78. De utenrikspolitiske forutsetninger' *Norsk Utenrikspolitisk Årbok 1973* p 30

28 Anxiety about United States—EEC bilateralism was also still being voiced for some time after the referendum, see for example Guttorm Hansen in *Arbeiderbladet* 4 February 1972 and *Norsk Utenrikspolitisk Årbok 1973* p 185; Paul Thyness *ibid* p 184; and Arne Arnesen, then secretary of state (or deputy foreign minister) at the foreign ministry, in *Norges sikkerhetspolitikk* ed Mimi Lønnum (Oslo 1974) pp 158—59

29 Anders C Sjaastad 'Atlanterhavssamarbeid i støpeskjeen — Norge i NATO' *Norsk Utenrikspolitisk Årbok 1973* pp 18—21

30 Sjaastad *Norsk Utenrikspolitisk Årbok 1974* p 27

31 Sjaastad *Norsk Utenrikspolitisk Årbok 1973* pp 18—25

32 For Norwegian views see J J Holst 'The 1973-crisis and intra-alliance relations' *NUPI-Notat* no 112 1975; Guttorm Hansen *Vest-Europa 30 år etter* (Den norske Atlanterhavskomité Oslo 1976) p 7

33 Beate Lindemann 'Europe and the Third World: the Nine at the United Nations' *The World Today* July 1976 pp 260—69

34 This point was made by foreign minister Knut Frydenlund in *Aftenposten* 14 May 1974

35 On 12 September 1975 *Aftenposten* reported a Norwegian initiative to intensify bilateral contacts following the British referendum in June.

36 *ibid* 18 October 1975

37 There were exceptions; see for example the editorials in *Aftenposten* 14 July 1976 and *Verdens Gang* 9 August 1976 after the EEC's decision to hold direct elections to the European assembly

38 Michael Palmer 'EEC: the road to better political co-operation' *The World Today* January 1976 pp 27—30

39 *Aftenposten* 12 September 1975

CHAPTER 10

1 For the background and issues see Evan Luard *The Control of the Sea-bed. A New International Issue* (London 1974), and by the same author 'The law of the sea conference' *International Affairs* no 2 vol 50 April 1974 pp 268—78; J E S Fawcett 'The law of the sea: issues at Caracas' *The World Today* June 1974 pp 239—46

2 For Norwegian policy see *St meld nr 40 (1973—74) FN-konferansen om havets folkerett; UD-informasjon* no 9 1973; *ibid* no 23 1973; Helge Vindenes 'The UN conference on the law of the sea — the basic problems from a Norwegian point of view' *Cooperation and Conflict* no 2 and 3 1974 pp 69—81; Ivan Kristoffersen *Havet-75. En bok om ressurser og kystfolk* (Oslo 1975); *Norges havretts- og ressurspolitikk* ed. Arne Treholt, Karl Nandrup Dahl, Einar Hysvaer, Ivar Nes

3 Kristoffersen *Havet-75* pp 9—19

4 *Norsk Utenrikspolitisk Årbok 1974* pp 209, 213—14

5 *Aftenposten* 23 April 1974

6 Kim Traavik 'Norge i havrettsforhandlingene' *Norsk Utenrikspolitisk Årbok 1974* pp 7—9

7 *Aftenposten* 28 August, 13 September, 17 October 1974; *Arbeiderbladet* 30 August 1974

8 *Aftenposten* 30 August 1974

9 *Financial Times* 22 August 1974

10 *The Times* 5 July 1974; for British interests and policy see R R Churchill 'United Kingdom' in *New directions in the law of the sea* ed R R Churchill, K R Simmonds and Jane Welch (London 1973) vol III pp 286—301

11 *ICJ Reports* 1974 pp 22—173

12 See the comments by Jens Evensen in *Arbeiderbladet* 27 August and 13 September 1974, Svenn Stray in *Aftenposten* 28 August 1974, and Professor Fleischer *Arbeiderbladet* 6 September 1974

13 Between 1968 and 1973 some 15 per cent of both the quantity and value of fish landed by Norwegian vessels was caught between twelve and fifty miles of the coasts of other countries, half of it off the United Kingdom, *Facts about the Norwegian Fishing Industry 1974*, published by Norges Fiskarlag p 9

14 Traavik *Norsk Utenrikspolitisk Årbok 1974* p 7

15 For a West German view of the role of the Evensen group in the conference

see Uwe Jenisch 'Seerecht und deutsche Meeresinteressen' *Aussenpolitik* no 1 1976 pp 6 and 12

16 *UD-informasjon* no 47 1974; *St forh* 29 January 1975 pp 2715—16

17 The Norwegians claimed that such no-trawling zones were permitted under the Geneva Convention on Fishing and Conservation of the Living Resources of the High Seas, 1958, which permitted states to establish non-discriminatory protection zones outside their fishing limits after negotiations with other countries, *St forh* 29 January 1975 p 2176; Michael Akehust *A Modern Introduction to International Law* Minerva series no 25 (London 1970) pp 228—29

18 *St prp nr 86 (1974—75) Om samtykke til inngåelse av en avtale mellom Norge og Sovjetunionen om samarbeid innen fiskerinæringen*

19 *Aftenposten* 4 November, 10 and 14 December 1974, 17 January 1975

20 Arne Olav Brundtland 'Noen hovedtrekk ved det norsk-sovjetiske forhold i 1974' *Norsk Utenrikspolitisk Årbok 1974* p 49

21 *Arbeiderbladet* 26 and 27 November 1974; *Aftenposten* 23 December 1974

22 *Financial Times* 20 March 1975

23 *Survey of Current Affairs* 4 July 1974 pp 265—66; *The Times* 6 March 1975

24 For an official Norwegian account of the negotiations see *St forh* 29 January 1975 pp 2715—23

25 *Aftenposten* 13 November 1974

26 For a Norwegian view of British policy during these negotiations see *Arbeiderbladet* 30 January 1975

27 *The Economist* 22 June 1974; *The Times* 31 January 1975

28 See *Aftenposten* 23 December 1974 for French policy during the negotiations

29 *ibid* 13 November 1974

30 According to *Arbeiderbladet* 7 and 8 January 1975 this was a French proposal

31 *Aftenposten* 13 December 1974

32 *ibid* 23 December 1974; *Arbeiderbladet* 28 November 1974

33 *The Times* 22 January 1975; *Aftenposten* 22 and 23 January 1975

34 *St forh* 21 October 1975 pp 223—24

35 Even before that, according to *Aftenposten* 21 December 1974

36 See *St forh* 29 January 1975 for Evensen's assessment of the situation

37 John R Stevenson and Bernard H Oxman 'The Third United Nations conference on the law of the sea: the 1975 Geneva session' *American Journal of International Law* vol 69 1975 pp 763—97

38 *Arbeiderbladet* 24 January 1975

39 *Aftenposten* 20 March and 21 April 1975

40 *St forh* 21 October 1975 pp 223—24

41 *Aftenposten* 20 August 1975

42 *UD-informasjon* no 54 1975; *St forh* 26 November 1975 pp 1187—94

43 Jenisch *Aussenpolitik* no 1 1976 pp 11—13

44 *St forh* 28 May 1976 pp 3771—77

45 *ibid* 1 December 1976 pp 1685—87

46 *ibid* 28 May 1976 p 3776

47 *Aftenposten* 15 October 1976; *St forh* 1 December 1976 pp 1688—89

48 *Aftenposten* 29 December 1976

49 See *ibid* 29 March 1976 for Evensen's speech at Henningsvaer. The idea of a 'common area' had already been suggested earlier, see for example *St forh* 24 March 1971 pp 2347—48

50 *Survey of Current Affairs* June 1975 p 230

51 *ibid* December 1975 pp 478—80. West Germany reached agreement with Iceland on 20 November, Belgium on 28 November 1975

52 *St forh* 28 May 1976 p 3775

53 *Arbeiderbladet* 24 January and 9 February 1976
54 *The Times* 3 February 1976; *The Sunday Times* 14 March 1976
55 For the development of commission thinking see *Financial Times* 27 November 1975
56 *Aftenposten* 10 February 1976
57 *The Times* 3 February 1976
58 *Survey of Current Affairs* June 1976 pp 251—52
59 *St forh* 28 May 1976 p 3776
60 For the details of these talks see *Aftenposten* 21 February, 13 March, 11 May, 2 and 5 June and 30 July 1976
61 *St forh* 28 May 1976 p 3775
62 Angelika Volle and William Wallace 'How common a fisheries policy?' *The World Today* February 1977 pp 66—68
63 *Financial Times* 29 June 1976
64 *Survey of Current Affairs* December 1976 p 421
65 On 10 December 1976 the Soviet Union announced its intention of establishing a 200-mile economic zone too, *Aftenposten* 11 December 1976
66 *ibid* 2 September 1976; *Norges Handels- og Sjøfartstidende* 29 November 1976
67 *Financial Times* 19 February and 24 September 1976
68 *Arbeiderbladet* 6 December 1976
69 *ibid* 22 December 1976
70 On 11 November 1977 the Norwegian government decided to sign an interim agreement with the Soviet Union regulating their fisheries relations in the 'grey zone' while discussions on the continental shelf boundary continued, *Norway News Bulletin* no 200 1977

Bibliography

OFFICIAL PUBLICATIONS

Uttalelser vedrørende Norges stilling til de europeiske fellesskap. Særskilt vedlegg 111 til St.meld. nr. 86 for 1966—67

St.meld. nr. 95 (1969—70) and St.meld. nr. 76 (1970—71) Undersøkelse etter og utvinning av undersjøiske naturforekomster på den norske kontinentalsokkel m.m.

St.meld. nr. 92 (1969—70) Om Norges forhold til de nordiske og europeiske markedsdannelser

Innstilling S. nr. 332 (1969—70) Innstilling fra utenriks- og konstitusjonskomiteen om Norges forhold til de nordiske og europeiske markedsdannelser (St.meld. nr. 92 1969—70)

Rapport om De Europeiske Fellesskap fra et utvalg nedsatt av Regjeringen 29. mars 1966 (Markedsutvalgets rapport vi) avgitt 21. april 1971

St.meld. nr. 90 (1970—71) Om Norges forhold til De Europeiske Fellesskap

Innst. S. nr. 333 (1970—71) Innstilling fra utenriks- og konstitusjonskomiteen om Norges forhold til De Europeiske Fellesskap (St.meld. nr. 90)

St.meld. 50 (1971—72) Om Norges tilslutning til De Europeiske Fellesskap

Innst. S. nr. 277 (1971—72) Innstilling fra utenriks- og konstitusjonskomiteen om Norges tilslutning til De Europeiske Fellesskap (St.meld. nr. 50)

St.prp. nr. 126 (1972—73) Om samtykke til ratifikasjon av Avtale mellom Norge og Det Europeiske Økonomiske Fellesskap og Avtale mellom Norge og medlemsstatene i Det Europeiske Kull- og Stålfellesskap og Det Europeiske Kull- og Stålfellesskap

Uttalelser vedrørende Norges avtaler med De Europeiske Fellesskap. Særskilt vedlegg 2 til St.prp. nr. 126 for 1972—73

Innst. S. nr. 296 (1972—73) Innstilling fra utenriks- og konstitusjonskomiteen om ratifikasjon av Avtale mellom Norge og Det Europeiske Økonomiske Fellesskap og Avtale mellom Norge og medlemsstatene i Det Europeiske Kull- og Stålfellesskap og Det Europeiske Kull- og Stålfellesskap

St.meld. nr. 25 (1973—74) Petroleumsvirksomhetens plass i det norske samfunn

St.meld nr. 30 (1973—74) Virksomheten på den norske kontinentalsokkel m.v.

St.meld. nr. 40 (1973—74) FN-konferansen om havets folkerett

St.meld. nr. 100 (1973—74) Energiforsyningen i Norge i fremtiden

St.meld. nr. 86 (1974—75) Om samtykke til inngåelse av en avtale mellom Norge og Sovjetunion om samarbeid innen fiskerinæringen

St.meld. nr. 67 (1974—75) Norsk industris utvikling og framtid

St.meld. nr. 75 (1976—77) Langtidsprogrammet 1978—81

BOOKS AND ARTICLES

Akehurst, Michael, *A Modern Introduction to International Law.* Minerva series No. 25, London 1970

Angell, Valter, 'Om skandinavisk inntreden i Fellesmarkedet uten Storbritannia' *Internasjonal Politikk* No. 5 1968 pp. 441—71

Angell, Valter, and Johan Jørgen Holst (eds.) *EF-Norges vei? Forhandlingsresultatet satt i perspektiv.* Oslo 1972

Angell, Valter, 'Norsk utenriksøkonomi under endrede forutsetninger' *Norsk Utenrikspolitisk Årbok* 1974 pp. 58—66

Brandt, Willy, *Begegnungen und Einsichten. Die Jahre 1960—75.* Hamburg 1976

Brox, Ottar, *Hva skjer i Nord-Norge?* Pax, 1966

Brox, Ottar, 'Hva hendte i Norge 25. sept. 1972?' *Internasjonal Politikk* nr. 4B — Supplement — 1972 pp. 771—82

Brundtland, Arne Olav, 'Noen hovedtrekk ved det norsk-sovjetiske forhold i 1974' *Norsk Utenrikspolitisk Årbok* 1974 pp. 41—57

Brunvand, Olav, *Fra samspill til sammenbrudd* Trondheim 1973

Christophersen, Jens A., 'The making of foreign policy in Norway' *Cooperation and Conflict* No. 1 1968 pp. 52—74

Christophersen, Jens A., 'Valget 1975. Tilbake til det normale?' *Samtiden* no. 1 1976 pp. 1—12

Churchill, R. R., K. R. Simmonds and Jane Welch (eds.) *New Directions in the Law of the Sea* 6 vols. London 1973—76

Converse, Philip E., and Henry Valen. 'Dimensions of cleavage and perceived party distances in Norwegian voting' *Scandinavian Political Studies* vol. 6 1971 pp. 107—52

Davidson, Ian, *Britain and the Making of Europe.* London 1971

De sier — vi svarer om EF'. Labour Party pamphlet

Derry, T. K., *A History of Modern Norway 1814—1972.* Oxford 1973

'Dette bør du vite OM EF. Argumentbok for motstandsbevegelsen' Oslo 1972

'Ditt valg. Hva betyr JA? Hva betyr NEI?' broadsheet from the Youth Campaign for EEC Membership (Ungdomskampanjen for EF)

Ekelund, Sigurd, *Norway in Europe. An Economic Survey.* Press Department of the Royal Ministry of Foreign Affairs Oslo 1970

Europa No. 10 December 1976 pp. 7—8, interview with K. B. Andersen, 'Danmark villig til at forpligte sig til forudgående udenrigspolitiske EF-konsultationer'

Facts about the Norwegian Fishing Industry 1974 published by Norges Fiskarlag

Fawcett, J. E. S., 'The law of the sea: issues at Caracas' *The World Today* June 1974 pp. 239—46

Folkebevegelsens melding om Norges forhold til De Europeiske Fellesskap (EF) (Motmelding til Regjeringens Stortingsmelding nr. 50, 1971—72)

Frydenlund, Knut, *Norsk utenrikspolitikk i etterkrigstidens internasjonale samarbeid* Oslo 1966

Frydenlund, Knut, 'Et nordisk alternativ?' *Internasjonal Politikk* No. 1 1968 pp. 48—52

Fullerton, Brian and Alan F. Williams *Scandinavia.* London 1972

Galtung, Johan *EF-en supermakt i verdenssamfunnet.* Oslo 1972

Gleditsch, Nils Petter, 'Generaler og fotfolk i utakt. EF-avgjørelsen i de tre skandinaviske land' *Internasjonal Politikk* 4B — Supplement — 1972 pp. 795—804

Gleditsch, Nils Petter, and Ottar Hellevik, *Kampen om EF.* Oslo 1977

Gundelach, Finn O., 'En sydvendt EF-politik må afbalanceres af en mere nordvendt' *Europa* No. 10 December 1976 pp. 4—6

Hansen, Guttorm, *Vest-Europa 30 år etter.* Den norske Atlanterhavskomité Oslo 1976

Hanssen, Halle Jörn, and Kåre Sandegren, 'Norway and Western economic integration' *Cooperation and Conflict* No. 1 1969 pp. 47—62

Hellevik, Ottar and Tord Høivik and Nils Petter Gleditsch 'Folkemeininga om EEC i 1971' *Syn og Segn* no. 2 1972 pp. 105—17

Hellevik, Ottar and Nils Petter Gleditsch, 'The Common Market decision in Norway: a clash between direct and indirect democracy' *Scandinavian Political Studies* vol. 8 1973 pp. 227—35

Heradstveit, Daniel, 'The red/green alliance in Norwegian politics: a strange partnership' in *Norway's NO to Europe*. International Studies Association 1975

Hodne, Fritz, *An Economic History of Norway 1815—1970*. Trondheim 1975

Holland, Arild, 'Norges handelsavtale med EF og norsk papirindustri' *Aktuelle Økonomiske og Handelspolitiske Spørsmål* No. 3 1976 pp. 32—38

Holst, Johan Jørgen, 'Langtidsplanen for forsvaret 1974—78. De utenrikspolitiske forutsetninger, *Norsk Utenrikspolitisk Årbok* 1973 pp. 26—32

Holst, Johan Jørgen, 'Norge og forhandlingene om det internasjonale energibyrået, IEA', *Norsk Utenrikspolitisk Årbok* 1974 pp. 67—79

Holst, Johan Jørgen, 'Norway's EEC referendum: lessons and implications' *The World Today* March 1975 pp. 114—20

Holst, Johan Jørgen, *Aktiv norsk Europapolitikk* NUPI-Notat no. 92 1975

Holst, Johan Jørgen, *The 1973-crisis and intra-alliance relations*. NUPI-Notat no. 112 1975

'*Hva er EEC?*' pamphlet published by the People's Movement. Oslo 1971

Hveem, Helge, *International Relations and World Images: a Study of Norwegian Foreign Policy Elites*. Oslo 1972

Høivik, Susan (ed.), *10 innlegg om EEC*. Oslo 1971

Høivik, Tord, Ottar Hellevik and Nils Petter Gleditsch 'Folkeopinion og EEC, *Samtiden* No. 4 1971 pp. 239—60

Jenish, Uwe, 'Seerecht und deutsche Meeresinteressen' *Aussenpolitik* No. 1 1976 pp. 3—27

Kielland, Arne, 'Skillelinjer i norsk politikk' *Samtiden* No. 6 1971 pp. 348—59

Kielland, Arne, *All makt? Dagbok fra Stortinget*. Oslo 1972

Kitzinger, Uwe, *Diplomacy and Persuasion. How Britain Joined the Common Market*. London 1973

Kleppe, Per, *Main Aspects of Economic Policy in Norway since the War* Press Department of the Royal Ministry of Foreign Affairs. Oslo 1968

Kleppe, Per, *EFTA-Nordek-EEC. Analyse av de nordiske ländernas integrationsproblem*. Stockholm 1970

Koritzinsky, Theo, *Velgere, partier og utenrikspolitikk. Analyse av norske holdninger 1945—70*. Oslo 1970

Kristoffersen, Ivan, *Havet-75. En bok om ressurser og kystfolk*. Oslo 1975

Kvam, Ragnar, *DNA mot splittelsen. Da venstrefløyen ble ekskludert og SF stiftet*. Trondheim 1973

Lange, Halvard, *Retningslinjer i norsk utenrikspolitikk*. Den norske Atlanterhavskomité Oslo 1960

Langholm, Sivert, 'On the concepts of center and periphery' *Journal of Peace Research* 8 Nos. 2—4 1971

Lie, Haakon, 'Hva var det egentlig som skjedde?' *Internasjonal Politikk* No. 4B — Supplement — 1972 pp. 783—94

Lie, Haakon, '. . . slik jeg ser det'. Oslo 1975

Lindemann, Beate, 'Europe and the Third World: the Nine at the United Nations' *The World Today* July 1976 pp. 260—69

Luard, Evan, 'The law of the sea conference' *International Affairs* No. 2 vol. 50 April 1974 pp. 268—78

Luard, Evan, *The Control of the Sea-bed. A New International Issue*. London 1974

Lyng, John, *Mellom øst og vest. Erindringer 1965—68*. Oslo 1976

Lønnum, Mimi (ed.), *Norges sikkerhetspolitikk*. Oslo 1974

Norge og EEC. Innstilling fra Venstres EEC-utvalg. Oslo 1971

Ørvik, Nils (ed.), *Fears and Expectations. Norwegian Attitudes towards European Integration*. Oslo 1972

Ørvik, Nils, 'Norwegian foreign policy. The impact of special relationships' in Ronald P. Barston (ed) *The Other Powers*. London 1973

'Oslo-Bonn' *Noroil* June 1976 pp. 25—32

Palmer, Michael, 'EEC: the road to better political co-operation' *The World Today* January 1976 pp. 25—30

Petersen, Nikolaj and Jørgen Elklit 'Denmark enters the European Communities' *Scandinavian Political Studies* vol. 8 1973 pp. 198—213

Prebensen, Chris, *Norway and NATO*. The Royal Ministry of Foreign Affairs Oslo 1974

Riste, Olav, *The Neutral Ally. Norway's Relations with Belligerent Powers during the First World War*. Oslo 1965

Rokkan, Stein and Torstein Hjellum, 'The Storting election of September 1965' *Scandinavian Political Studies* vol. 1 1966 pp. 237—46

Rokkan, Stein, and Henry Valen 'Regional contrasts in Norwegian politics' in Erik Allardt and Stein Rokkan (eds.) *Mass Politics*. New York 1970

Rostoft, Alice 'Valutauro og valutapolitikk' *Penger og Kreditt* No. 1 1973 pp. 21—28

Saetra, Hartvig, *Den økopolitiske sosialismen*. Pax 1973

Singleton, F., 'Finland, Comecon, and the EEC' *The World Today* February 1974 pp. 64—72

Sjaastad, Anders C., 'Atlanterhavssamarbeid i støpeskjeen — Norge i NATO' *Norsk Utenrikspolitisk Årbok* 1973 pp. 15—25

Sjaastad, Anders C., 'Norge i Euro-gruppen' *Norsk Utenrikspolitisk Årbok* 1974 pp. 26—40

Sjaastad, Anders C., 'Økonomi og politikk i Atlanterhavssamarbeidet' *Internasjonal Politikk* No. 2B 1974 pp. 597—618

Sørebø, Herbjørn (ed.) *Ja eller nei til NATO*. Oslo 1968

Solstad, Arve, 'The Norwegian coalition system' *Scandinavian Political Studies* vol. 4 1969 pp. 160—67

Sparring, Åke (ed.), *Kommunismen i Norden*. Oslo 1965

Stevenson, John R. and Bernard H. Oxman, 'The third United Nations conference on the law of the sea: the 1975 Geneva session' *American Journal of International Law* vol. 69 1975 pp. 763—97

Storing, James A., *Norwegian Democracy*. Oslo 1963

Sundar, Egil, 'Folkeavstemningen og politikernes ansvar' *Internasjonal Politikk* No. 1 Jan/March 1973 pp. 123—26

'The tanker crisis . . . and its effect on Norway' *The OECD Observer* No. 79 Jan/Feb. 1976

'*Til Arbeiderpartiets velgere*' broadsheet from the Labour Information Committee against Membership of the EEC

Traavik, Kim, 'Norge i havrettsforhandlingene' *Norsk Utenrikspolitisk Årbok* 1974 pp. 5—17

Treholt, Arne and Karl Nandrup Dahl, Einar Hysvear, Ivar Nes (eds.) *Norges havretts- og ressurspolitikk*. Oslo 1976

Udgaard, Nils Morten, *Great Power Politics and Norwegian Foreign Policy*. Oslo 1973

Underdal, Arild, 'Diverging roads to Europe' *Cooperation and Conflict* Nos. 1/2 1975 pp. 65—76

Unneberg, Bjørn, 'Grønt valg' *Samtiden* No. 8 1973 pp. 477—83

Valen, Henry, and D. Katz, *Political Parties in Norway*. Oslo 1964

Valen, Henry and Stein Rokkan, 'The election to the Norwegian Storting in September 1969' *Scandinavian Political Studies* vol. 5 1970 pp. 287—300

Valen, Henry and W. Martinussen (eds.) *Velgere og politiske frontlinjer*. Oslo 1972

Valen, Henry, 'Local elections in the shadow of the Common Market' *Scandinavian Political Studies* vol. 7 1972 pp. 272—82

Valen, Henry, 'Norway: «No» to EEC' *Scandinavian Political Studies* vol. 8 1973 pp. 214—26

Valen, Henry, and Stein Rokkan, 'The election to the Storting in September 1973' *Scandinavian Political Studies* vol. 9 1974 pp. 205—18

Valen, Henry and Stein Rokkan, 'Cleavage structures and mass polities in a European periphery: Norway' in R. Rose (ed.) *Electoral Behaviour: a Comparative Handbook.* New York 1974

Valen, Henry, 'The local elections of September 1975' *Scandinavian Political Studies* vol. 11 1976 pp. 168—84

Vassbotn, Per, *Lekkasje og forlis: om regjeringen Bortens fall,* Oslo 1971

Vindenes, Helge, 'The UN conference on the law of the sea — the basic problems from a Norwegian point of view' *Cooperation and Conflict* Nos. 2 and 3 1974 pp. 69—81

Vindsetmo, Emil, 'Norsk markedspolitikks både/og — enkelte hovedsynspunkter' in *Norge i Europa. Norge i forhandlingsposisjon* vol. 1 Oslo 1970

Volle, Angelika and William Wallace, 'How common a fisheries policy?' *The World Today* February 1977 pp. 62—72

Wicklund, Claes, 'The zig-zag course of the Nordek negotiations' *Scandinavian Political Studies* vol. 5 1970 pp. 307—36

Wold, Knut Getz, 'Den økonomiske situasjon' *Penger og Kreditt* No. 1 for 1973, 1974, 1976 and 1977

Young, Simon Z., *Terms of Entry. Britain's Negotiations with the European Community 1970—72.* London 1973

Index

tension of the fishing limit: 226, 228—247

Labour Movement, 26

Labour Movement Information Committee against Norwegian Membership of the EEC, 152, 153, 166, formation of —: 150

Labour Party, 10, 24, 25, 27, 28, 29, 31, 44, 59, 65, 87, 96, 108, 119, 120, 165, 168, 172, 194, 197, 199, 202; history of —: 33—35; — and EEC: 47, 48, 49, 50, 52, 54, 57, 81, 85, 100—105, 131, 136, 137, 138, 140, 147—148, 149, 150, 151, 152, 153—157, 159, 160, 163, 165—166, 168; — and NORDEK: 68, 70, 76—78, 79, 129; — and the negotiations for membership of the EEC: 113, 119, 128—130, 131, 132, 133, 136; — and the treaty of accession: 136; mistakes by — during the campaign: 11; — about the referendum result: 192; — and the resignation of the government 1972: 170; — and the negotiations for Free Trade Agreement: 158, 170, 171—172, 175, 177; — after the referendum: 193—194; — and the policy towards EEC after the referendum: 181, 182, 191, 202, 205, 206—209, 224; — after the 1973 general election: 198, 201, 203; — European policy after 1973: 206—225; — and the Alcan crisis: 200—201; foreign policy of —: 102, 193, 200, 206—225; economic policy of —: 22; — and NATO: 37, 38, 102, 212—214; — and IEA: 210—211; — and the election of chairman 1975: 193, 199—200; — and Socialist Electoral Alliance: 181, 193, 197, 198, 200—201, 203, 210, 229; — and the extension of the fishing limit: 226—227, 229, 230, 239, 245, 246; — and the 1971 local election: 134—135; — and the 1973 general election: 193, 195—196, 197; — and the 1975 local election: 203, 239; — and the 1977 general election: 204, 205; — in public opinion polls: 101, 104, 108, 128, 156, 198—199, 201, 203, 211, 238
See also Labour Government and

Labour Movement Information Committee

Labour's National Conference in May 1971, 128—129

Labour's Special National Conference on the EEC in April 1972, 150, 153—156

Labour's Youth Organisation 154; — and EEC: 47, 105; — and NATO: 213; — and the election of Chairman of the party and prime minister (1973): 194; — and extension of the fishing limit: 230

Landsmål Movement, The Norwegian 26, 27, 28, 34; — and EEC: 159, 162

Lange, Anders (Chairman of Anders Lange's Party 1973—1974), 193, 195

Lange, Halvard (Minister of Foreign Affairs, 1946—1965), 44, 46, 78

Language, Norwegian — and EEC membership: 146—147, 162

Law of the Sea
See UNCLOS

Left-wing socialists, 12, 25, 58, 87; — and EEC: 48, 49, 55, 59, 151, 163; — about the referendum result: 192; — and the Free Trade Agreement: 178, 180; — after the referendum: 191; — and NATO: 36, 37
See also Socialist People's Party, Communist Party and Socialist Electoral Alliance

'Letter Affair', The, 91

Liberal Party, 24, 25, 26, 29, 30, 31, 32, 33, 44, 58, 160, 165, 168; history of —: 27—28; — and EEC: 48, 49, 50, 52, 71, 84, 87, 88—90, 101, 106, 135, 136—137, 151, 154, 155, 163, 192; — and NORDEK: 72—73, 74, 75, 79; — and the end of the coalition (1971): 110, 111; — and the negotiations for membership of the EEC: 130, 131, 132, 133; — about the referendum result: 192; — and the formation of a new coalition (1972): 170—171; splitting of the —: 171, 192; — and policy towards EEC after referendum: 205; — and extension of the fishing limit: 230; — and NATO: 38; — and the 1971 local election: 134; — and the 1973 general elec-

284

83, 96, 97, 98; — and the treaty of accession: 119, 126, 135; — and alternatives to membership: 131; — and the date of the referendum: 150; — and the binding of the referendum: 133—134, 154; — and the formation of a new coalition (1972): 170; — and the Free Trade Agreement: 169, 171, 172, 179, 180, 186—187; — and the policy towards EEC after the referendum: 181; — and the 1973 general election: 194, 195, 196
See also 'Yes to EEC'
Public opinion polls, 137; — about EEC: 10, 40, 50, 55, 106, 108—109, 134, 141, 156, 168, 169; — about the fairness of a referendum: 161; — about foreign policy after 1973: 209; — about non-socialist co-operation 1975; 202; Centre Party in —: 86, 108; Liberal Party in —: 89, 151; Labour in —: 101, 104, 108, 128, 156, 198—199, 201, 203, 211, 238; Socialist People's Party in —: 108; Socialist Electoral Alliance in —: 199, 201; Non-socialist parties in —: 199; — about NATO: 213
Pulp, Norwegian export of —: 19

Referendum, The, 40, 46; — binding or not: 133—134, 154; the date of —: 149; polls about the fairness of —: 161; the government linking its fate to the result of —: 154—155, 158—159; the result of —: 10, 41, 159—168; interpretations of the result of —: 11—14, 161—168, 192
Referendum Campaign, 105; March 1971 — Jan. 1972: 128—137; Jan.—Sept. 1972: 148—159; arguments during the —: 137—148
Regional policy, Norwegian, 15—16, 58—59; — and membership of the EEC: 86, 88, 144, 145, 151, 180
Report on relations with EEC, The, Government's (June 1971), 130—131
Rossbach, Hans Hammond (Chairman of the Liberal Party 1976—) 89

SALT (Strategic Arms Limitation Talks) 60
Scandinavian Defence Pact, 37
School politics, Norwegian, 30
Security policy, Norwegian, 16, 36—39, 41, 42, 43, 46, 48, 51; — and NORDEK: 66, 78; — and EEC membership: 103, 137, 138, 139—142, 144, 157—158, 164, 205; —, EEC and Norway after 1973: 220—222
See also NATO
Seip, Helge (Chairman of the Liberal Party 1969—1972 and of the New People's Party 1972—1975), 33, 51, 109, 151, 170, 192
Seip, Jens Arup (historian), 137
Shipping, Norwegian, 15, 16, 18, 47, 48, 161, 164; — and EEC: 46, 101, 130, 142, 143, 144, 158; — supporting membership of the EEC: 124, 137; — and the Free Trade Agreement: 176, 177, 179—180, — after the referendum: 184, 185, 187; Norway, EEC and — after 1973: 188, 217; — and UNCLOS: 227, 228, 229
Silisium carbide — and the Free Trade Agreement: 178
Skaanland, Hermod (Deputy Governor of the Bank of Norway), 135
Social policy, Norwegian, 25; — and EEC: 103, 144, 180
Socialist Electoral Alliance 181, 193, 197, 198; — and the Alcan crisis: 200—201; — and extension of the fishing limit: 229, 230; — and Labour: 197, 198, 200, 203, 210, 224; — and the 1973 general election: 194, 195, 196, 197; — transforming to a party 1975: 200; — in public opinion polls: 199, 201
See also Socialist Left Party
Socialist Left Party, 201; — and policy towards EEC after the referendum: 205; — and Labour: 203; — and the 1975 local election: 203, 238, 239; — and the 1977 general election: 204—205
See also Socialist Electoral Alliance
Socialist People's Party (SSP), 24, 27, 34—35, 119, 134, 135, 136, 201; — and EEC: 48, 49, 50, 54, 101, 147; — and NORDEK: 76, 78—79; — and NATO: 38; — and Labour:

101, 196; — and the Socialist Electoral Alliance: 181, 193, 200; — and the 1971 local election: 134—135; — in public opinion polls: 108, 199

See also Left-wing socialists and Socialist Electoral Alliance

Soviet Union, 37, 65, 200; Norwegian border with —: 16; — military forces in the north and Norwegian membership of the EEC: 140; — and the northern areas of Norway: 214; — and extension of Norwegian fishing limit: 238, 240, 241, 244; — and agreement with Norway about the no-trawling zones: 233; — and the boundary line between Norway and — in the Barents Sea: 214, 215, 231—232, 240, 246—247; — and the Arctic Cod Quota Agreement with Norway and Britain: 230, 233; — fishing limits and EEC: 243; — and extension of Iceland's fishing limit: 239; — and UNCLOS: 230, 232

Spaak, Ferdinand (Energy Director of the EEC Commission), 157

Spain — and EEC: 223

Statfjord, 184, 185

Steen, Reiulf (Chairman of Labour Party 1975—   ), 194, 199, 200

Svalbard —, Norway and the Soviet Union: 214

Sweden, 16, 21, 26, 27, 37, 38, 40, 49, 74, 78, 100, 107; Norwegian export to: 18, 68, 170; — and EEC: 19, 20, 54, 67, 68, 72, 73, 74, 92, 104, 112, 137, 143, 167, 173, 174, 177, 186, 219; — and NORDEK: 60, 68, 71, 73, 75, 77

Switzerland — and EEC: 173, 174

Teetotaller Movement, Norwegian, 27, 28, 34; — and EEC: 159, 162

Timber, Norwegian export of —: 42

Trade, Norwegian, 15, 48, 161; foreign —: 18—23 pass., 39, 46, 47; — and EEC: 130, 144; foreign — after the referendum: 185, 187, 211

See also Exports, EFTA, NORDEK, Free Trade Agreement

Trade Unions, Norwegian, 29; — and EEC: 10, 48, 105, 124, 137, 153, 156

Treaty of Rome, The, 48, 49, 53, 57, 58, 61, 82, 94, 103, 120

Turkey —, NATO and EEC: 223

UNCLOS (United Nations Conference on the Law of the Sea), 125, 179, 215, 226, 233, 234, 240, 242, 244, 247; — at Caracas (1974): 227—230, 231, 232, 237; — at Geneva (1975): 238; — in New York (1976): 240

UNCTAD (United Nations Conference on Trade and Development) 215

United Nations, 39; Norway and —: 43; — and EEC: 222

United Nations Conference on the Law of the Sea
See UNCLOS

United Nations Conference on Trade and Development
See UNCTAD

USA (United States of America) 37; — and Norway: 44, 46—47, 161; — and Norwegian security policy: 42, 140, 141, 212; — troops in Western Europe: 60; foreign policy of —: 37, 59; — extension of fishing limit: 239, 240, 241; — and UNCLOS: 230; — and the boundary line between Norway and the Soviet Union in the Barents Sea: 247; — and EEC: 141, 145, 216; —, EEC and NATO: 207, 213, 221, 222; —, Norway and IEA: 210, 211

Vaarvik, Dagfinn (Minister of Wages and Prices 1965—1971, Minister of Foreign Affairs 1972—1973 and Chairman of the Centre Party 1973—1977), 51, 194, 202, 205

Vietnam, -war: 37, 59, 106

Werner Plan
See Economic and Monetary Union in the EEC

West Germany, 58, 64, 75; — and the Free Trade Agreement between Norway and EEC: 175; — and energy and industrial co-operation with Norway: 189, 225; — and the Norwegian no-trawling zones: 233—237; — and extension of fishing limits: 240, 244; East policy of —: 60; — and NATO: 141; — and United Nations: 222

288